HYMNS

OF THE

CHURCH MILITANT.

"These are they which came out of great tribulation, and have washed their robes, and made them white in the blood of the Lamb."—Rev. vii. 14.

NEW YORK:
ROBERT CARTER & BROTHERS,
No. 530 BROADWAY.

1858.

STEREOTYPED BY
T. B. SMITH & SON,
82 & 84 Beekman-st., N. Y.

PRINTED BY
E. O. JENKINS,
24 Frankfort St.

PREFACE.

THIS is simply a book of hymns for private use. They are chosen from many sources; are of many countries; and were written, some of them, centuries ago. Perhaps I cannot better tell what the book really is, than by a title which I once thought of giving it—Hymns *of* and *for* the Church Militant. The pages will, I think, prove such description true. They are not fuller of trial than of consolation.

I wished to bring together all the really fine hymns, and none others; but I found that I must admit a little class of general favourites, so long known and loved that they are beyond criticism—like the faces of old friends.

Of many a hymn I wish I could know the history—so sure do I feel that some special circumstances called it forth; and every hint that I have found makes me wish to know more. Thus the hymn on page 218, was found treasured up in a chest in some poor cottage in England, —that on page 615 is a French hymn, written in Paris during the cholera summer of 1832; and who can read "The Battle Song of Gustavus Adolphus," (p. 253) and not feel stirred to know that it was sung by his army before every battle? While many another is the war-cry of unknown combatants, in unseen strife. The old leaf whereon I found "The Saviour's Merit," (p. 351,) was so worn through with use, though the rest of the book was perfect, that some few words had to be supplied. To me, the hymns have been like a vision of the "great cloud of witnesses."

It is perhaps well that I cannot put in words all the pleasure this hymn-work has given me, nor just what I think of its results,—I fear the gentlest charity would call me at least eccentric. But I may tell (since I am but usher to the book) I may tell some of its titles to favour, and some of the grand truths which its pages *collectively* teach.

It has brought most vividly before my eyes, some of those Bible facts which before I knew rather by faith. For these are not assembly hymns, nor paraphrases, nor hymns written to order,—they are the living words of deep Christian experience.

And they tell that the Church is one. In prose, one denomination will war with another,—war, and strive—as some of the disciples did—for a place above the rest. The Church Militant is to outward eyes, often a Church divided against itself—every banner attacking every other, forgetful that the great standard of the Prince of Peace floats over all.

Yet this is but a difference of head—look here at their hearts. Read Luther and some old Catholic monk, side by side,—read Wesley, and all he ever opposed, or who ever opposed him. They fight still, but it is with themselves, with sin, with unbelief. They work out that other word—"through much tribulation." O friends—whether christian or unchristian—see what a hidden war doth rage in the midst of the Church; and find kinder cause than hypocrisy, for a ruffled temper and an unsteady walk! Even Christian gave way a little, when "Apollyon wounded him in his head, his hand, and foot."

The Church are one here also—they suffer in mind, in

body, in estate; with sometimes no sign of life but this —they would lie in the Slough of Despond for ever, rather than climb out on any side but that which is towards the Celestial City. "For they desire a better country, even an heavenly." And herein again they are one—"as sorrowing, yet alway rejoicing,"—as esteeming "the reproach of Christ greater riches than the treasures of Egypt." With one voice they sing,

"Heavenward the waves I'll breast
Till in heaven I am at rest."

Heavenward with Christ—after him. His headship over the Church is wonderfully set forth in their songs. They ever say with the old martyr—"None but Christ!" All eyes are looking unto Jesus, and waiting for him; and while one says of the loss of all things—

"Pass away, earthly joy,
Jesus is mine!"

another answers that without him all things are worth nought,—

"What have I in this barren land?
My Jesus is not here."

"One Lord, one faith, one baptism"—the building of their faith may cover more or less ground, but its corner-stone is the same.

I have read with great edification the prefaces of sundry collectors, who say, that wherever it seemed desirable to alter a hymn, the thing was done "without the slightest hesitation!" For me, I have tried to give the author's own words, and all of them. There is always a fresh beauty in the free growth of a fine thing (even though it be a little unruly) which no strange hand can trim into better shape. But the pruning knives have been so many, that I long ago gave up the hope of finding *all* the lopped branches. In three or four instances I have wittingly left out what seemed to me objectionable verses.

Of well-known hymn writers, I could sometimes get an old edition and copy from that; but with the thousand nameless hymns, I could but compare and take which version I liked best. Often indeed (especially where the alterations had sprung from that great root of alteration —a lower tone of Christianity than that of the hymn) the original words asserted their own right without a question; and many times the hymn had to be *collected* from various books,—I have had twelve open before me at one time, for one hymn.

I have admitted a few hymns, which I well knew would be called unlearned and even rough; yet there was something in their strong faith, or its strong expression, which I was not willing to leave out. It was fair, too, that all parts of the Church should be represented. And for any general favourites that are wanting, I can only say, look at my number of pages.

As to names—whenever I found such as were well authenticated, I have put them in the index. Where the name was doubtful I preferred to leave a blank.

ANNA WARNER.

NEW YORK, Feb. 9, 1858.

These Hymns are here brought together for the Help of the Christian's life --- the Joy and Comfort of the Sick Room --- the Hope of the Doubting, and the Rest of the Weary in Heart. Under His Blessing, who has Promised to His People that "in the Days of Famine They shall be Satisfied."

Thou shalt remember all the way which the Lord thy God led thee these forty years in the wilderness, to humble thee, and to prove thee, to know what was in thine heart, whether thou wouldest keep his commandments, or no.

Deut. viii. 2.

HYMNS

OF

THE CHURCH MILITANT.

The Kingdoms are but One.

HAPPY the souls to Jesus joined,
  And saved by grace alone:
Walking in all his ways, they find
  Their heaven on earth begun.
The church triumphant in thy love,
  Their mighty joys we know:
They sing the Lamb in hymns above,
  And we in hymns below.

Thee in thy glorious realm they praise,
  And bow before thy throne;
We in the kingdom of thy grace;
  The kingdoms are but one.
The holy to the holiest leads,
  And thence our spirits rise;
For he that in thy statutes treads,
  Shall meet thee in the skies.

Nearer Home.

One sweetly solemn thought
  Comes to me o'er and o'er—
I'm nearer home to-day
  Than I ever have been before.

Nearer my Father's house,
  Where the many mansions be;
Nearer the great white throne,
  Nearer the jasper sea;

Nearer the bound of life,
  Where we lay our burdens down;—
Nearer leaving the cross—
  Nearer gaining the crown.

But lying darkly between,
  Winding down through the night,
Is the dim and unknown stream
  That leads me at last to the light.

Closer, closer my steps
  Come to the dark abysm;
Closer death to my lips
  Presses the awful chrysm.

Saviour, perfect my trust,
  Strengthen the might of my faith;
Let me feel as I would when I stand
  On the rock of the shore of death;

Feel as I would when my feet
Are slipping over the brink:
For it may be I'm nearer home—
Nearer now, than I think!

The Charge.

A CHARGE to keep I have,
A God to glorify;
A never-dying soul to save,
And fit it for the sky.

To serve the present age,
My calling to fulfil,
O may it all my powers engage,
To do my Master's will.

Arm me with jealous care
As in thy sight to live;
And O, thy servant, Lord, prepare,
A strict account to give.

Help me to watch and pray,
And on thyself rely;
Assured, if I my trust betray,
I shall forever die.

David and Goliath.

By whom was David taught
To aim the dreadful blow,
When he Goliath fought,
And laid the Gittite low?
No sword nor spear the stripling took,
But chose a pebble from the brook.

'Twas Israel's God and king
Who sent him to the fight;
Who gave him strength to sling,
And skill to aim aright.
Ye feeble saints, your strength endures,
Because young David's God is yours.

Who ordered Gideon forth,
To storm th' invaders' camp,
With arms of little worth,
A pitcher and a lamp?
The trumpets made his coming known,
And all the host was overthrown.

Oh! I have seen the day,
When with a single word,
God helping me to say,
'My trust is in the Lord',
My soul has quelled a thousand foes,
Fearless of all that could oppose.

But unbelief, self-will,
Self-righteousness and pride,

How often do they steal
My weapons from my side!
Yet David's Lord and Gideon's Friend
Will help his servant to the end.

The Name of Jesus.

How sweet the name of Jesus sounds
In a believer's ear!
It soothes his sorrows, heals his wounds,
And drives away his fear.

It makes the wounded spirit whole,
And calms the troubled breast;
'Tis manna to the hungry soul,
And to the weary, rest.

Dear name! the rock on which I build,
My shield and hiding-place;
My never-failing treasury, filled
With boundless stores of grace.

By thee, my prayers acceptance gain,
Although with sin defiled;
Satan accuses me in vain,
And I am owned a child.

Jesus, my Shepherd, Husband, Friend,
My Prophet, Priest, and King,
My Lord, my Life, my Way, my End,
Accept the praise I bring.

Weak is the effort of my heart,
And cold my warmest thought;
But when I see thee as thou art,
I'll praise thee as I ought.

Till then, I would thy love proclaim
With every fleeting breath;
And may the music of thy name
Refresh my soul in death!

Upward.

NEARER, my God, to thee,
Nearer to thee!
E'en though it be a cross
That raiseth me;
Still all my song shall be,
Nearer, my God, to thee,
Nearer to thee!

Though like the wanderer,
The sun gone down,
Darkness be over me,
My rest a stone;
Yet in my dreams I'll be
Nearer, my God, to thee,
Nearer to thee!

There let my way appear
Steps unto heaven;

All that thou sendest me,
  In mercy given;
Angels to beckon me
Nearer, my God, to thee,
  Nearer to thee!

Then with my waking thoughts
  Bright with thy praise,
Out of my stony griefs
  Bethel I'll raise;
So by my woes to be
Nearer, my God, to thee,
  Nearer to thee!

Or if on joyful wing,
  Cleaving the sky,
Sun, moon, and stars forgot,
  Upward I fly;
Still, all my song shall be,
Nearer, my God, to thee!
  Nearer to thee!

The Safety of Trusting.

THY ways, O Lord, with wise design,
  Are framed upon thy throne above,
And every dark or bending line
  Meets in the centre of thy love.

With feeble light, and half obscure,
  Poor mortals thy arrangements view,
Not knowing that they all are sure,
  And, though mysterious, just and true.

Thy flock, thy own peculiar care,
  Though now they seem to roam un-eyed,
Are led by power and goodness where
  They best and safest may abide.

They neither know nor trace the way,
  But guided by thy piercing eye,
None of their feet to ruin stray,
  Nor shall the weakest fail or die.

My favoured soul shall meekly learn
  To lay her reason at thy throne;
Too weak thy secrets to discern,
  I'll trust thee for my guide alone.

A Psalm of Praise.

YE holy angels bright,
  Who stand before God's throne,
And dwell in glorious light,
    Praise ye the Lord, each one.
      You there, so nigh,
        Are much more meet
        Than we, the feet,
      For things so high.

You blessed souls at rest,
  That see your Saviour's face,
Whose glory, even the least,
  Is far above our grace;

God's praises sound,
As in his sight,
With sweet delight,
You do abound.

All nations of the earth
Extol the world's great King,
With melody and mirth
His glorious praises sing;
For he still reigns,
And will bring low
The proudest foe
That him disdains.

Sing forth Jehovah's praise
Ye saints that on him call;
Magnify him always
His holy churches all;
In him rejoice,
And thus proclaim
His holy name
With sounding voice.

My soul, bear thou thy part;
Triumph in God above;
With a full-tunéd heart,
Sing thou the songs of love.
Thou art his own,
Whose precious blood,
Shed for thy good,
His love made known.

He did in love begin,
Renewing thee by grace,
Forgiving all thy sin,
Showed thee his pleaséd face.
He did thee heal
By his Son's merit,
And by his Spirit
For glory seal.

In saddest thoughts and grief,
In sickness, fears, and pain,
I cried for his relief,
And it was not in vain.
He heard with speed;
And still I found
Mercy abound,
In time of need.

Let not his praises grow
On prosperous heights alone;
But in the vales below
Let his great love be known.
Let no distress
Curb and control
My wingéd soul,
And praise suppress.

Let not the fear or smart
Of his chastising rod,
Take off my fervent heart
From praising my dear God.

Whate'er I feel,
Still let me bring
This offering,
And to him kneel.

Though I lose friends and wealth,
And bear reproach and shame;
Though I lose ease and health,
Still let me praise God's name.
That fear and pain
Which would destroy
My thanks and joy,
Do thou restrain.

Though human help depart,
And flesh draw near to dust,
Let faith keep up my heart,
To love God true and just:
And all my days
Let no disease
Cause me to cease
His joyful praise.

Though sin would make me doubt,
And fill my soul with fears,
Though God seems to shut out
My daily cries and tears:
By no such frost
Of sad delays,
Let thy sweet praise
Be nipped and lost.

Away, distrustful care!
  I have thy promise, Lord,
To banish all despair,
  I have thy oath and word.
    And therefore I
      Shall see thy face,
      And there thy grace
    Shall magnify.

Though sin and death conspire
  To rob thee of thy praise,
Still towards thee I'll aspire,
  And thou dull hearts canst raise.
    Open thy door;
      And when grim death
      Shall stop this breath,
    I'll praise thee more.

With thy triumphant flock
  Then I shall numbered be;
Built on th' eternal rock,
  His glory we shall see.
    The heavens so high
      With praise shall ring,
      And all shall sing
    In harmony.

The sun is but a spark
  From the eternal light:
Its brightest beams are dark
  To that most glorious sight:

There the whole choir,
With one accord,
Shall praise the Lord
For evermore.

Perseverance.

My soul, be on thy guard,
Ten thousand foes arise;
The hosts of sin are pressing hard
To draw thee from the skies.

O watch, and fight, and pray;
The battle ne'er give o'er;
Renew it boldly every day,
And help divine implore.

Ne'er think the victory won,
Nor once at ease sit down;
The work of faith will not be done
Till thou hast got thy crown.

Then persevere till death
Shall bring thee to thy God;
He'll take thee, at thy parting breath,
To his divine abode.

Prayer Answered by Crosses.

I ASKED the Lord that I might grow
  In faith, and love, and every grace;
Might more of his salvation know,
  And seek more earnestly his face.

'Twas he who taught me thus to pray,
  And he, I trust, has answered prayer;
But it has been in such a way
  As almost drove me to despair.

I hoped that in some favoured hour
  At once he'd answer my request,
And by his love's constraining power,
  Subdue my sins and give me rest.

Instead of this, he made me feel
  The hidden evils of my heart,
And let the angry powers of hell
  Assault my soul in every part.

Yea, more—with his own hand he seemed
  Intent to aggravate my woe;
Crossed all the fair designs I schemed,
  Blasted my gourds, and laid me low.

"Lord, why is this?" I trembling cried,
  "Wilt thou pursue thy worm to death?"
"'Tis in this way," the Lord replied,
  "I answer prayer for grace and faith.

"These inward trials I employ,
From self and pride to set thee free,
And break thy schemes of earthly joy,
That thou may'st seek thy all in me."

"Thy Will be Done."

My God, my Father, while I stray
Far from my home, in life's rough way,
Oh teach me from my heart to say,
"Thy will be done."

Though dark my path, and sad my lot,
Let me "be still" and murmur not;
Or breathe the prayer, divinely taught,
"Thy will be done."

What though in lonely grief I sigh
For friends beloved, no longer nigh?
Submissive still I would reply,
"Thy will be done."

If thou shouldst call me to resign
What most I prize, it ne'er was mine:
I only yield thee what was thine;
"Thy will be done."

Should pining sickness waste away
My life in premature decay,
My Father! still I strive to say,
"Thy will be done."

If but my fainting heart be blest
With thy sweet Spirit for its guest,
My God! to thee I leave the rest,
"Thy will be done."

Renew my will from day to day;
Blend it with thine, and take away
All that now makes it hard to say,
"Thy will be done."

Then, when on earth I breathe no more
The prayer half mixed with tears before,
I'll sing, upon a happier shore,
"Thy will be done."

The Will of God.

I WORSHIP thee, sweet will of God!
And all thy ways adore,
And every day I live I seem
To love thee more and more.

Thou wert the end, the blessed rule
Of Jesu's toils and tears;
Thou wert the passion of his heart
Those three and thirty years.

And he hath breathed into my soul
A special love of thee,
A love to lose my will in his,
And by that loss be free.

I love to see thee bring to nought
  The plans of wily men;
When simple hearts outwit the wise,
  O thou art loveliest then!

The headstrong world, it presses hard
  Upon the church full oft;
And then how easily thou turn'st
  The hard ways into soft.

I love to kiss each print where thou
  Hast set thine unseen feet;
I cannot fear thee, blessed will!
  Thine empire is so sweet.

When obstacles and trials seem
  Like prison-walls to be,
I do the little I can do,
  And leave the rest to thee.

I know not what it is to doubt;
  My heart is ever gay;
I run no risk, for, come what will,
  Thou always hast thy way.

I have no cares, O blessed will!
  For all my cares are thine;
I live in triumph, Lord! for thou
  Hast made thy triumphs mine.

And when it seems no chance nor change
  From grief can set me free,
Hope finds its strength in helplessness,
  And gayly waits on thee.

Man's weakness, waiting upon God,
  Its end can never miss,
For men on earth no work can do
  More angel-like than this.

Ride on, ride on triumphantly,
  Thou glorious will! ride on;
Faith's pilgrim sons behind thee take
  The road that thou hast gone.

He always wins who sides with God,
  To him no chance is lost;
God's will is sweetest to him when
  It triumphs at his cost.

Ill that he blesses is our good,
  And unblest good is ill,
And all is right that seems most wrong,
  If it be his sweet will!

Question.

AM I an Israelite indeed,
  Without a false disguise?
Have I renounced my sins, and left
  My refuges of lies?

Say, does my heart unchanged remain,
  Or is it formed anew?
What is the rule by which I walk,
  The object I pursue?

Cause me, O God of truth and grace,
  My real estate to know;
If I am wrong, oh set me right!
  If right, preserve me so.

Twenty-third Psalm.

GOD, who the universe doth hold
            In his fold,
Is my shepherd kind and heedful,
Is my shepherd, and doth keep
            Me, his sheep,
Still supplied with all things needful.

He feedeth me in fields which lie
            Fresh and green,
Mottled with spring's flowery painting,
Through which creep, with murmuring crooks,
            Crystal brooks
To refresh my spirit's fainting.

When my soul from heaven's way
            Went astray,
With earth's vanities seduced,
For his name's sake, kindly he,
            Wandering me,
To his holy fold reduced.

Yea, though I stray through death's dark vale,
            Where his pale
Shades did on each side enfold me,

Dreadless, having thee for guide,
Should I bide,
For thy rod and staff uphold me.

Thou my board with messes large
Dost surcharge;
My bowls full of wine thou pourest,
And before mine enemies'
Envious eyes,
Balm upon my head thou showerest.

Neither dures thy bounteous grace
For a spaee,
But it knows nor bound nor measure;
So my days, to my life's end,
Shall I spend
In thy courts with heavenly pleasure.

What Think Ye of Christ?

WHAT think you of Christ? is the test
To try both your state and your scheme;
You cannot be right in the rest,
Unless you think rightly of him.
As Jesus appears in your view,
As he is belovéd or not,
So God is disposéd to you,
And mercy or wrath is your lot.

Some take him a creature to be,
A man or an angel at most;

Sure these have not feelings like me,
  Nor know themselves wretched and lost.
So guilty, so helpless am I,
  I durst not confide in his blood,
Nor on his protection rely,
  Unless I were sure he is God.

Some call him a Saviour, in word,
  But mix their own works with his plan,
And hope he his help will afford,
  When they have done all that they can:
If doings prove rather too light,
  (A little, they own, they may fail)
They purpose to make up full weight
  By casting his name in the scale.

Some style him the pearl of great price,
  And say he's the fountain of joys,
Yet feed upon folly and vice,
  And cleave to the world and its toys;
Like Judas, the Saviour they kiss,
  And while they salute him, betray;
Ah! what will profession like this
  Avail in the terrible day?

If asked what of Jesus I think?
  Though still my best thoughts are but poor,
I say he's my meat and my drink,
  My life, and my strength, and my store,
My Shepherd, my Husband, my Friend,
  My Saviour from sin and from thrall,
My hope from beginning to end,
  My portion, my Lord, and my All.

Pleading for Pardon.

SHOW pity, Lord, O Lord forgive,
Let a repentant rebel live:
Are not thy mercies large and free?
May not a sinner trust in thee?

My crimes are great, but can't surpass
The power and glory of thy grace;
Great God, thy nature hath no bound,
So let thy pardoning love be found.

O wash my soul from every sin,
And make my guilty conscience clean;
Here on my heart the burden lies,
And past offences pain mine eyes.

My lips with shame my sins confess,
Against thy law, against thy grace:
Lord, should thy judgment grow severe,
I am condemned, but thou art clear.

Should sudden vengeance seize my breath,
I must pronounce thee just in death;
And if my soul were sent to hell,
Thy righteous law approves it well.

Yet save a trembling sinner, Lord,
Whose hope, still hovering round thy word,
Would light on some sweet promise there,
Some sure support against despair.

He hath Borne our Griefs.

SURELY Christ thy griefs hath borne,
Weeping soul, no longer mourn;
View him bleeding on the tree,
Pouring out his life for thee;
There thy every sin he bore,
Weeping soul, lament no more.

All thy crimes on him were laid;
See, upon his blameless head
Wrath its utmost vengeance pours,
Due to my offence and yours;
Wounded in our stead he is,
Bruised for our iniquities.

Weary sinner, keep thine eyes
On the atoning sacrifice;
There the incarnate Deity,
Numbered with transgressors, see;
There, his Father's absence mourns,
Nailed, and bruised, and crowned with thorns.

See thy God his head bow down,
Hear the Man of Sorrows groan!
For thy ransom there condemned,
Stripped, derided, and blasphemed;
Bleed the guiltless for th' unclean,
Made an offering for thy sin.

Cast thy guilty soul on him,
Find him mighty to redeem;

At his feet thy burden lay,
Look thy doubts and cares away;
Now by faith the Son embrace,
Plead his promise, trust his grace.

Lord, thy arm must be revealed,
Ere I can by faith be healed!
Since I scarce can look to thee,
Cast a gracious eye on me;
At thy feet myself I lay,
Shine, O shine, my fears away.

The Morning Joy.

MARY to her Saviour's tomb
 Hasted at the early dawn;
Spice she brought and sweet perfume,
 But the Lord she loved was gone.
For awhile she weeping stood,
 Struck with sorrow and surprise,
Shedding tears, a plenteous flood,
 For her heart supplied her eyes.

Jesus, who is always near,
 Though too often unperceived,
Came his drooping child to cheer,
 Kindly asking, "Why she grieved?"
Though at first she knew him not,
 When he called her by her name,
Then her griefs were all forgot,
 For she found he was the same.

Grief and sighing quickly fled
  When she heard his welcome voice;
Just before, she thought him dead,
  Now, he bids her heart rejoice.
What a change his word can make,
  Turning darkness into day!
You who weep for Jesus' sake,
  He will wipe your tears away.

He who came to comfort her,
  When she thought her all was lost,
Will for your relief appear,
  Though you now are tempest-tost.
On his word your burden cast,
  On his love your thoughts employ;
Weeping for a while may last,
  But the morning brings the joy.

The Refuge.

JESUS! I come to thee,
  A sinner doomed to die;
My only refuge is thy cross,
  Here at thy feet I lie.

Can mercy reach my case,
  And all my sins remove?
Break, O my God! this heart of stone,
  And melt it by thy love.

Too long my soul has gone
  Far from my God astray;
I've sported on the brink of hell,
  In sin's delusive way.

But, Lord! my heart is fixed,
  I hope in thee alone;
Break off the chains of sin and death,
  And bind me to thy throne.

Thy blood can cleanse my heart,
  Thy hand can wipe my tears;
Oh! send thy blessed Spirit down
  To banish all my fears.

Then shall my soul arise,
  From sin and Satan free;
Redeemed from hell and every foe,
  I'll trust alone in thee.

Our Peace.

HARK! the voice of love and mercy
  Sounds aloud from Calvary;
Rending rocks the words attesting,
  Shaking earth and veilèd sky;
    "It is finished!"
  Was the Saviour's dying cry.

That which prophets long predicted,
  That which legal sacrifice

Only shadowed, not effected,
  That which justice satisfies,
    Now is finished!
  So the dying Saviour cries.

Finished, all the types and shadows
  Of the ceremonial law;
Finished, all that God had promised,
  Death and hell no more shall awe.
    "It is finished!"
  Saints, from hence your comfort draw.

Now redemption is completed,
  Sin atoned, the curse removed,
Satan, death, and hell, defeated,
  As his rising fully proved;
    All is finished:
  Here our hopes may rest unmoved.

O the life, the peace, the pleasure,
  Which these charming words afford!
Heavenly blessings, without measure,
  Flow to us through Christ the Lord.
    "It is finished!"
  Let our joyful songs record.

Tune your harps anew, ye seraphs,
  Sound aloud Immanuel's fame;
All creation swell the chorus,
  These delightful words proclaim,
    "It is finished!"
  Glory to his worthy name!

The King of Glory.

Our Lord is risen from the dead;
  Our Jesus is gone up on high;
The powers of hell are captive led,—
  Dragged to the portals of the sky:
There his triumphant chariot waits,
  And angels chant the solemn lay;—
Lift up your heads, ye heavenly gates;
  Ye everlasting doors, give way!

Loose all your bars of massy light,
  And wide unfold the ethereal scene;
He claims these mansions as his right;
  Receive the King of glory in!
Who is the King of glory? who?
  The Lord, that all our foes o'ercame;—
The world, sin, death, and hell o'erthrew;—
  And Jesus is the Conqueror's name.

Lo! his triumphant chariot waits,
  And angels chant the solemn lay;
Lift up your heads, ye heavenly gates;
  Ye everlasting doors, give way!
Who is the King of glory? who?
  The Lord, of glorious power possessed;—
The King of saints and angels too;—
  God over all, forever blest!

Increase our Faith.

When sins and fears prevailing rise,
And fainting hope almost expires,
Jesus, to thee I lift mine eyes,
To thee I breathe my soul's desires.

Art thou not mine, my dearest Lord?
And can my hope, my comfort die,
Fixed on thy everlasting word,
That word which built the earth and sky?

If my immortal Saviour lives,
Then my immortal life is sure;
This word a firm foundation gives,
Here let me build and rest secure.

Here let my faith unshaken dwell;
Immovable the promise stands;
Not all the powers of earth or hell
Can e'er dissolve the sacred bands.

Here, O my soul, thy trust repose;
Since Jesus is forever mine,
Not death itself, that last of foes,
Shall break a union so divine.

The True Riches.

Lord, I delight in thee,
And on thy care depend;
To thee in every trouble flee,
My best, my only friend.

When nature's streams are dry,
  Thy fulness is the same;
With this will I be satisfied,
  And glory in thy name.

Should I a drop bemoan,
  Who have a fountain near,
A fountain which will ever run
  With waters sweet and clear?

There can no good be found
  But may be found in thee;
I must have all things and abound,
  While God is God to me.

O for a stronger faith
  To look within the veil,
To credit what my Saviour saith,
  Whose word can never fail!

Who made my heaven secure,
  Will here all good provide;
While Christ is rich, can I be poor?
  What can I want beside?

I cast my care on thee,
  I triumph and adore;
Henceforth my great concern shall be
  To love and please thee more.

Follow Me.

WITNESS, ye men and angels now,
Before the Lord we speak;
To him we make our solemn vow,
A vow we dare not break;

That long as life itself shall last,
Ourselves to Christ we yield;
Nor from his cause will we depart,
Nor ever quit the field.

We trust not in our native strength,
But on his grace rely,
That, with returning wants, the Lord
Will all our need supply.

O guide our doubtful feet aright,
And keep us in thy ways;
And while we turn our vows to prayers,
Turn thou our prayers to praise.

God with Me.

MY God is with me every place—
Firmly does the promise stand—
On land or sea, with present grace,
Still to aid us near at hand.
If you ask, "Who is with thee?"
God is here— my God with me!

No depth, nor prison, nor the grave,
  Can exclude him from his own;
His cheering presence shall I have,
  If in crowds, or all alone.
In whatever state I be,
Everywhere is God with me!

My God for me! I dare to say,
  God is the portion of my soul!
Nor need I tremble in dismay
  When around me troubles roll.
If you ask, "What comforts thee?"
It is this—God is for me!

Ah! faith has seen him cradled lie,
  Here on earth a weeping child;
Has seen him for my vileness die—
  He, the sinless, undefiled!
And thus I know it true to be,
God, my Saviour, is for me!

In life, in death, with God so near,
  Every battle I shall win,
Shall boldly press through dangers here,
  Triumph over every sin!
"What!" you say, "a victor be?"
No, not I, but God in me!

The Defence of Zion.

As birds their infant brood protect,
And spread their wings to shelter them,
Thus saith the Lord to his elect,
"So will I guard Jerusalem."

And what is then Jerusalem,
This darling object of his care?
Where is its worth in God's esteem?
Who built it? who inhabits there?

Jehovah founded it in blood,
The blood of his incarnate Son;
There dwell the saints, once foes to God,
The sinners whom he calls his own,

There, though besieged on every side,
Yet much beloved, and guarded well,
From age to age they have defied
The utmost force of earth and hell.

Let earth repent, and hell despair,
This city has a sure defence;
Her name is called "The Lord is there;"
And who has power to drive him thence?

Zion.

Glorious things of thee are spoken,
Zion, city of our God!
He whose word cannot be broken,
Formed thee for his own abode.

On the Rock of ages founded,
  What can shake thy sure repose?
With salvation's walls surrounded,
  Thou may'st smile at all thy foes.

See! the streams of living waters,
  Springing from eternal love,
Well supply thy sons and daughters,
  And all fears of want remove:
Who can faint while such a river
  Ever flows their thirst t' assuage?
Grace, which like the Lord, the giver,
  Never fails from age to age.

Round each habitation hovering,
  See the cloud and fire appear,
For a glory and a covering,
  Showing that the Lord is near.
Thus deriving from their banner
  Light by night, and shade by day,
Safe they feed upon the manna
  Which he gives them when they pray.

Blest inhabitants of Zion,
  Washed in the Redeemer's blood!
Jesus, whom their souls rely on,
  Makes them kings and priests to God.
'Tis his love his people raises
  Over self to reign as kings,
And as priests, his solemn praises
  Each for a thank-offering brings.

Saviour, if of Zion's city
  I through grace a member am,
Let the world deride or pity,
  I will glory in thy Name.
Fading is the worldling's pleasure,
  All his boasted pomp and show;
Solid joys and lasting treasure
  None but Zion's children know.

The Recompense of the Reward.

My soul, with all thy wakened powers,
  Survey the heavenly prize,
Nor let these glittering toys of earth
  Allure thy wandering eyes.

The splendid crown which Moses chose
  Still beams around his brow;
While soon the king of Egypt's pride
  Was taught in death to bow.

The joys and treasures of a day
  I cheerfully resign;
Rich in the everlasting store
  Secured by grace divine.

Let fools my wiser choice deride,
  Angels and God approve;
Nor scorn of men, nor rage of hell,
  My steadfast soul shall move.

With ardent eye, that bright reward
I daily will survey;
And in the glorious prospect lose
The sorrows of the way.

The End of our Faith.

LOOK up to yonder world,
See myriads round the throne;
Each bears a golden harp,
And wears a golden crown:
With zeal they strike
The sacred lyre,
And strive to raise
Their praises higher.

Believing in his name,
They in his footsteps trod;
His righteousness their hope,
Their only plea his blood;
Lo, now they reign
With him above,
Behold his face
And sing his love.

And shall we not aspire
Like them our course to run?
The crown if we would wear,
That crown must first be won;
Divinely taught,
They showed the way;
First to believe
And then obey.

Early will I Seek Thee.

O God! thou art my God alone,
Early to thee my soul shall cry,
A pilgrim in a land unknown,
A thirsty land, whose springs are dry.

O that it were as it hath been,
When praying in the holy place,
Thy power and glory I have seen,
And marked the footsteps of thy grace.

Yet through this rough and thorny maze
I follow hard on thee, my God;
Thine hand, unseen, upholds my ways,
I safely tread where thou hast trod.

Thee in the watches of the night
When I remember on my bed,
Thy presence makes the darkness light,
Thy guardian wings are round my head.

Better than life itself thy love,
Dearer than all beside to me,
For whom have I in heaven above,
Or what on earth, compared with thee?

Praise with my heart, my mind, my voice,
For all thy mercy I will give;
My soul shall still in God rejoice,
My tongue shall bless thee while I live.

Night Thought.

How can I sleep while angels sing,
  When all the saints on high
Cry "Glory" to the eternal King,
  The Lamb that once did die:
When guardian angels fill the room,
  And hovering round my bed,
Do clap their wings, in love to him
  Who is my glorious Head?

Such joyful spirits never sleep,
  Their love is ever new;
Then, O my soul, no longer cease
  To love and praise him too;
For I, of all the race that fell,
  Or all the heavenly host,
Have greatest cause, with humbler soul,
  To love and praise him most.

Did God the Father love men so,
  As to give up his Son
To be a ransom, and redeem
  Them from the sins they'd done?
Did Jesus leave the Father's breast,
  That heaven of heavens on high,
To come to earth, this world of woe,
  For guilty worms to die?

No longer then will I lie here,
  But rise and praise and pray!
And join to sing, while I enjoy
  A glimpse of heavenly day.

Lord, give me strength to die to sin,
To run the Christian race:
To live to God, and glorify
The riches of his grace.

Pressing Toward the Mark.

THEE will I love, my strength and tower,
Thee will I love, my joy and crown,
Thee will I love with all my power,
In all my works, and thee alone:
Thee will I love, till that pure fire
Fills my whole soul with strong desire.

In darkness willingly I strayed,
I sought thee, yet from thee I roved;
For wide my wandering thoughts were spread,
Thy creatures more than thee I loved:
And now, if more at length I see,
'Tis through thy light, and comes from thee.

I thank thee, uncreated Sun,
That thy bright beams on me have shined;
I thank thee, who hast overthrown
My foes, and healed my wounded mind;
I thank thee, whose enlivening voice
Bids my freed heart in thee rejoice.

Uphold me in the doubtful race,
Nor suffer me again to stray;

Strengthen my feet with steady pace
  Still to press forward in thy way;
My soul and flesh, O Lord of might,
Fill, satiate, with thy heavenly light.

Give to mine eyes refreshing tears;
  Give to my heart chaste, hallowed fires;
Give to my soul, with filial fears,
  The love that all heaven's host inspires,
That all my powers, with all their might,
In thy sole glory may unite.

Thee will I love, my joy, my crown;
  Thee will I love, my Lord my God;
Thee will I love beneath thy frown
  Or smile, thy sceptre or thy rod;
What though my heart and flesh decay,
Thee shall I love in endless day.

Come with Us.

SINNER, what has earth to show
Like the joys believers know?
Is thy path, of fading flowers,
Half so bright, so sweet, as ours?

Doth a skilful, healing friend,
On thy daily path attend,
And, where thorns and stings abound,
Shed a balm on every wound?

When the tempest rolls on high,
Hast thou still a refuge nigh?
Can, O can thy dying breath
Summon one more strong than death?

Canst thou, on that awful day,
Fearless tread the gloomy way,
Plead a glorious ransom given,
Burst from earth and soar to heaven?

The Ark.

THE deluge, at the Almighty's call,
In what impetuous streams it fell,
Swallowed the mountains in its rage,
And swept a guilty world to hell.

In vain the tallest sons of pride
Fled from the close pursuing wave;
Nor could their mightiest towers defend,
Nor swiftness 'scape, nor courage save.

How dire the wreck! how loud the roar!
How shrill the universal cry
Of millions in the last despair,
Re-echoed from the lowering sky!

Yet Noah, humble, happy saint,
Surrounded with the chosen few,
Sat in his ark, secure from fear,
And sang the grace that steered him through.

So may I sing, in Jesus safe,
While storms of vengeance round me fall,
Conscious how high my hopes are fixed,
Beyond what shakes this earthly ball.

Enter thine ark while patience waits,
Nor ever quit that sure retreat;
Then the wide flood which buries earth,
Shall waft thee to a fairer seat.

Nor wreck nor ruin there is seen;
There not a wave of trouble rolls;
But the bright rainbow round the throne,
Seals endless life to all their souls.

Freely Ye have Received.

WHEN this passing world is done,
When has sunk yon glaring sun,
When we stand with Christ in glory,
Looking o'er life's finished story,
Then, Lord, shall I fully know—
Not till then—how much I owe.

When I hear the wicked call
On the rocks and hills to fall,
When I see them start and shrink
On the fiery deluge-brink,
Then, Lord, shall I fully know—
Not till then—how much I owe.

When I stand before the throne,
Dressed in beauty not my own,
When I see thee as thou art,
Love thee with unsinning heart,
Then, Lord, shall I fully know—
Not till then—how much I owe.

When the praise of heaven I hear,
Loud as thunder to the ear,
Loud as many waters' noise,
Sweet as harp's melodious voice,
Then, Lord, shall I fully know—
Not till then—how much I owe.

Even on earth, as through a glass,
Darkly, let this glory pass;
Make forgiveness feel so sweet,
Make thy Spirit's help so meet;
Even on earth, Lord, make me know
Something of how much I owe.

Chosen, not for good in me;
Wakened up from wrath to flee;
Hidden in the Saviour's side;
By the Spirit sanctified;
Teach me, Lord, on earth to show
By my love, how much I owe.

Oft I walk beneath the cloud,
Dark as midnight's gloomy shroud;
But when fear is at the height,
Jesus comes, and all is light;

Blessed Jesus! bid me show
Doubting saints how much I owe.

When in flowery paths I tread,
Oft by sin I'm captive led;
Oft I fall, but still arise—
The Spirit comes, the tempter flies:
Blessed Spirit! bid me show
Weary sinners all I owe.

Oft the nights of sorrow reign—
Weeping, sickness, sighing, pain;
But a night thine anger burns,
Morning comes and joy returns;
God of comforts, bid me show
To thy poor how much I owe.

A Perfect Heart, the Redeemer's Throne.

O FOR a heart to praise my God,
 A heart from sin set free;
A heart that always feels thy blood,
 So freely spilt for me;

A heart resigned, submissive, meck—
 My great Redeemer's throne,
Where only Christ is heard to speak,
 Where Jesus reigns alone.

O for a lowly, contrite heart,
  Believing, true, and clean;
Which neither life nor death can part
  From him that dwells within:

A heart in every thought renewed,
  And full of love divine;
Perfect, and right, and pure, and good,
  A copy, Lord, of thine.

Fruit of thy gracious lips, on me
  Bestow that peace unknown;
The hidden manna, and the tree
  Of life, and the white stone.

Thy nature, gracious Lord, impart;
  Come quickly from above;
Write thy new name upon my heart,
  Thy new, best name of love.

Hatred of Sin.

HOLY Lord God! I love thy truth,
  Nor dare thy least commandment slight;
Yet pierced by sin, the serpent's tooth,
  I mourn the anguish of the bite.

But though the poison lurks within,
  Hope bids me still with patience wait;
Till death shall set me free from sin,
  Free from the only thing I hate.

Had I a throne above the rest,
  Where angels and archangels dwell,
One sin, unslain, within my breast,
  Would make that heaven as dark as hell.

The prisoner sent to breathe fresh air,
  And blessed with liberty again,
Would mourn were he condemned to wear
  One link of all his former chain.

But oh! no foe invades the bliss,
  Where glory crowns the Christian's head:
One view of Jesus as he is,
  Will strike all sin for ever dead.

Longing for Heaven.

O WHEN shall I see Jesus,
  And reign with him above;
And from that flowing fountain
  Drink everlasting love?
When shall I be delivered
  From this vain world of sin,
And with my blessed Jesus,
  Drink endless pleasures in?

But now I am a soldier,
  My Captain's gone before,
He's given me my orders,
  And bid me not give o'er;

And since he has proved faithful,
  A righteous crown he'll give,
And all his valiant soldiers
  Eternal life shall have.

Through grace I am determined
  To conquer, though I die;
And then away to Jesus,
  On wings of love I'll fly.
Farewell to sin and sorrow,
  I bid you all adieu;
Then O my friends prove faithful,
  And on your way pursue.

Whene'er you meet with troubles
  And trials on your way,
O cast your care on Jesus,
  And don't forget to pray.
Gird on the heavenly armour
  Of faith, and hope, and love;
Then, when the combat's ended,
  He'll carry you above.

Self-consecration.

LORD, in the strength of grace,
  With a glad heart and free,
Myself, my residue of days,
  I consecrate to thee.

Thy ransomed servant, I
  Restore to thee thine own;
And from this moment live or die
  To serve my God alone.

The Garden-Hymn.

THE Lord into his garden comes,
The spices yield their rich perfumes,
  The lilies grow and thrive;
Refreshing showers of grace divine,
From Jesus flow to every vine,
  And make the dead revive.

This makes the dry and barren ground
In springs of water to abound,
  And fruitful soil become;
The desert blossoms like the rose,
When Jesus conquers all his foes,
  And makes his people one.

The glorious time is rolling on,
The gracious work is now begun,
  My soul a witness is;
Come taste and see the pardon free
To all mankind, as well as me;
  Who comes to Christ may live.

The worst of sinners here may find
A Saviour pitiful and kind,
  Who will them all relieve:

None are too late if they repent;
Out of one sinner legions went,
  Jesus did him receive.

Come, brethren, you that love the Lord,
Who taste the sweetness of his word,
  In Jesus' ways go on;
Our troubles and our trials here,
Will only make us richer there,
  When we arrive at home.

We feel that heaven is now begun,
It issues from the shining throne,
  From Jesus' throne on high;
It comes like floods, we can't contain,
We drink, and drink, and drink again,
  And yet we still are dry.

But when we come to reign above,
And all surround the throne of love,
  We'll drink a full supply;
Jesus will lead his armies through,
To living fountains where they flow,
  That never will run dry.

There we shall reign, and shout, and sing,
And make the upper regions ring,
  When all the saints get home;
Come on, come on, my brethren dear,
Soon we shall meet together, there,
  For Jesus bids us come.

No Man can Serve Two Masters.

FAREWELL, vain world, I bid adieu,
  Your glories I despise;
Your friendship I no more pursue,
  Your flatteries are but lies.

You promise happiness in vain,
  Nor can you satisfy;
Your highest pleasures turn to pain,
  And all your treasures die.

Had I the Indies, east and west,
  And riches of the sea;
Without my God I could not rest,
  For he is all to me

Then let my soul rise far above,
  By faith I'll take my wing
To the eternal realms of love,
  Where saints and angels sing.

There's love and joy that will not waste,
  There's treasures that endure;
There's pleasures that will always last,
  When time shall be no more.

Heaven and Earth.

UP to the fields where angels lie,
  And living waters gently roll,
Fain would my thoughts leap out and fly,
  But sin hangs heavy on my soul.

Thy wondrous blood, dear dying Christ,
  Can make this load of guilt remove;
And thou canst bear me where thou fly'st,
  On thy kind wings, celestial Dove!

O might I once mount up and see
  The glories of th' eternal skies,
What little things these worlds would be!
  How despicable to my eyes!

Had I a glance of thee, my God,
  Kingdoms and men would vanish soon;
Vanish as though I saw them not,
  As a dim candle dies at noon.

Then they might fight, and rage, and rave,
  I should perceive their noise no more
Than we can hear a shaking leaf,
  While rattling thunders round us roar.

Great All in All! eternal King!
  Let me but view thy lovely face,
And all my powers shall bow and sing
  Thine endless grandeur and thy grace.

The Way.

How shall I get there? who will aid?
And who will carry me to life?
Ah no one, Lord, can set me free
From sin, but thee.
All my help on thee is laid:
The seeker of the lost, thou art,
The blesser of the wretched heart:
Help, Jesus, take my part!

Lord, all my sins distress me sore,
And fears of death my soul dismay;
O Lord of life have pity now,
Hear, and save thou.
Let them disturb my peace no more!
For well thou knowest all my need;
I know it too, though less indeed:
Help, Jesus, hear me plead!

Thou speakest to me: Tremble not!
Thou callest: See, I am the life!
Therefore my heart to thee doth call,
Thou canst give all!
O let me never be forgot!
In death be near, my fears to drown;
In grief before me, as a crown;
Help, Jesus, the cast down!

Art thou the Shepherd of the weak?
Then in thy hands myself I lay;

Art thou the healer of the soul?
Then make me whole!
For I am perilously sick:
Now to my sins thy blood apply;
Physician, Saviour, hear my cry;
Help, Jesus, or I die!

I know I do not what I ought;
How can I stand before thy face?
These things distress me, thou dost see:
O can it be,
That I, unclean in word and thought,
Should be set free and purified?
And sin no more in me abide?
Yea, I thank God, Christ died!

Jesus I Love.

JESUS, I love thy charming name,
'Tis music to mine ear;
Fain would I sound it out so loud
That earth and heaven should hear.

Yes, thou art precious to my soul,
My transport, and my trust;
Jewels to thee are gaudy toys,
And gold is sordid dust.

All my capacious powers can wish,
In thee doth richly meet;
Nor to mine eyes is light so dear,
Nor friendship half so sweet.

Thy grace still dwells upon my heart,
And sheds its fragrance there;
The noblest balm of all its wounds,
The cordial of its care.

I'll speak the honors of thy name
With my last laboring breath;
Then, speechless, clasp thee in mine arms,
The antidote of death.

No Condemnation.

Who shall the Lord's elect condemn?
'Tis God that justifies their souls;
And mercy, like a mighty stream,
O'er all their sins divinely rolls.

Who shall adjudge the saints to hell?
'Tis Christ that suffered in their stead;
And, their salvation to fulfil,
Behold him rising from the dead.

He lives! he lives! and sits above,
For ever interceding there;
Who shall divide us from his love,
Or what should tempt us to despair?

Shall persecution, or distress,
Famine, or sword, or nakedness?
He that hath loved us, bears us through,
And makes us more than conquerors too.

Faith hath an overcoming power,
It triumphs in the dying hour;
Christ is our life, our joy, our hope,
Nor can we sink with such a prop.

Not all that men on earth can do,
Nor powers on high, nor powers below,
Shall cause his mercy to remove,
Or wean our hearts from Christ our love.

Jesus my All.

Why should I fear the darkest hour,
Or tremble at the tempter's power?
Jesus vouchsafes to be my tower.

Though hot the fight, why quit the field?
Why must I either flee or yield,
Since Jesus is my mighty shield?

When creature comforts fade and die,
Worldlings may weep, but why should I?
Jesus still lives, and still is nigh.

Though all the flocks and herds were dead,
My soul a famine need not dread,
For Jesus is my living bread.

I know not what may soon betide,
Or how my wants shall be supplied;
But Jesus knows, and will provide.

Though sin would fill me with distress,
The throne of grace I dare address,
For Jesus is my righteousness.

Though faint my prayers and cold my love,
My steadfast hope shall not remove,
While Jesus intercedes above.

Against me earth and hell combine,
But on my side is power divine;
Jesus is all, and he is mine.

Rejoice Alway.

REJOICE, the Lord is King;
  Your Lord and King adore:
Mortals, give thanks and sing,
  And triumph evermore.
Lift up your hearts, lift up your voice,
Rejoice, again I say, rejoice.

Jesus, the Saviour reigns,
  The God of truth and love;
When he had purged our stains,
  He took his seat above.
Lift up your hearts, lift up your voice,
Rejoice, again I say, rejoice.

He sits at God's right hand
  Till all his foes submit,

And bow to his command,
And fall beneath his feet.
Lift up your hearts, lift up your voice,
Rejoice, again I say, rejoice.

His kingdom cannot fail,
He rules o'er earth and heaven;
The keys of death and hell
Are to our Jesus given.
Lift up your hearts, lift up your voice,
Rejoice, again I say, rejoice.

He all his foes shall quell,
Shall all our sins destroy;
And every bosom swell
With pure seraphic joy.
Lift up your hearts, lift up your voice,
Rejoice, again I say, rejoice.

Rejoice in glorious hope;
Jesus, the Judge, shall come,
And take his servants up
To their eternal home.
We soon shall hear the archangel's voice,
The trump of God shall sound rejoice!

The Passing of Time.

How swift the torrent rolls,
That bears us to the sea!
The tide that bears our thoughtless souls
To vast eternity!

Our fathers, where are they,
  With all they called their own?
Their joys, and griefs, and hopes, and cares,
  And wealth and honour gone.

But joy or grief succeeds
  Beyond our mortal thought;
While the poor remnant of their dust
  Lies in the grave forgot.

There, where the fathers lie,
  Must all the children dwell;
Nor other heritage possess,
  But such a gloomy cell.

God of our fathers, hear,
  Thou everlasting Friend!
While we, as on life's utmost verge,
  Our souls to thee commend.

Of all the pious dead,
  May we the footsteps trace;
Till with them, in the land of light,
  We dwell before thy face.

A Trust-song.

NOT so darkly, not so deep,
  O my soul, now be thou stirred;
God is thy joy—let others keep
  The wealth and rank he has conferred.
Thou hast all in him, indeed;
Hast thou God, thou hast no need.

Not one child of mortal birth
Can lay claim to earthly treasure;
All that live on this poor earth
Are but guests at God's good pleasure:
Shall he not dispense at will
Goods which his own house do fill?

Therefore think not in thy heart
Earth shall ever be thy own;
Let thy thoughts from earth depart—
Seek thy wealth in heaven alone:
Heavenly riches cannot rust,
Heavenly joy sinks not to dust.

He is foolish, he is dead,
Who doth clasp earth in his hand,
When God offers him instead,
The treasures of th' enduring land.
So that my soul may live forever,
Drive on, earth-clouds, I fear ye never!

There behold, laid up in store,
All that hearts can satisfy;
When thou reachest the grave-door,
Earthly goods *behind* thee lie:
Mortal joys and mortal care
Enter not with mortals there.

But the wealth of a true soul,
Love to God and his sweet peace,
These will stand while ages roll;
Ages will their worth increase:
All beside, death may destroy,
But the soul shall keep its joy.

Let it sink into thy heart,
  And thy murmuring will subdue;
God doth every hour impart
  Benefits for ever new.
Yes, the sands may numbered be,
So cannot his gifts to thee!

And he is the full content
  Of each faithful Christian soul;
When thy prayers to him are sent,
  Leave the end to his control:
Let him grant what he sees best,
And say no to all the rest.

Now lift up thy troubled face!
  Call thy faith, and bid it shine;
Faith can light the darkest place,—
  Still those weary sighs of thine!
When the world was wrapped in night,
Israel had their dwellings light.

Set a boundary for thy will,
  As a child of heaven should;
Tune thy harp with praises still,
  To thy God, for ever good!
For his mercy puts to shame
All that thy deserts could claim.

Struggling through thy busy life,
  Set the Lord before thee ever;
Every hour of peace or strife
  Is from him—then murmur never.
Are things adverse? let them be!
God and heaven remain to thee!

The Church Militant

LEARNING THE CHURCH TRIUMPHANT'S SONG.

SING we the song of those who stand
Around the eternal throne,
Of every kindred, clime, and land,
A multitude unknown.

Life's poor distinctions vanish here;
To-day, the young, the old,
Our Saviour and his flock appear
One Shepherd and one fold.

Toil, trial, suffering, still await
On earth the pilgrim throng;
Yet learn we, in our low estate,
The Church triumphant's song.

"Worthy the Lamb for sinners slain,"
Cry the redeemed above,
"Blessing and honour to obtain,
And everlasting love."

"Worthy the Lamb!" on earth we sing,
"Who died our souls to save;
Henceforth, O Death! where is thy sting?
Thy victory, O Grave?"

Then, hallelujah! power and praise
To God in Christ be given;
May all who now this anthem raise,
Renew the strain in heaven!

Redeeming Love.

Now begin the heavenly theme,
Sing aloud in Jesus' name;
Ye who his salvation prove,
Triumph in redeeming love.

Ye who see the Father's grace
Beaming in the Saviour's face,
As to Canaan on ye rove,
Praise and bless redeeming love.

Mourning souls, dry up your tears,
Banish all your guilty fears;
See your guilt and curse remove,
Cancelled by redeeming love.

Ye, alas! who long have been
Willing slaves of death and sin,
Now from bliss no longer rove,
Stop, and taste redeeming love.

Welcome all by sin opprest,
Welcome to his sacred rest;
Nothing brought him from above,
Nothing but redeeming love.

When his Spirit leads us home,
When we to his glory come,
We shall all the fulness prove
Of our Lord's redeeming love.

He subdued th' infernal powers,
Those tremendous foes of ours;
From their cursed empire drove,
Mighty in redeeming love.

Hither, then, your music bring;
Strike aloud each joyful string:
Mortals, join the host above,
Join to praise redeeming love.

Perfection.

O HOW the thought of God attracts
And draws the heart from earth,
And sickens it of passing shows,
And dissipating mirth!

'Tis not enough to save our souls,
To shun the eternal fires;
The thought of God will rouse the heart
To more sublime desires.

God only is the creature's home,
Though long and rough the road;
Yet nothing less can satisfy
The love that longs for God.

O utter but the name of God,
Down in your heart of hearts,
And see how from the world at once
All tempting light departs.

A trusting heart, a yearning eye,
  Can win their way above;
If mountains can be moved by faith,
  Is there less power in love?

How little of that road, my soul!
  How little hast thou gone!
Take heart, and let the thought of God
  Allure thee further on.

The freedom from all wilful sin,
  The Christian's daily task;
O these are graces far below
  What longing love would ask!

Dole not thy duties out to God,
  But let thy hand be free:
Look long at Jesus; his sweet blood,
  How was it dealt to thee?

The perfect way is hard to flesh;
  It is not hard to love;
If thou wert sick for want of God,
  How swiftly wouldst thou move!

Good is the cloister's silent shade,
  Cold watch and pining fast;
Better the mission's wearing strife,
  If there thy lot were cast.

Yet none of these perfection needs;
  Keep thy heart calm all day,
And catch the words the Spirit there
  From hour to hour may say.

O keep thy conscience sensitive;
No inward token miss;
And go where grace entices thee:
Perfection lies in this.

Be docile to thy unseen Guide;
Love him as he loves thee;
Time and obedience are enough,
And thou a saint shalt be!

Prayer for the Spirit.

Come, Holy Spirit, come,
Let thy bright beams arise;
Dispel the sorrow from our minds,
The darkness from our eyes.

Convince us of our sin;
Then lead to Jesus' blood;
And to our wondering view reveal
The secret love of God.

Revive our drooping faith;
Our doubts and fears remove;
And kindle in our breasts the flame
Of never-dying love.

'Tis thine to cleanse the heart,
To purify the soul,
To pour fresh life in every part,
And new create the whole.

Dwell, Spirit, in our hearts;
Our minds from bondage free;
Then shall we know, and praise, and love,
The Father, Son, and thee.

Self-Examination.

WHAT strange perplexities arise!
What anxious fears and jealousies!
What crowds in doubtful light appear;
How few, alas, approved and clear!

And what am I? My soul awake,
And an impartial survey take:
Does no dark sign, no ground of fear,
In practice or in heart appear?

What image does my spirit bear?
Is Jesus formed and living there?
Say, do his lineaments divine
In thought, in word, and action shine?

Searcher of hearts, O search me still;
The secrets of my soul reveal;
My fears remove, let me appear
To God and my own conscience clear!

Scatter the clouds which o'er my head
Thick glooms of dubious terrors spread;
Lead me into celestial day,
And to myself, myself display.

May I at that blest world arrive,
Where Christ through all my soul shall live,
And give full proof that he is there,
Without one gloomy doubt or fear!

The New Creation.

Love divine, all love excelling,
  Joy of heaven, to earth come down;
Fix in us thy humble dwelling,
  All thy faithful mercies crown.
Jesus, thou art all compassion,—
  Pure, unbounded love thou art;
Visit us with thy salvation;
  Enter every trembling heart.

Breathe, O breathe thy loving Spirit
  Into every troubled breast;
Let us all in thee inherit;
  Let us find that second rest.
Take away the love of sinning;
  Alpha and Omega be;
End of faith, as its beginning,
  Set our souls at liberty.

Come, almighty to deliver,
  Let us all thy life receive;
Suddenly return, and never,
  Never more thy temples leave:

Thee we would be always blessing;
  Serve thee as thy host above;
Pray, and praise thee without ceasing,
  Glory in thy perfect love.

Carry on thy new creation;
  Happy, holy, may we be;
Let us see our whole salvation
  Perfectly secured by thee:
Change from glory into glory,
  Till in heaven we take our place—
Till we cast our crowns before thee,
  Lost in wonder, love, and praise.

The Hope of our High Calling.

WHAT is our calling's glorious hope,
  But inward holiness?
For this, to Jesus I look up;
  I calmly wait for this.

I wait till he shall touch me clean—
  Shall life and power impart;
Give me the faith that casts out sin,
  And purifies the heart.

This is the dear redeeming grace,
  For every sinner free;
Surely it shall on me take place,
  The chief of sinners—me.

From all iniquity, from all,
  He shall my soul redeem;
In Jesus I believe, and shall
  Believe myself to him.

When Jesus makes my heart his home,
  My sin shall all depart;
And, lo! he saith, I quickly come
  To fill and rule thy heart.

Be it according to thy word;
  Redeem me from all sin:
My heart would now receive thee, Lord;
  Come in, my Lord, come in!

Rest.

I REST with thee, Lord! Whither should I go?
  I feel so blest, within thy home of love!
The blessings purchased by thy pain and woe,
  To thy poor child thou sendest from above.
O never let thy grace depart from me;
So shall I still abide, my Lord, with thee.

I rest with thee! Eternal life the prize
  Thou wilt bestow, when faith's good fight is won:
What can earth give, but vain regrets and sighs,
  To the poor heart whose passing bliss is done?
For lasting joys, I fleeting ones resign,
Since Jesus calls me his, and he is mine.

I rest with thee! No other place of rest
  Can now attract, no other portion please:
The soul, of heavenly treasure once possessed,
  All earthly glory with indifference sees.
Poor world, farewell! thy splendors tempt no more,
The power of grace I feel, and thine is o'er.

I rest with thee! With thee whose wondrous love
  Descends to seek the lost, the fallen raise;
Oh! that my whole of future life might prove
  One hallelujah, one glad song of praise!
So shall I sing, as time's last moments flee,
Now, and for ever, Lord, I rest with thee!

Trust in the Lord.

God is my strong salvation,
  What foe have I to fear?
In darkness and temptation
  My light, my help is near;
Though hosts encamp around me,
  Firm to the fight I stand:
What terror can confound me,
  With God at my right hand?

Place on the Lord reliance,
  My soul with courage wait;
His truth be thine affiance,
  When faint and desolate:

His might thine heart shall strengthen,
  His love thy joy increase;
Mercy thy days shall lengthen,
  "The Lord will give thee peace."

The Christian Walk.

O HAPPY souls, from heaven born
  While yet they sojourn here;
Who all their days begin with God,
  And spend them in his fear.

So may our thoughts ascend to God
  As dawns the morning ray,
Ponder with love the sacred page,
  And grateful homage pay.

'Midst hourly cares may love present
  Its incense at his throne;
And while the world our hands employs,
  Our hearts be his alone.

In painful duties, days of grief,
  When by temptations tried,
We still will in the Lord be strong,
  And in his love confide.

Each night we'll lean our weary head
  On his paternal breast,
And safely folded in his arms,
  Resign our powers to rest.

A life like this, is heaven on earth:
Thus let my days be passed!
Nor shall I then impatient wish,
Nor shall I fear, the last.

The Mercy-Seat.

From every stormy wind that blows,
From every swelling tide of woes,
There is a calm, a sure retreat,
'Tis found beneath the mercy-seat.

There is a place where Jesus sheds
The oil of gladness on our heads;
A place than all beside more sweet:
It is the blood-bought mercy-seat.

There is a scene where spirits blend,
Where friend holds fellowship with friend;
Though sundered far, by faith they meet
Around one common mercy-seat.

Ah! whither could we flee for aid,
When tempted, desolate, dismayed?
Or how the hosts of hell defeat,
Had suffering saints no mercy-seat?

There, there on eagles' wings we soar,
And sin and sense molest no more;
And heaven comes down our souls to greet,
Where glory crowns the mercy-seat.

The Pilgrim's Guide and Guardian.

GUIDE me, O thou great Jehovah,
Pilgrim through this barren land;
I am weak, but thou art mighty,
Hold me with thy powerful hand:
Bread of heaven,
Feed me till I want no more.

Open, Lord, the crystal fountain
Whence the healing waters flow;
Let the fiery, cloudy pillar
Lead me all my journey through:
Strong Deliverer,
Be thou still my strength and shield.

When I tread the verge of Jordan,
Bid my anxious fears subside;
Bear me through the swelling current,
Land me safe on Canaan's side:
Songs of praises
I will ever give to thee.

An Evening Psalm.

LORD, thou wilt hear me when I pray,
I am for ever thine;
I fear before thee all the day,
Nor would I dare to sin.

And when I rest my weary head,
From cares and business free;
'Tis sweet conversing on my bed
With my own heart and thee.

I pay this evening sacrifice,
And when my work is done,
Great God, my faith, my hope relies
Upon thy grace alone.

Thus with my thoughts composed to peace,
I'll give mine eyes to sleep;
Thy hand in safety keeps my days,
And will my slumbers keep.

I will Praise Thee Every Day.

FATHER of spirits! hear our prayer;
Our life, our hope, our comforter,
Our strong abode:
To thee our grateful hearts we raise,
And humbly, gladly, hymn thy praise,
Preserver, God!

Thy gentle hand hath smoothed our way,
Fed and sustained us day by day;
In thee we move:
O may thy mercies, Lord, inspire
Our hearts with gratitude, and fire
Our souls with love.

Trust in Him at all Times.

God is the refuge of his saints,
  When storms of sharp distress invade;
Ere we can offer our complaints,
  Behold him present with his aid.

Let mountains from their seats be hurled
  Down to the deep, and buried there;
Convulsions shake the solid world;
  Our faith shall never yield to fear.

Loud may the troubled ocean roar—
  In sacred peace our souls abide;
While every nation, every shore,
  Trembles and dreads the swelling tide.

There is a stream whose gentle flow
  Supplies the city of our God;
Life, love, and joy, still gliding through,
  And watering our divine abode.

That sacred stream, thy holy word,
  Our grief allays, our fear controls;
Sweet peace thy promises afford,
  And give new strength to fainting souls.

Zion enjoys her monarch's love,
  Secure against a threatening hour;
Nor can her firm foundations move,
  Built on his truth, and armed with power.

He Led Them on Safely.

O ISRAEL, who is like to thee?
A people saved and called to be
Peculiar to the Lord!
Thy shield, he guards thee from the foe;
Thy sword, he fights thy battles too,
Himself thy great reward.

Fear not, though many should oppose,
For God is stronger than thy foes,
And makes thy cause his own;
The promised land before thee lies,
Go and possess the glorious prize,
Reserved for thee alone.

In glory there the King appears,
He wipes away his people's tears,
And makes their sorrows cease;
From toil and strife they there repose,
And dwell, secure from all their foes,
In everlasting peace.

Fair emblem of a better rest,
Of which believers are possessed
Beyond material space;
Methinks I see the heavenly shore
Where sin and sorrow are no more,
And long to reach the place.

Nor shall I always absent be
From him my soul desires to see

Within the realms of light:
Ere long, my Lord will rend the veil,
And not a cloud shall then conceal
His glory from my sight.

I will Fear no Evil.

Thy way, not mine, O Lord,
However dark it be;
Lead me by thine own hand,
Choose out the path for me.

Smooth let it be or rough,
It will be still the best;
Winding or straight, it matters not,
It leads me to thy rest.

I dare not choose my lot,
I would not, if I might;
Choose thou for me, my God,
So shall I walk aright.

The kingdom that I seek
Is thine, so let the way
That leads to it be thine,
Else I must surely stray.

Take thou my cup, and it
With joy or sorrow fill,
As best to thee may seem:
Choose thou my good and ill.

Choose thou for me my friends,
  My sickness or my health;
Choose thou my cares for me,
  My poverty or wealth.

Not mine, not mine the choice,
  In things or great or small;
Be thou my guide, my strength,
  My wisdom and my all.

They Left all, and Followed Him.

WHAT poor despiséd company
  Of travellers are these,
That walk in yonder narrow way,
  Along that rugged maze?

Ah, these are of a royal line,
  All children of a king,
Heirs of immortal crowns divine,
  And lo! for joy they sing.

Why do they then appear so mean,
  And why so much despised?
Because of their rich robes unseen
  The world is not apprised.

But some of them seem poor, distressed,
  And lacking daily bread?
Yet they 're of boundless wealth possessed,
  With hidden manna fed.

Why do they shun the pleasing path
  That worldlings love so well?
Because that is the road to death,
  The open way to hell.

But why keep they that narrow road,
  That rugged, thorny maze?
Why that's the way their Leader trod
  They love to keep his ways.

What, is there then no other road
  To Salem's happy ground?
Christ is the only way to God,
  No other can be found.

The Covenanter's Scaffold Song.

Sing with me! sing with me!
Weeping brethren, sing with me!
For now an open heaven I see,
And a crown of glory laid for me.
How my soul this earth despises!
How my heart and spirit rises!
Bounding from the flesh I sever!
World of sin, adieu for ever!

Sing with me! sing with me!
Friends in Jesus, sing with me!
All my sufferings, all my woe,
All my griefs, I here forego.

Farewell terrors, sighing, grieving,
Praying, hearing, and believing,
Earthly trust and all its wrongings,
Earthly love and all its longings.

Sing with me! sing with me!
Blessed spirits, sing with me!
To the Lamb our songs shall be,
Through a glad eternity!
Farewell, earthly morn and even,
Sun, and moon, and stars of heaven;
Heavenly portals ope before me,
Welcome, Christ, in all his glory!

The Lord our Righteousness.

JESUS, thy blood and righteousness
My beauty are, my glorious dress;
'Midst flaming worlds, in these arrayed,
With joy shall I lift up my head.

When from the dust of earth I rise
To claim my mansion in the skies;
E'en then shall this be all my plea,
"Jesus hath lived and died for me."

Bold shall I stand in that great day,
For who aught to my charge shall lay?
Fully absolved through thee I am,
From sin and fear, from guilt and shame.

The holy, meek, unspotted Lamb,
Who from the Father's bosom came,—
Who died for me, e'en me to atone,—
Now for my Lord and God I own.

Thus Abraham, the friend of God,
Thus all the armies bought with blood,
Saviour of sinners thee proclaim,—
Sinners, of whom the chief I am.

Lord, I believe thy precious blood,
Which at the mercy-seat of God
For ever doth for sinners plead,
For me, e'en for my soul was shed.

Lord, I believe were sinners more
Than sands upon the ocean shore,
Thou hast for all a ransom paid,
For all a full atonement made.

This spotless robe the same appears
When ruined nature sinks in years;
No age can change its glorious hue,
The grace of Christ is ever new.

O let the dead now hear thy voice,
Now bid thy banished ones rejoice;
Their beauty this, their glorious dress,
JESUS, THE LORD OUR RIGHTEOUSNESS!

Heavenly Rest.

When I can read my title clear
 To mansions in the skies,
I'll bid farewell to every fear,
 And wipe my weeping eyes.

Should earth against my soul engage,
 And hellish darts be hurled,
Then I can smile at Satan's rage,
 And face a frowning world.

Let cares like a wild deluge come,
 And storms of sorrow fall;
May I but safely reach my home,
 My God, my heaven, my all.

There shall I bathe my weary soul
 In seas of heavenly rest,
And not a wave of trouble roll
 Across my peaceful breast.

Luther's Prayer.

Our God, our Father, with us stay,
And make us keep thy narrow way;
Free us from sin and all its power;
Give us a joyful dying hour;
Deliver us from Satan's arts,
And let us build our hopes on thee,
Down in our very heart of hearts!

O God, may we true servants be!
And serve thee ever perfectly.
Help us, with all thy children here,
To fight and flee with holy fear;
Flee from temptation, and to fight
With thine own weapons for the right;
Amen, amen, so let it be!
So shall we ever sing to thee,
Hallelujah!

The Other Side Jordan.

DARK and thorny is the desert
Through which pilgrims make their way;
Yet beyond this vale of sorrow
Lie the fields of endless day:
Fiends, loud howling through the desert,
Make them tremble as they go,
And the fiery darts of Satan
Often bring their courage low.

O young soldiers, are you weary
Of the roughness of the way?
Does your strength begin to fail you,
And your vigour to decay?
Jesus, Jesus will go with you;
He will lead you to his throne;
He who dyed his garments for you,
And the wine-press trod alone;

He, whose thunder shakes creation;
  He, who bids the planets roll;
He, who rides upon the tempest,
  And whose sceptre rules the whole.
Round him are ten thousand angels,
  Ready to obey command;
They are always hovering round you,
  Till you reach the heavenly land.

There, on flowery hills of pleasure,
  Lie the fields of endless rest;
Love, and joy, and peace for ever
  Reign and triumph in your breast.
Who can paint the scene of glory
  Where the ransomed dwell on high?
They on golden harps for ever
  Sound redemption through the sky.

There's a million flaming seraphs
  Fly across the heavenly plain;
There they sing immortal praises:
  Glory, glory is their strain.
But methinks a sweeter concert
  Makes the heavenly arches ring;
And the song is heard in Zion,
  Which the angels cannot sing.

O their crowns! how bright they sparkle;
  Such as monarchs never wear;
They are gone to richer pastures,
  Jesus is their Shepherd there:

Hail! ye happy, happy spirits,
  Death no more shall make you fear;
Grief nor sorrow, pain nor anguish,
  Shall no more distress you there.

Arise, Shine.

O Zion, tune thy voice,
  And raise thy hands on high;
Tell all the world thy joys,
  And boast salvation nigh.
    Cheerful in God,
      Arise and shine,
      While rays divine
    Stream all abroad.

He gilds thy mourning face
  With beams that cannot fade;
His all-resplendent grace
  He pours around thy head:
    The nations round,
      Thy form shall view,
      With lustre new
    Divinely crowned.

In honour to his name
  Reflect that sacred light,
And loud that grace proclaim,
  Which makes thy darkness bright:
    Pursue his praise,
      Till sovereign love,
      In worlds above,
    The glory raise.

There, on his holy hill,
  A brighter sun shall rise,
And with his radiance fill
  Those fairer, purer skies;
    While round his throne
      Ten thousand stars
      In nobler spheres,
    His influence own.

Christ's Kingdom.

JESUS shall reign where'er the sun
Does his successive journeys run;
His kingdom stretch from shore to shore,
Till moons shall wax and wane no more.

Behold! the islands with their kings,
And Europe her best tribute brings;
From north to south the princes meet
To pay their homage at his feet.

There Persia, glorious to behold,
There India, shines in eastern gold;
And barbarous nations at his word
Submit, and bow, and own their Lord.

For him shall endless prayer be made,
And princes throng to crown his head;
His name, like sweet perfume, shall rise
With every morning sacrifice.

People and realms of every tongue
Dwell on his love with sweetest song;
And infant voices shall proclaim
Their early blessings on his name.

Blessings abound where'er he reigns;
The prisoner leaps to lose his chains;
The weary find eternal rest,
And all the sons of want are blest.

Where he displays his healing power,
Death and the curse are known no more;
In him the tribes of Adam boast
More blessings than their father lost.

Let every creature rise, and bring
Peculiar honours to our King;
Angels descend with songs again,
And earth repeat the loud Amen.

Praise to Christ.

AWAKE, and sing the song
  Of Moses and the Lamb;
Wake, every heart and every tongue,
  To praise the Saviour's name.

Sing of his dying love;
  Sing of his rising power;
Sing, how he intercedes above
  For those whose sins he bore.

Sing, till we feel our hearts
  Ascending with our tongues;
Sing, till the love of sin departs,
  And grace inspires our songs.

Sing on your heavenly way,
  Ye ransomed sinners, sing!
Sing on, rejoicing every day,
  In Christ th' exalted King.

Soon shall we hear him say,
  "Ye blessèd children, come;"
Soon will he call us hence away,
  And take his wanderers home.

Soon shall our raptured tongue
  His endless praise proclaim,
And sweeter voices tune the song
  Of Moses and the Lamb.

The Hiding-Place.

HAIL, sovereign love, that first began
The scheme to rescue fallen man!
Hail, matchless, free, eternal grace,
That gave my soul a hiding-place!

Against the God that rules the sky
I fought with hand uplifted high;
Despised his rich abounding grace,
Too proud to seek a hiding-place.

Inwrapt in thick Egyptian night,
And fond of darkness more than light,
Madly I ran the sinful race,
Secure without a hiding-place.

But thus th' eternal counsel ran,
"Almighty love—arrest that man:"
I felt the arrows of distress,
And found I had no hiding-place.

Indignant justice stood in view,
To Sinai's fiery mount I flew;
But justice cried, with frowning face,
"This mountain is no hiding-place."

Ere long a heavenly voice I heard,
And mercy's angel-form appeared;
She led me on, with gentle pace,
To Jesus, as my hiding-place.

On him almighty vengeance fell
That must have sunk a world to hell;
He bore it for the chosen race,
And so became their hiding-place.

Should storms of sevenfold vengeance roll,
And shake the globe from pole to pole,
No flaming bolt shall daunt my face,
For Jesus is my hiding-place.

A few more rolling suns, at most,
Will land me safe on Canaan's coast,
Where I shall sing the song of grace,
And see my glorious hiding-place.

Forget not.

O BLESS the Lord, my soul!
Let all within me join,
And aid my tongue to bless his name,
Whose favours are divine.

O bless the Lord, my soul!
Nor let his mercies lie
Forgotten in unthankfulness,
And without praises die.

'T is he forgives thy sins,
'T is he relieves thy pain,
'T is he that heals thy sicknesses,
And makes thee young again.

He crowns thy life with love,
When ransomed from the grave;
He that redeemed my soul from hell,
Hath sovereign power to save.

He fills the poor with good,
He gives the sufferer rest;
The Lord hath judgments for the proud,
And justice for th' opprest.

His wondrous works and ways
He made by Moses known,
But sent the world his truth and grace
By his belovéd Son.

Unchangeable Love.

If Jesus is ours
We have a true friend,
His goodness endures
The same to the end;
Our comforts may vary,
Our frames may decline;
We cannot miscarry,
Our aid is divine.

Though God may delay
To show us his light,
And heaviness may
Endure for a night,
Yet joy in the morning
Shall surely abound;
No shadow of turning
In Jesus is found.

Then tune every string
To Jesus's name!
With angels we 'll sing
The song of the Lamb:
Thee, every believer
Shall joyfully praise,
Thou bountiful giver
Of glory and grace.

A Psalm for the Lord's Day.

SWEET is the work, my God, my King,
To praise thy name, give thanks, and sing;
To show thy love by morning light,
And talk of all thy truth at night.

Sweet is the day of sacred rest;
No mortal cares shall seize my breast:
O may my heart in tune be found,
Like David's harp of solemn sound!

My heart shall triumph in my Lord,
And bless his works, and bless his word;
Thy works of grace, how bright they shine!
How deep thy counsels, how divine!

Fools never raise their thoughts so high;
Like brutes they live, like brutes they die;
Like grass they flourish, till thy breath
Blasts them in everlasting death.

But I shall share a glorious part,
When grace hath well refined my heart;
And fresh supplies of joy are shed,
Like holy oil, to cheer my head.

Sin, my worst enemy before,
Shall vex my eyes and ears no more;
My inward foes shall all be slain,
Nor Satan break my peace again.

Then shall I see, and hear, and know,
All I desired or wished below;
And every power find sweet employ
In that eternal world of joy.

Christ's Resurrection.

HARK! the herald angels say,
Christ, the Lord, is risen to-day!
Raise your joys and triumphs high,
Let the glorious tidings fly.

Love's redeeming work is done!
The battle 's fought, the victory won!
Lo, the sun's eclipse is o'er;
Lo, he sets in blood no more.

Vain the stone, the watch, the seal—
Christ has burst the gates of hell;
Death in vain forbids his rise;
Christ has opened Paradise.

Lives again our glorious King,
"Where, O death, is now thy sting?"
Once he died our souls to save,
"Where's thy victory, boasting grave?"

What though once we perished all,
Partners of our parents' fall;—
Second life we shall receive,
And in Christ for ever live.

Sunday in a Sick Room.

THOUSANDS, O Lord of Hosts! this day
  Around thine altar meet;
And tens of thousands throng to pay
  Their homage at thy feet.

They see thy power and glory there
  As I have seen them too;
They read, they hear, they join in prayer,
  As I was wont to do.

They sing thy deeds, as I have sung,
  In sweet and solemn lays;
Were I among them, my glad tongue
  Might learn new themes of praise.

For thou art in the midst to teach,
  When on thy name they call;
And thou hast blessings, Lord, for each—
  Hast blessings, Lord, for all.

I, of such fellowship bereft,
  In spirit turn to thee;
Oh hast thou not a blessing left,
  A blessing, Lord, for me?

The dew lies thick on all the ground;
  Shall my poor fleece be dry?
The manna rains from heaven around;
  Shall I of hunger die?

Behold thy prisoner;—loose my bands,
  If 'tis thy gracious will;
If not,—contented in thy hands,
  Behold thy prisoner still!

I may not to thy courts repair,
  Yet here thou surely art;
Lord, consecrate a house of prayer
  In my surrendered heart.

To faith reveal the things unseen,
  To hope the joys untold;
Let love, without a veil between,
  Thy glory now behold.

O make thy face on me to shine,
  That doubt and fear may cease;
Lift up thy countenance benign
  On me, and give me peace.

None upon Earth I desire besides Thee.

How tedious and tasteless the hours
  When Jesus no longer I see;
Sweet prospects, sweet birds, and sweet flowers,
  Have lost all their sweetness to me;
The midsummer sun shines but dim,
  The fields strive in vain to look gay,
But when I am happy in him,
  December's as pleasant as May.

His name yields the richest perfume,
  And sweeter than music his voice;

His presence disperses my gloom,
  And makes all within me rejoice;
I should, were he always so nigh,
  Have nothing to wish or to fear;
No mortal so happy as I,
  My summer would last all the year.

Content with beholding his face,
  My all to his pleasure resigned,
No changes of season or place
  Would make any change in my mind:
While blest with a sense of his love,
  A palace a toy would appear,
And prisons would palaces prove,
  If Jesus would dwell with me there.

Dear Lord, if indeed I am thine,
  If thou art my sun and my song,
Say, why do I languish and pine,
  And why are my winters so long?
O drive these dark clouds from my sky,
  Thy soul-cheering presence restore;
Or take me unto thee on high,
  Where winter and clouds are no more.

It Shall be Well.

WHAT cheering words are these!
  Their sweetness who cau tell?
In time, and to eternity,
  'Tis with the righteous well.

In every state secure,
Kept by Jehovah's eye,
'Tis well with them while life endures,
And well when called to die.

'Tis well when joys arise,
'Tis well when sorrows flow;
'Tis well when darkness veils the skies,
And strong temptations blow.

'Tis well when on the mount
They feast on dying love;
And 'tis as well, in God's account,
When they the furnace prove.

'Tis well when, at his throne,
They wrestle, weep, and pray;
'Tis well when at his feet they groan,
Yet bring their wants away.

'Tis well when Jesus calls:
"From earth and sin arise;
Join with the host of virgin souls
Made to salvation wise."

The Good Shepherd.

YES! our Shepherd leads, with gentle hand,
Through the dark pilgrim-land,
His flock so dearly bought,
So long and fondly sought.
Hallelujah!

When in clouds and mist the weak ones stray,
He shows again the way,
And points to them afar
A bright and guiding star.
Hallelujah!

Tenderly he watches from on high
With an unwearied eye;
He comforts and sustains
In all their fears and pains.
Hallelujah!

Through the parched desert he will guide
To the green fountain-side;
Through the dark, stormy night,
To a calm land of light.
Hallelujah!

Yes! his "little flock" are ne'er forgot;
His mercy changes not;
Our home is safe above,
Within his arms of love.
Hallelujah!

Wait.

THE saints should never be dismayed,
Nor sink in hopeless fear;
For when they least expect his aid,
The Saviour will appear.

This Abraham found; he raised the knife;
  God saw, and said, "Forbear!
Yon ram shall yield his meaner life:
  Behold the victim there."

Once David seemed Saul's certain prey;
  But hark! the foe's at hand;
Saul turns his arms another way,
  To save th' invaded land.

When Jonah sunk beneath the wave,
  He thought to rise no more;
But God prepared a fish to save,
  And bear him to the shore.

Blessed proofs of power and grace divine
  That meet us in his word!
May every deep-felt care of mine
  Be trusted with the Lord.

Wait for his seasonable aid,
  And though it tarry, wait:
The promise may be long delayed,
  But cannot come too late.

Peace I Leave with You.

Source of my life's refreshing springs,
  Whose presence in my heart sustains me,
Thy love appoints me pleasant things,
  Thy mercy orders all that pains me.

If loving hearts were never lonely,
  If all they wish might always be,
Accepting what they look for only,
  They might be glad, but not in thee.

Well may thy own beloved, who see
  In all their lot their Father's pleasure,
Bear loss of all they love, save thee,
  Their living, everlasting Treasure.

Well may thy happy children cease
  From restless wishes, prone to sin,
And, in thy own exceeding peace,
  Yield to thy daily discipline.

We need as much the cross we bear,
  As air we breathe—as light we see;
It draws us to thy side in prayer,
  It binds us to our strength in thee.

Content.

THOU restless soul!
  How long wilt thou torment me?
  And when shall I prevent thee?
Be still, and yield to my control.
  How long shall thoughts of care
  So wander here and there?
Now on my Saviour all thy burdens roll.

My Lord, my guard,
Who dost through life attend me,
And everywhere defend me,
So that my foes press not too hard;
I trust thy gracious will,
Now, Lord, my murmurs still;
Thy mercies only, let me now regard.

When back again
Storms come to try their power
Lord Jesus, in that hour
So thou wilt at my side remain,
I will in sorrow sing,
To thee my service bring,
And leave my way with thee to make it plain.

I look to thee;
Help thou my weak believing,
All help from thee receiving,
So shall my trust rise up to thee
With every weary breath;
And when thou sendest death,
Then, O, my God, thine own I 'll ever be.

Praise the Lord.

All people that on earth do dwell,
Sing to the Lord with cheerful voice;
Him serve with mirth, his praise forth tell;
Come ye before him and rejoice.

Know that the Lord is God indeed;
  Without our aid he did us make:
We are his flock, he doth us feed,
  And for his sheep he doth us take.

O enter thou his gates with praise,
  Approach with joy his courts unto;
Praise, laud, and bless his name always,
  For it is seemly so to do.

For why? the Lord our God is good,
  His mercy is for ever sure;
His truth at all times firmly stood,
  And shall from age to age endure.

Praising Him.

WHO sings with such rejoicing,
  In tones so loud and sweet?
A lamb from Jesus' pasture,
  A soul at Jesus' feet:
A sinner who through favour
  Is counted as a child,
When he had long lamented
  His heart all sin-defiled.

Here am I ever blessèd,
  Here ever satisfied;
The joys cannot be numbered
  That grow on every side:

My sins are all forgiven,
  My heart is made anew,
I go from earth to heaven,
  And Jesus bears me through.

For this I love and praise him,
  And tell it unto all;
I will gladly do or suffer
  As I hear my Jesus call:
And when my foes come round me,
  They cannot stop my song;
His love doth never fail me,
  And joy doth make me strong.

Come here, all earth's proud children,
  Here is eternal good!
Come here, ye needy sinners,
  Here is reviving food!
Renouncing all rebellion,
  To him allegiance vow,
And make a friend of Jesus—
  Come, all is ready now!

Thou, God, Seest Me.

O God, unseen, but not unknown,
  Thine eye is ever fixed on me;
I dwell beneath thy secret throne,
  Encompassed by the Deity.

Throughout this universe of space,
  To nothing am I long allied,
For flight of time and change of place,
  My strongest, dearest bonds divide.

Parents I had, but where are they?
  Friends whom I knew I know no more;
Companions, once that cheered my way,
  Have dropped behind or gone before.

Now I am one amidst a crowd
  Of life and action hurrying round;
Now left alone—for, like a cloud,
  They came, they went, and are not found.

Even from myself I sometimes part:
  Unconscious sleep is nightly death;
Yet surely by my couch thou art,
  To prompt my pulse, inspire my breath.

Of all that I have done or said,
  How little can I now recall;
Forgotten things to me are dead.
  With thee they live—thou know'st them all.

Thou hast been with me from the womb,
  Witness to every conflict here;
Nor wilt thou leave me at the tomb—
  Before thy bar I must appear.

The moment comes—the only one
  Of all my time to be foretold;
Yet when, and how, and where, can none
  Among the race of men unfold.

The moment comes, when strength shall fail,
  When, health and hope and courage flown,
I must go down into the vale
  And shade of death, with thee alone.

Alone with thee! in that dread strife
  Uphold me in mine agony,
And gently be this dying life
  Exchanged for immortality.

Then, when the unbodied spirit lands
  Where flesh and blood hath never trod,
And in the unveiled presence stands,
  Of thee, my Saviour and my God,

Be mine eternal portion this,
  Since thou wert always here with me,
That I may view thy face in bliss,
  And be for evermore with thee.

God our Preserver.

UPWARD I lift mine eyes,
  From God is all my aid—
The God who built the skies,
  And earth and nature made:
      God is the tower
        To which I fly;
        His grace is nigh
      In every hour.

My feet shall never slide,
  And fall in fatal snares,

Since God, my guard and guide,
  Defends me from my fears:
    Those wakeful eyes,
      That never sleep,
      Shall Israel keep
    When dangers rise.

No burning heats by day,
  Nor blasts of evening air,
Shall take my health away,
  If God be with me there:
    Thou art my sun,
      And thou my shade,
      To guard my head
    By night or noon.

Hast thou not given thy word
  To save my soul from death?
And I can trust my Lord
  To keep my mortal breath:
    I'll go and come,
      Nor fear to die,
      Till from on high
    Thou call me home.

The Lord my Banner.

If God be on my side,
  Then let who will oppose,
For oft, ere now, to him I cried,
  And he hath quelled my foes.

If Jesus be my friend,
  If God doth love me well,
What matters all my foes intend,
  Though strong they be, and fell.

Here I can firmly rest,
  I dare to boast of this,
That God, the highest and the best,
  My Friend and Father is.
From dangerous snares he saves;
  Where'er he bids me go,
He checks the storms and calms the waves,
  Nor lets aught work me woe.

I rest upon the ground
  Of Jesus and his blood,
For 'tis through him that I have found
  The true eternal Good.
Nought have I of mine own,
  Nought in the life I lead:
What Christ hath given me, that alone
  Is worth all love indeed.

His Spirit in me dwells,
  O'er all my mind he reigns,
All care and sadness he dispels,
  And soothes away all pains;
He prospers, day by day,
  His work within my heart,
Till I have strength and faith to say,
  Thou, God, my Father art!

When weakness on me lies,
  And tempts me to despair,
He speaketh words and utters sighs
  Of more than mortal prayer;
But what no tongue can tell,
  Thou, God, canst hear and see,
Who readest in the heart full well
  If aught there pleaseth thee.

He whispers in my breast
  Sweet words of holy cheer,
How he who seeks in God his rest,
  Shall ever find him near;
How God hath built above
  A city fair and new,
Where eye and heart shall see and prove
  What faith hath counted true.

There is prepared on high
  My heritage, my lot;
Though here on earth I fail and die,
  My heaven shall fail me not.
Though here my days are dark,
  And oft my tears must rain,
Where'er my Saviour's light I mark,
  All things grow bright again.

Who joins him to that Lord
  Whom Satan flies and hates,
Shall find himself despised, abhorred;
  For him the burden waits

Of mockery and shame,
  Heaped on his guiltless head;
And crosses, trials, cruel blame,
  Shall be his daily bread.

I knew it long ere now,
  Yet am I not afraid;
The God to whom I pledged my vow
  Will surely send me aid.
At cost of all I have,
  At cost of life and limb,
I cling to God, who yet shall save,
  I will not turn from him.

The world may fail and flee,
  Thou standest fast for ever;
Not fire, or sword, or plague, from thee
  My trusting soul shall sever.
No hunger, and no thirst,
  No poverty or pain,
Let mighty princes do their worst,
  Shall fright me back again.

No joys that angels know,
  No throne or wide-spread fame,
No love or loss, no fear or woe,
  No grief of heart or shame—
Man cannot aught conceive
  Of pleasure or of harm,
That e'er could tempt my soul to leave
  Her refuge in thine arm.

My heart for gladness springs,
  It cannot more be sad,

10

For very joy it laughs and sings,
  Sees nought but sunshine glad.
The sun that glads mine eyes
  Is Christ, the Lord I love,
I sing for joy of that which lies
  Stored up for us above.

Thy Favour is Life.

PASS away, earthly joy,
    Jesus is mine!
Break, every mortal tie,
    Jesus is mine!
Dark is the wilderness;
Distant the resting-place;
Jesus alone can bless:
    Jesus is mine!

Tempt not my soul away,
    Jesus is mine!
Here would I ever stay,
    Jesus is mine!
Perishing things of clay,
Born but for one brief day,
Pass from my heart away:
    Jesus is mine!

Fare ye well, dreams of night,
    Jesus is mine!
Mine is a dawning bright,
    Jesus is mine!

All that my soul has tried
Left but a dismal void;
Jesus has satisfied:
Jesus is mine!

Farewell, mortality,
Jesus is mine!
Welcome, eternity,
Jesus is mine!
Welcome, a Saviour's breast,
Welcome, ye scenes of rest,
Welcome, ye mansions blest:
Jesus is mine!

More than Conquerors.

'Tis finished, 'tis done, the spirit is fled;
The pris'ner is gone, the Christian is dead;
The Christian is living, through Jesus's love,
And gladly receiving a kingdom above.

All honor and praise are Jesus's due:
Supported by grace he fought his way through;
Triumphantly glorious through Jesus's zeal,
And more than victorious o'er sin, death, and hell.

Then let us record the conquering name;
Our Captain and Lord with shoutings proclaim;
Who trust in his passion, and follow our Head,
To certain salvation we all shall be led.

O Jesus! lead on thy militant care;
And give us the crown of righteousness there,
Where, dazzled with glory, the seraphim gaze,
Or prostrate adore thee, in silence of praise.

Come, Lord, and display thy sign in the sky,
And bear us away to mansions on high:
The kingdom be given, the purchase divine,
And crown us in heaven eternally thine.

Sleep.

SLEEP well, thou little guest of earth,
Thou hast the Lord for friend;
Sleep soft, for thou art blest,
In Jesus' hand at rest,
He gives thee blessings without end.

Come on! to such sweet heaven-joy
May he our souls prepare.
Like children if we be,
We shall that glory see,
Then death is only entrance there.

Now sleep, sleep soft, and fear thou nought,
The judgment hath no dread;
Safe in the grave's dark night
Death cannot thee affright,
Jesus himself doth watch thy bed.

O well for thee! so safe, so sure,
Until eternity;
Jesus defends thy sleep,
Jesus sure watch will keep;
How sweet, how soft thy rest shall be!

To-Day.

To-morrow, Lord, is thine,
Lodged in thy sovereign hand;
And if its sun arise and shine,
It shines by thy command.

The present moment flies,
And bears our life away;
O make thy servants truly wise,
That they may live to-day.

Since on this wingéd hour
Eternity is hung,
Waken, by thine almighty power,
The aged and the young.

One thing demands our care;
O be it still pursued!
Lest, slighted once, the season fair
Should never be renewed.

To Jesus may we fly
Swift as the morning light,
Lest life's young golden beams should die
In sudden, endless night.

Be ye Perfect.

O THAT the Lord would guide my ways
To keep his statutes still!
O that my God would grant me grace
To know and do his will.

O send thy Spirit down to write
Thy law upon my heart!
Nor let my tongue indulge deceit,
Nor act the liar's part.

From vanity turn off my eyes;
Let no corrupt design,
Nor covetous desires, arise
Within this soul of mine.

Order my footsteps by thy word,
And make my heart sincere;
Let sin have no dominion, Lord,
But keep my conscience clear.

My soul hath gone too far astray,
My feet too often slip,
Yet since I 've not forgot thy way,
Restore thy wandering sheep.

Make me to walk in thy commands,
'Tis a delightful road;
Nor let my head, or heart, or hands,
Offend against my God.

Time.

O TIME, how few thy value weigh!
How few will estimate a day!
Days, months, and years are rolling on,
The soul neglected and undone.

In painful cares, or empty joys,
Our life its precious hours employs,
While death stands watching at our side,
Eager to stop the living tide.

Was it for this, ye mortal race,
Your Maker gave you here a place?
Was it for this his thoughts designed
The frame of your immortal mind?

For nobler cares, for joys sublime,
He fashioned all the sons of time;
Pilgrims on earth, but soon to be
The heirs of immortality.

This season of your being, know,
Is given to you your seed to sow;
Wisdom and folly's differing grain,
In future worlds is bliss and pain.

Then let me every day review,
Idle or busy, search it through;
And while probation's minutes last,
Let every day amend the past.

Why will ye Die?

SINNERS! turn—why will ye die?
God, your Maker, asks you why:
God, who did your being give,
Made you with himself to live;
He the fatal cause demands;
Asks the work of his own hands—
Why, ye thankless creatures, why
Will ye cross his love and die?

Sinners, turn—why will ye die?
God, your Saviour, asks you why:
He who did your souls retrieve,
Died himself, that ye might live.
Will ye let him die in vain?
Crucify the Lord again?
Why, ye ransomed sinners, why
Will ye slight his grace, and die?

Sinners, turn—why will ye die?
God, the Spirit, asks you why:
He who all your lives hath strove,
Urged you to embrace his love;
Will ye not his grace receive?
Will ye still refuse to live?
O ye dying sinners, why,
Why will ye forever die?

Without Holiness.

CAN sinners hope for heaven
Who love this world so well?
Or dream of future happiness
While on the road to hell?

Shall they hosannas sing
With an unhallowed tongue?
Shall palms adorn the guilty hand
Which does its neighbour wrong?

Can sin's deceitful way
Conduct to Zion's hill?
Or those expect with God to reign,
Who disregard his will?

Thy grace, O God, alone,
Can a good hope afford!
The pardoned and renewed shall see
The glory of the Lord.

Heavenward.

HEAVENWARD our road doth lie,
And as strangers journey we,
O thou promised land on high,
Through the wilderness to thee!
We are but a pilgrim band,
Yonder is our Fatherland.

Heavenward then rise, my soul,
  If to heaven thou art heir;
Let not earth thy love control,
  Lay not up thy riches there:
One who God hath seen and known
Thenceforth turns to him alone.

Heavenward! God saith to me,
  By his word and by his grace;
Shows me where my rest shall be,
  Calls me on to view his face:
When this word is in my heart
Earth and I already part.

Heavenward! my faith doth show
  From afar the shining gates,
And my heart springs up to know
  All that in their folding waits:
Sun and stars too faintly shine
After yonder gleam divine.

Heavenward shall death, at last,
  In his hand my spirit bear;
Safe, at home, all troubles past,
  I shall reign for ever there!
Jesus that same way hath gone,
I with joy may follow on.

Heavenward, ah heavenward!
  This my daily choice shall be;
Earth's sweet voices are unheard,
  I would heaven's glory see:
Heavenward the waves I'll breast
Till in heaven I am at rest.

The Comforter.

OUR blest Redeemer, ere he breathed
His last farewell,
A guide, a Comforter, bequeathed
With us to dwell.

He came in tongues of living flame,
To teach, subdue;
All powerful as the wind he came,
As viewless too.

He comes, his graces to impart;
A willing guest,
While he can find one humble heart
Wherein to rest.

He breathes that gentle voice we hear,
As breeze of even,
That checks each fault, that calms each fear,
And speaks of heaven.

And all the good that we possess,
His gift we own;
Yea, every thought of holiness,
And victory won.

Spirit of purity and grace,
Our weakness see;
O make our hearts thy dwelling-place,
And worthier thee.

Walking with God.

God of the morning, at whose voice
The cheerful sun makes haste to rise,
And, like a giant, doth rejoice
To run his journey through the skies:

From the fair chambers of the east
The circuit of his race begins,
And without weariness or rest,
Round the whole earth he flies and shines.

O like the sun may I fulfil
Th' appointed duties of the day;
With ready mind and active will
March on and keep the heavenly way.

But I shall rove, and lose the race,
If God, my Sun, should disappear,
And leave me in this world's wide maze
To follow every wandering star.

Lord, thy commands are clean and pure,
Enlightening our beclouded eyes;
Thy threatenings just, thy promise sure,
Thy gospel makes the simple wise.

Give me thy counsel for my guide,
And then receive me to thy bliss;
All my desires and hopes beside
Are faint and cold compared with this.

Obedience.

Th' importance of a sacred rite
  Depends upon the Lord;
For he' s a Being infinite,
  And awful is his word.

If he a trifle shall command
  His creatures to fulfil,
'Tis not a trifle to withstand
  Or counteract his will.

Adam might think the thing but small,
  And ventured to transgress;
But it produced a dreadful fall
  To all the human race.

'Twas but a little wherein Saul
  His God did disobey;
But what reward had he for all
  The labour of that day?

The prophet, unto Bethel sent
  With messages express,
Was by a furious lion rent
  For eating at the place.

The man who did refuse to smite
  The prophet of the Lord,
Was slain for his presumptuous slight
  Of the mysterious word.

Naaman contemns, with proud disdain,
  To wash in Jordan's flood,
Concluding that it would be vain,
  Or others were as good.

These may appear but little things
  To do, or not to do;
But see what grievous evil springs
  When not attended to.

Our business is to learn to know
  Our great Redeemer's will,
And with alacrity to go
  His pleasure to fulfil.

Whether the thing be great or small,
  It matters not to us;
He is the Potter, and we all
  Are vessels for his use.

Dependence.

To keep the lamp alive,
  With oil we fill the bowl;
'Tis water makes the willow thrive,
  And grace that feeds the soul.

The Lord's unsparing hand
  Supplies the living stream;
It is not at our own command,
  But still derived from him.

Beware of Peter's word,
  Nor confidently say,
"I never will deny thee, Lord,"
  But "Grant I never may."

Man's wisdom is to seek
  His strength in God alone;
And e'en an angel would be weak,
  Who trusted in his own.

Retreat beneath his wings,
  And in his grace confide;
This more exalts the King of kings
  Than all your work beside.

In Jesus is our store:
  Grace issues from his throne;
Whoever says, "I want no more,"
  Confesses he has none.

Saturday Evening.

SAFELY through another week
  God has brought us on our way,
Let us now a blessing seek
  On the approaching Sabbath-day:
Day of all the week the best,
Emblem of eternal rest.

Mercies, multiplied each hour,
  Through the week our praise demand;

Guarded by Almighty power,
  Fed and guided by his hand.
Though ungrateful we have been,
Only made returns of sin.

While we pray for pardoning grace
  Through the dear Redeemer's name,
Show thy reconciléd face;
  Shine away our sin and shame.
From our worldly care set free,
May we rest this night with thee.

When the morn shall bid us rise,
  May we feel thy presence near!
May thy glory meet our eyes
  When we in thy house appear!
There afford us, Lord, a taste
Of our everlasting feast.

May thy gospel's joyful sound
  Conquer sinners, comfort saints—
Make the fruits of grace abound;
  Bring relief for all complaints:
Thus may all our Sabbaths prove,
Till we join the Church above!

The Morning of a Lord's Day.

EARLY, my God, without delay,
  I haste to seek thy face;
My thirsty spirit faints away
  Without thy cheering grace.

So pilgrims on the scorching sand,
  Beneath a burning sky,
Long for a cooling stream at hand;
  And they must drink or die.

I've seen thy glory and thy power
  Through all thy temple shine;
My God, repeat that heavenly hour
  That vision so divine!

Not all the blessings of a feast
  Can please my soul so well
As when thy richer grace I taste,
  And in thy presence dwell.

Not life itself, with all her joys,
  Can my best passions move,
Or raise so high my cheerful voice,
  As thy forgiving love.

Thus till my last expiring day
  I'll bless my God and King;
Thus will I lift my hands to pray,
  And tune my lips to sing.

The Eternal Sabbath.

LORD of the Sabbath, hear our vows
On this thy day, in this thy house;
And own, as grateful sacrifice,
The songs which from the desert rise.

Thine earthly Sabbaths, Lord, we love,
But there' s a nobler rest above;
To that our labouring souls aspire
With ardent pangs of strong desire.

No more fatigue, no more distress,
Nor sin nor hell shall reach the place;
No groans to mingle with the songs
Which warble from immortal tongues.

No rude alarms of raging foes;
No cares to break the long repose;
No midnight shade, no clouded sun,
But sacred, high, eternal noon.

O long-expected day, begin;
Dawn on these realms of woe and sin;
Fain would we leave this weary road,
And sleep in death to rest with God.

The Anchor.

I KNOW in whom I believe,
And that he doth live on high;
When down in the dust I lie
He will my spirit receive.

I know unto whom I flee
When all else totters and falls;
Who heareth my trembling calls,
And reacheth his hand to me.

I know my faith's resting-place;
I know when this earth grows dim
I shall forever see him,
My Lord! even face to face.

He will dry away my tears,
So comforting and so kind!
And in him my restless mind
Shall be still through endless years!

I know by whom I shall rise
When I am glorified;
I shall stand at Jesus' side,
With a life that never dies.

Sure and Steadfast.

The promises I sing,
Which sovereign love hath spoke;
Nor will the eternal King
His words of grace revoke;
They stand secure
And steadfast still;
Not Zion's hill
Abides so sure.

The mountains melt away
When once the Judge appears,

And sun and moon decay,
  That measure mortals' years;
    But still the same,
      In radiant lines,
      The promise shines
    Through all the flame.

Their harmony shall sound
  Through my attentive ears,
When thunders cleave the ground,
  And dissipate the spheres;
    'Midst all the shock
      Of that dread scene,
      I stand serene,
    Thy word my rock.

By Faith we Know.

O FAITH! thou workest miracles
  Upon the hearts of men,
Choosing thy home in those same hearts
  We know not how or when.

To one thy grave unearthly truths
  A heavenly vision seem;
While to another's eye they are
  A superstitious dream.

To one the deepest doctrines look
  So naturally true,
That when he learns the lesson first
  He hardly thinks it new.

To other hearts the selfsame truths
No light or heat can bring;
They are but puzzling phrases strung
Like beads upon a string.

O gift of gifts! O grace of Faith!
My God! how can it be
That thou, who hast discerning love,
Shouldst give that gift to me?

There was a place, there was a time,
Whether by night or day,
Thy Spirit came and left that gift,
And went upon his way.

How many hearts thou mightst have had
More innocent than mine!
How many souls more worthy far
Of that sweet touch of thine!

Ah Grace! into unlikeliest hearts
It is thy boast to come;
The glory of thy light to find
In darkest spots a home.

How will they die, how will they die,
How bear the cross of grief,
Who have not got the light of faith,
The courage of belief?

The crowd of cares, the weightiest cross,
Seem trifles less than light,—
Earth looks so little and so low
When faith shines full and bright.

O happy, happy that I am!
  If thou canst be, O Faith!
The treasure that thou art in life,
  What wilt thou be in death?

Thy choice, O God of goodness, then
  I lovingly adore;
O give me grace to keep thy grace,
  And grace to merit more!

The Sinner to Christ.

MY spirit longeth for thee
  To dwell within my breast;
Although I am unworthy
  Of so divine a guest!

Of so divine a guest
  Unworthy though I be;
Yet hath my heart no rest
  Until it come to thee!

Until it come to thee,
  In vain I look around;
In all that I can see,
  No rest is to be found!

No rest is to be found
  But in thy bleeding love:
O! let my wish be crowned,
  And send it from above!

Dies Iræ.

The day of wrath! that dreadful day,
When heaven and earth shall pass away!
What power shall be the sinner's stay?
How shall he meet that dreadful day?

When, shrivelling like a parchèd scroll,
The flaming heavens together roll;
When louder yet, and yet more dread,
Swells the high trump that wakes the dead:

Oh on that day, that wrathful day,
When man to judgment wakes from clay;
Be thou, O Christ, the sinner's stay,
Though heaven and earth shall pass away.

Without Power.

How sad our state by nature is!
Our sin how deep it stains!
And Satan holds our captive minds
Fast in his slavish chains.

But there 's a voice of sovereign grace
Sounds from the sacred word,
Ho, ye despairing sinners, come,
And trust upon the Lord.

My soul obeys th' almighty call,
  And runs to this relief;
I would believe thy promise, Lord,
  O help my unbelief.

To the dear fountain of thy blood,
  Incarnate God, I fly;
Here let me wash my spotted soul
  From crimes of deepest dye.

Stretch out thine arm, victorious King,
  My reigning sins subdue;
Drive the old dragon from his seat,
  With his apostate crew.

A guilty, weak, and helpless worm,
  On thy kind arms I fall;
Be thou my strength and righteousness,
  My Jesus, and my all.

Christ and His Righteousness

No more, my God, I boast no more
  Of all the duties I have done;
I quit the hopes I held before
  To trust the merits of thy Son.

Now, for the love I bear his name,
  What was my gain I count my loss;
My former pride I call my shame,
  And nail my glory to his cross.

12

Yes, and I must and will esteem
All things but loss for Jesus' sake;
O may my soul be found in him,
And of his righteousness partake!

The best obedience of my hands
Dares not appear before thy throne;
But faith can answer thy demands
By pleading what my Lord has done.

What is your Life?

THOU God of glorious majesty,
To thee, against myself, to thee,
A worm of earth, I cry;
A half-awakened child of man,
An heir of endless bliss or pain,
A sinner born to die.

Lo! on a narrow neck of land,
'Twixt two unbounded seas, I stand,
Secure, insensible;
A point of time, a moment's space,
Removes me to that heavenly place,
Or shuts me up in hell.

O God, my inmost soul convert,
And deeply on my thoughtful heart
Eternal things impress;
Give me to feel their solemn weight,
And tremble on the brink of fate,
And wake to righteousness.

Before me place, in dread array,
The pomp of that tremendous day
  When thou with clouds shalt come
To judge the nations at thy bar;
And tell me, Lord, shall I be there
  To meet a joyful doom?

Be this my one great business here,
With serious industry and fear
  Eternal bliss t' ensure;
Thine utmost counsel to fulfil,
And suffer all thy righteous will,
  And to the end endure.

Then, Saviour, then my soul receive,
Transported from this vale, to live
  And reign with thee above,
Where faith is sweetly lost in sight,
And hope in full, supreme delight,
  And everlasting love.

Save, Lord, or I Perish.

O Jesus, in pity draw near;
  Come quickly to help a lost soul;
To comfort a mourner, appear,
  And make a poor penitent whole:
The balm of thy mercy apply
  (Thou seest the sore anguish I feel);
Save, Lord, or I perish, I die;
  O save, or I sink into hell.

I sink, if thou longer delay
Thy pardoning mercy to show;
Come quickly, and kindly display
The power of thy passion below:
By all thou hast done for my sake,
One drop of thy blood I implore;
Now, now let it touch me, and make
The sinner a sinner no more.

The Christian Race.

AWAKE, my soul, stretch every nerve,
And press with vigour on;
A heavenly race demands thy zeal,
And an immortal crown.

A crowd of witnesses around
Hold thee in full survey;
Forget the steps already trod,
And onward urge thy way.

'Tis God's all-animating voice
That calls thee from on high;
'Tis his own hand presents the prize
To thine aspiring eye;—

That prize, with peerless glories bright,
Which shall new lustre boast,
When victors' wreaths and monarchs' gems
Shall blend in common dust.

Blest Saviour, introduced by thee,
 Have I my race begun;
And crowned with victory, at thy feet
 I 'll lay my honours down.

Not unto Us.

The countless multitude on high,
 Who tune their songs to Jesus' name,
All merit of their own deny,
 And Jesus' worth alone proclaim.

Firm, on the ground of sovereign grace,
 They stand before Jehovah's throne;
The only song in that blest place
 Is, "Thou art worthy, thou alone."

With spotless robes of purest white,
 And branches of triumphal palm,
They shout, with transports of delight,
 The ceaseless, universal psalm:

"Salvation's glory all be paid
 To him who sits upon the throne,
And to the Lamb, whose blood was shed;
 Thou, thou art worthy, thou alone."

Christ our Sacrifice.

Not all the blood of beasts
  On Jewish altars slain,
Could give the guilty conscience peace,
  Or wash away the stain.

But Christ, the heavenly Lamb,
  Takes all our sins away;
A sacrifice of nobler name,
  And richer blood, than they.

My faith would lay her hand
  On that dear head of thine,
While like a penitent I stand,
  And there confess my sin.

My soul looks back to see
  The burdens thou didst bear
When hanging on the cursèd tree,
  And hopes her guilt was there.

Believing, we rejoice
  To see the curse remove;
We bless the Lamb with cheerful voice,
  And sing his bleeding love.

The Good Physician.

How lost was my condition
  Till Jesus made me whole!
There is but one Physician
  Can cure a sin-sick soul!

Next door to death he found me,
  And ransomed from the grave,
To tell to all around me
  His wond'rous power to save.

The worst of all diseases
  Is light compared with sin;
On every part it seizes,
  But rages most within:
'Tis palsy, plague, and fever,
  And madness—all combined;
And none but a believer
  The least relief can find.

From men great skill professing,
  I thought a cure to gain;
But this proved more distressing,
  And added to my pain:
Some said that nothing ailed me,
  Some gave me up for lost;
Thus every refuge failed me,
  And all my hopes were crossed.

At length this great Physician—
  How matchless is his grace!—
Accepted my petition,
  And undertook my case:
First gave me sight to view him,
  For sin my eyes had sealed,
Then bade me look unto him:
  I looked, and I was healed.

A dying, risen Jesus,
  Seen by the eye of faith,

At once from anguish frees us,
And saves the soul from death:
Come then to this Physician,
His help he'll freely give,
He makes no hard condition,
'Tis only—look, and live.

The New Covenant Sealed.

"THE promise of my Father's love
Shall stand for ever good;"
He said—and gave his soul to death,
And sealed the grace with blood.

To this dear covenant of thy word
I set my worthless name;
I seal the engagement to my Lord,
And make my humble claim.

Thy light, and strength, and pardoning grace
And glory shall be mine;
My life and soul, my heart and flesh,
And all my powers are thine.

I call that legacy my own,
Which Jesus did bequeath;
'Twas purchased with a dying groan,
And ratified in death.

Sweet is the memory of his name
  Who blest us in his will;
And to the test'ment of his love
  Made his own life the seal!

Praise.

KING of glorie, King of peace,
      I will love thee:
And that love may never cease,
      I will move thee.

Thou hast granted my request,
      Thou hast heard me:
Thou didst note my working breast,
      Thou hast spared me.

Wherefore with my utmost art
      I will sing thee,
And the cream of all my heart
      I will bring thee.

Though my sinnes against me cried,
      Thou didst clear me;
And alone, when they replied,
      Thou didst heare me.

Seven whole dayes, not one in seven,
      I will praise thee.
In my heart, though not in heaven,
      I can raise thee.

Thou grew'st soft and moist with tears,
Thou relentedst;
And when Justice called for fears,
Thou dissentedst.

Small it is, in this poore sort,
To enroll thee:
Even eternitie is too short
To extoll thee.

Hope Thou in God.

O MY soul, what means this sadness?
Wherefore art thou thus cast down?
Let thy griefs be turned to gladness;
Bid thy restless fears be gone:
Look to Jesus,
And rejoice in his dear name.

What though Satan's strong temptations
Vex and grieve thee day by day;
And thy sinful inclinations
Often fill thee with dismay:
Thou shalt conquer,
Through the Lamb's redeeming blood.

Though ten thousand ills beset thee,
From without and from within;
Jesus saith he 'll ne'er forget thee,
But will save from hell and sin:
He is faithful
To perform his gracious word.

Though distresses now attend thee,
  And thou tread'st the thorny road,
His right hand shall still defend thee;
  Soon he'll bring thee home to God!
    Therefore praise him—
Praise the great Redeemer's name.

O that I could now adore him
  Like the heavenly host above,
Who forever bow before him,
  And unceasing sing his love!
    Happy songsters!
When shall I your chorus join?

Thou art Worthy.

GLORY to God on high!
Let earth and skies reply;
  Praise ye his name:
His love and grace adore,
Who all our sorrows bore;
Sing loud for evermore,
  Worthy the Lamb.

Jesus, our Lord and God,
Bore sin's tremendous load;
  Praise ye his name:
Tell what his arm hath done,
What spoils from death he won;
Sing his great name alone:
  Worthy the Lamb.

While they around the throne
Cheerfully join in one,
  Praising his name:
Those who have felt his blood
Sealing their peace with God,
Sound his dear name abroad:
  Worthy the Lamb.

Join, all ye ransomed race,
Our holy Lord to bless;
  Praise ye his name:
In him we will rejoice,
And make a joyful noise,
Shouting with heart and voice,
  Worthy the Lamb.

What though we change our place,
Yet we shall never cease
  Praising his name:
To him our songs we bring,
Hail him our gracious King,
And without ceasing sing,
  Worthy the Lamb.

Then let the hosts above,
In realms of endless love,
  Praise his dear name:
To him ascribéd be
Honour and majesty,
Through all eternity:
  Worthy the Lamb.

The Leopard, his Spots.

How helpless guilty nature lies,
Unconscious of its load!
The heart, unchanged, can never rise
To happiness and God.

The will perverse, the passions blind,
In paths of ruin stray;
Reason, debased, can never find
The safe, the narrow way.

Can aught beneath a power divine
The stubborn will subdue?
'Tis thine, almighty Saviour, thine,
To form the heart anew.

'Tis thine the passions to recall,
And bid them upward rise;
And make the scales of errour fall
From reason's darkened eyes.

To chase the shades of death away,
And bid the sinner live;
A beam of heaven, a vital ray,
Tis thine alone to give.

O change these wretched hearts of ours,
And give them life divine!
Then shall our passions and our powers,
Almighty Lord, be thine.

Wilt Thou be Made Clean?

Come to Calvary's holy mountain,
Sinners ruined by the fall;
Here a pure and healing fountain
Flows to you, to me, to all,
In a full, perpetual tide,
Opened when our Saviour died.

Come in poverty and meanness,
Come defiled, without, within;
From infection and uncleanness,
From the leprosy of sin,
Wash your robes, and make them white:
Ye shall walk with God in light.

Come, in sorrow and contrition,
Wounded, impotent, and blind;
Here the guilty, free remission,
Here the troubled, peace may find;
Health this fountain will restore,
He that drinks shall thirst no more.

He that drinks shall live forever;
'Tis a soul-renewing flood:
God is faithful—God will never
Break his covenant in blood;
Signed when our Redeemer died,
Sealed when he was glorified.

Lord, I Believe.

UNTO thine altar, Lord,
A broken heart I bring;
And wilt thou graciously accept
Of such a worthless thing?

To Christ, the bleeding Lamb,
My faith directs its eyes;
Thou mayst reject that worthless thing,
But not his sacrifice.

When he gave up his life
The law was satisfied;
And now to its severer claims,
I answer, "Jesus died."

The Evil that I Would Not.

JESUS my God, my All in all,
Display thy power, unveil thy face:
Wilt thou not hear when sinners call?
Is not thy reign a reign of grace?

A thousand times my tongue hath said,
"Bought with a price, I'm not my own;"
A thousand times my soul hath fled
And sought relief before thy throne.

But now I grope as in the night,
  I can't believe, I dare not trust;
My path is hedged, I see no light,
  My hopes are prostrate in the dust.

With fears that all experience past
  Has been delusive, false, and vain,
I dread, lest falling short at last,
  I never shall the prize obtain.

When to the cross I wish to fly,
  And see the blood of sprinkling flow,
To Sinai's mount, not Calvary,
  A legal spirit bids me go.

Striving to stretch my withered arms,
  I fain would give myself away;
But sins and guilt excite alarms,
  And check a near approach to thee.

O! if already I've believed,
  If Christ and I indeed are one,
Then prove thyself my Help and Shield,
  Or let the work be now begun.

Show me a token, Lord, for good,
  And let me know that I am thine;
Dispel my doubts, disperse the cloud,
  And on my soul benignant shine.

Now let thy Spirit from above
  Bear witness to my troubled heart;
Now shed abroad my Father's love,
  And filial confidence impart.

Then shall my foes, who hate me, see
That God is faithful to his saints;
That he hath heard and helpéd me,
And changed to praise my sad complaints.

The Key of the Morning and the Lock of Night.

Come to the morning prayer,
Come let us kneel and pray;
Prayer is the Christian pilgrim's staff
To walk with God all day.

At noon, beneath the Rock
Of Ages rest and pray;
Sweet is that shadow from the heat
When the sun smites by day.

At eve, shut to the door,
Round the home altar pray,
And finding there "the house of God,"
At "heaven's gate" close the day.

When midnight seals our eyes,
Let each in spirit say,
"I sleep, but my heart waketh, Lord,
With thee to watch and pray."

Power of Prayer.

In themselves as weak as worms,
  How can poor believers stand,
When temptations, foes, and storms
  Press them close on every hand?

Weak, indeed, they feel they are,
  But they know the throne of grace;
And the God who answers prayer
  Helps them when they seek his face.

Though the Lord awhile delay,
  Succour they at length obtain;
He who taught their hearts to pray
  Will not let them cry in vain.

Wrestling prayer can wonders do,
  Bring relief in deepest straits;
Prayer can force a passage through
  Iron bars and brazen gates.

Hezekiah, on his knees,
  Proud Assyria's host subdued;
And when smitten with disease,
  Had his life by prayer renewed.

Peter, though confined and chained,
  Prayer prevailed and brought him out;
When Elijah prayed it rained,
  After three long years of drought.

We can likewise witness bear
  That the Lord is still the same;
Though we feared he would not hear,
  Suddenly deliverance came.

For the wonders he has wrought
  Let us now our praises give;
And by sweet experience taught,
  Call upon him while we live.

The Morning Light.

JESUS, Sun of righteousness,
  Brightest beam of love divine,
With thy early morning rays
  Do thou on our darkness shine;
And dispel with purest light
All our night!

As on drooping herb or flower
  Falls the soft, refreshing dew,
Let thy Spirit's grace and power
  All our weary souls renew;
Showers of blessing over all
Softly fall!

Like the sun's reviving ray,
  May thy love, with tender glow,
All our coolness melt away,
  Warm and cheer us forth to go,
Gladly serve thee and obey
All the day!

O our only Hope and Guide!
Never leave us nor forsake:
Keep us ever at thy side
Till the eternal morning break;
Moving on to Zion's hill,
Homeward still!

Lead us all our days and years
In thy straight and narrow way;
Lead us through the vale of tears
To the land of perfect day,
Where thy people, fully blest,
Safely rest!

At Evening Time it Shall be Light.

We journey through a vale of tears
By many a cloud o'ercast;
And worldly cares and worldly fears
Go with us to the last.

Not to the last! Thy word hath said,
Could we but read aright,
Poor pilgrim, lift in hope thy head;
At eve it shall be light!

Though earthborn shadows now may shroud
Thy stormy path awhile;
God's blessèd word can part each cloud,
And bid the sunshine smile.

Only believe in living faith,
  His love and power divine;
And ere thy sun shall set in death,
  His light shall round thee shine.

When tempest clouds are dark on high,
  His bow of love and peace
Shines sweetly in the vaulted sky—
  A pledge that storms shall cease.

Hold on thy way with hope unchilled,
  By faith and not by sight,
And thou shalt own his word fulfilled;
  At eve it shall be light!

Heaven.

NOR eye hath seen, nor ear hath heard,
  Nor sense nor reason known,
What joys the Father has prepared
  For those who love the Son.

But the good Spirit of the Lord
  Reveals a heaven to come:
The beams of glory in his word,
  Allure and guide us home.

Pure are the joys above the sky,
  And all the region peace;
No wanton lips nor envious eye
  Can see or taste the bliss.

Those holy gates forever bar
  Pollution, sin, and shame;
None shall obtain admittance there
  But followers of the Lamb.

He keeps the Father's book of life,
  There all their names are found;
The hypocrite in vain shall strive
  To tread the heavenly ground.

The Heavenly Mariner.

THROUGH tribulations deep
  The way to glory is;
This stormy course I keep
  On these tempestuous seas:
By waves and winds I 'm tossed and driven,
Freighted with grace, and bound for heaven.

Sometimes temptations blow
  A dreadful hurricane,
And high the waters flow,
  And o'er the sides break in;
But still my little ship out-braves
The blustering winds and surging waves.

When I, in my distress,
  My anchor, Hope, can cast
Within the promises,
  It holds my vessel fast:
Safely she then at anchor rides,
Midst stormy blasts and swelling tides.

If a dead calm ensues,
And heaven no breezes give,
The oar of prayer I use,
And try, and toil, and strive;
Through storms and calms, for many a day,
I make but very little way.

But when a heavenly breeze
Springs up and fills my sail,
My vessel goes with ease
Before the pleasant gale;
And runs as much an hour or more
As in a month or two before.

Hid by the clouds from sight,
The sun doth not appear;
Nor can I in the night
Behold the moon or stars;
Sometimes for days and weeks, or more,
I cannot see the sky and shore.

As at the time of noon
My quadrant faith I take,
To view my Christ, my Sun,
If he the clouds should break:
I'm happy when his face I see,
I know then whereabouts I be.

Ere I can reach heaven's coast
I must a gulf pass through,
Which fatal proves to most,
For all this passage go;
But all death's waves can't me o'erwhelm,
If God himself is at my helm.

When through this gulf I get,
  Though rough, it is but short;
The pilot angels meet
  And bring me into port;
And when I land on that blest shore
I shall be safe for evermore.

Home in View.

As when the weary traveller gains
  The height of some o'erlooking hill,
His heart revives, if 'cross the plains
  He eyes his home, though distant still.

While he surveys the much-loved spot
  He slights the space that lies between;
His past fatigues are now forgot,
  Because his journey's end is seen.

Thus when the Christian pilgrim views
  By faith his mansion in the skies,
The sight his fainting strength renews,
  And wings his speed to reach the prize.

The thought of home his spirit cheers;
  No more he grieves for troubles past,
Nor any future trial fears
  So he may safe arrive at last.

'Tis there, he says, I am to dwell
  With Jesus in the realms of day;
Then I shall bid my cares farewell,
  And he shall wipe my tears away.

Jesus, on thee our hope depends,
To lead us on to thine abode:
Assured our home will make amends
For all our toil while on the road.

The Christian Mourner's Prospect of Death.

THE hour, the hour, the parting hour
That takes from this dark world its power,
And lays at once the thorn and flower
On the same withering bier, my soul!
The hour that ends all earthly woes,
And gives the wearied soul repose;
How soft, how sweet that last long close
Of mortal hope and fear, my soul!

How sweet, while on this broken lyre
The melodies of time expire,
To feel it strung with chords of fire
To praise the immortal One, my soul!
And while our farewell tears we pour
To those we leave on this cold shore,
To feel that we shall weep no more,
Nor dwell alone in heaven, my soul!

How sweet, while waning fast away
The stars of this dim world decay,
To hail, prophetic of the day,
The golden dawn arise, my soul!

To feel we only sleep to rise
In sunnier lands and fairer skies;
To bind again our broken ties
In ever-living love, my soul!

The hour, the hour, so pure and calm,
That bathes the wounded soul in balm,
And round the pale brow twines the palm
That shuns this wintry clime, my soul!
The hour that draws o'er earth and all
Its briars and blooms the mortal pall;
How soft, how sweet that evening-fall
Of fears, and grief, and time, my soul!

Submission.

Be still, my soul! the Lord is on thy side;
Bear patiently the cross of grief and pain;
Leave to thy God to order and provide—
In every change he faithful will remain.
Be still, my soul! thy best, thy heavenly Friend,
Through thorny ways leads to a joyful end.

Be still, my soul! thy God doth undertake
To guide the future, as he has the past:
Thy hope, thy confidence let nothing shake,
All now mysterious shall be bright at last.
Be still, my soul! the waves and winds still know
His voice who ruled them while he dwelt below.

Be still, my soul! when dearest friends depart,
  And all is darkened in the vale of tears,
Then shalt thou better know his love, his heart,
  Who comes to soothe thy sorrow and thy fears.
Be still, my soul! thy Jesus can repay,
From his own fulness, all he takes away.

Be still, my soul! the hour is hastening on
  When we shall be for ever with the Lord—
When disappointment, grief, and fear are gone,
  Sorrow forgot, love's purest joys restored.
Be still, my soul! when change and tears are past,
All safe and blessèd we shall meet at last.

Be still, my soul! begin the song of praise
  On earth, believing, to thy Lord on high;
Acknowledge him in all thy works and ways,
  So shall he view thee with a well-pleased eye.
Be still, my soul! the Sun of life divine
Through passing clouds shall but more brightly shine.

God our Shepherd.

THE Lord my Shepherd is,
  I shall be well supplied;
Since he is mine, and I am his,
  What can I want beside?

He leads me to the place
  Where heavenly pasture grows;
Where living waters gently pass,
  And full salvation flows.

If e'er I go astray,
He doth my soul reclaim,
And guides me in his own right way,
For his most holy name.

While he affords his aid,
I cannot yield to fear;
Though I should walk through death's dark shade,
My Shepherd 's with me there.

In spite of all my foes,
Thou dost my table spread;
My cup with blessings overflows,
And joy exalts my head.

The bounties of thy love
Shall crown my following days;
Nor from thy house will I remove,
Nor cease to speak thy praise.

Nothing Shall Hurt You.

DEAR Lord, though bitter is the cup
Thy gracious hand pours out to me,
I cheerfully will drink it up;
That cannot hurt which comes from thee.

'Tis filled with thy unchanging love,
And not a drop of wrath is there;
The saints, forever blessed above,
Were often most afflicted here.

From Jesus thy incarnate Son,
  I'll learn obedience to thy will;
And humbly kiss the chastening rod,
  When its severest strokes I feel.

Lord, Help Me.

THE way seems dark about me—overhead
The clouds have long since met in gloomy spread,
And when I looked to see the day break through,
Cloud after cloud came up with volume new.

And in that shadow I have passed along,
Feeling myself grow weak as it grew strong,
Walking in doubt, and searching for the way,
And often at a stand—as now to-day.

And if before me on the path there lies
A spot of brightness from imagined skies,
Imagined shadows fall across it too,
And the far future takes the present's hue.

Perplexities do throng upon my sight,
Like scudding fog-banks, to obscure the light;
Some new dilemma rises every day,
And I can only shut my eyes and pray.

Lord, I am not sufficient for these things.
Give me the light that thy sweet presence brings;
Give me thy grace, give me thy constant strength—
Lord, for my comfort now appear at length.

It may be that my way doth seem confused,
Because my heart of thy way is afraid;
Because my eyes have constantly refused
To see the only opening thou hast made.

Because my will would cross some flowery plain
Where thou hast thrown a hedge from side to side;
And turneth from the stony walk of pain,
Its trouble or its ease not even tried.

If thus I try to force my way along,
The smoothest road encumbered is for me;
For were I as an angel swift and strong,
I could not go unless allowed by thee.

And now I pray thee, Lord, to lead thy child—
Poor wretched wanderer from thy grace and love—
Whatever way thou pleasest through the wild,
So it but take her to thy home above.

For Victory.

Jesus, help conquer!
My spirit is sinking,
Deep waters of sorrow go over my head;
Weeping, and trembling,
And fearing, and shrinking,
I watch for the day, and night cometh instead.
Bitter the cup
I am hourly drinking—
How thorny the path that I hourly tread!

Jesus, help conquer!
For, fainting and weary,
Scarcely my hands can their weapons sustain;
The way seems so desolate,
Painful, and dreary—
How shall I ever to heaven attain?
Jesus, great Captain!
If thou be not near me,
How shall I ever the victory gain?

Jesus, help conquer!
Earth holds out her lure,
And mortal affections yearn after the prize:
Scarcely my heart
Can the struggle endure;
Scarce can I lift up my tear-blinded eyes.
Jesus, Redeemer!
Thy promise is sure—
Speak to my spirit, and bid me arise.

Jesus, help conquer!
There is not an hour
Of sorrow or joy but is ordered by thee;
Thou dost cut down,
Who hast planted the flower—
Tempest or calm at thy bidding shall be.
Look on my sorrow,
And give me the power
Humbly to wait till thou comfortest me.

Jesus, help conquer!
Lord, turn not away!
See with what power the billows increase!

Give me thy love
For my comfort and stay,
Then shall my trembling and murmuring cease.
Then shall my spirit
Grow strong for the fray—
Then shall my weary heart rest in thy peace.

Jesus, help conquer!
I cry unto thee!
Hardly my heart its petitions can frame:
All is so dark
And so painful to me,
All I can utter, sometimes, is thy name.
Jesus, help conquer!
My portion now be,
Though all else should change, be thou ever the same.

Providence.

When all thy mercies, O my God,
My rising soul surveys,
Transported with the view, I'm lost
In wonder, love, and praise.

O how shall words, with equal warmth,
The gratitude declare
That glows within my ravished heart!
But thou canst read it there.

To all my weak complaints and cries
  Thy mercy lent an ear,
Ere yet my feeble thoughts had learnt
  To form themselves in prayer.

Unnumbered comforts to my soul
  Thy tender care bestowed,
Before my infant heart conceived
  From whom those comforts flowed.

When in the slippery paths of youth
  With heedless steps I ran,
Thine arm, unseen, conveyed me safe,
  And led me up to man.

Through hidden dangers, toils, and deaths,
  It gently cleared my way,
And through the pleasing snares of vice,
  More to be feared than they.

When worn with sickness, oft hast thou
  With health renewed my face,
And when in sin and sorrow sunk,
  Revived my soul with grace.

Thy bounteous hand, with worldly bliss
  Has made my cup run o'er,
And in a kind and faithful friend
  Has doubled all my store.

Ten thousand thousand precious gifts
  My daily thanks employ,
Nor is the least a cheerful heart
  That tastes those gifts with joy.

Through every period of my life
  Thy goodness I'll pursue,
And after death, in distant worlds
  The glorious theme renew.

When nature fails, and day and night
  Divide thy works no more,
My ever-grateful heart, O Lord,
  Thy mercy shall adore.

Through all eternity to thee
  A joyful song I'll raise;
For oh! eternity 's too short
  To utter all thy praise.

Grace.

GRACE! 'tis a charming sound,
  Harmonious to my ear;
Heaven with the echo shall resound,
  And all the earth shall hear!

Grace first contrived a way
  To save rebellious man,
And all the steps that grace display,
  Which drew the wondrous plan.

Grace taught my wandering feet
  To tread the heavenly road;
And new supplies each hour I meet,
  While pressing on to God.

Grace all the work shall crown
Through everlasting days;
It lays in heaven the topmost stone,
And well deserves the praise.

Keep not Silence.

SOUND, sound the truth abroad,
Bear ye the word of God
Through the wide world;
Tell what our Lord has done,
Tell how the day was won;
And from his lofty throne
Satan is hurled.

Far over sea and land,
'Tis our Lord's own command,
Bear ye his name;
Bear it to every shore,
Regions unknown explore,
Enter at every door—
Silence is shame.

Speed on the wings of love;
Jesus, who reigns above,
Bids us to fly:
They who his message bear,
Should neither doubt nor fear;
He will their friend appear,
He will be nigh.

When on the mighty deep,
He will their spirits keep,
Stayed on his word;
When in a foreign land,
No other friend at hand,
Jesus will by them stand—
Jesus, their Lord.

Ye, who forsaking all
At your loved Master's call,
Comforts resign;
Soon will the work be done;
Soon will the prize be won;
Brighter than yonder sun
Then shall ye shine.

The Rebel's Surrender.

LORD, thou hast won, at length I yield;
My heart, by mighty grace compelled,
Surrenders all to thee;
Against thy terrors long I strove,
But who can stand against thy love?
Love conquers even me.

All that a wretch could do, I tried,
Thy patience scorned, thy power defied,
And trampled on thy laws;
Scarcely thy martyrs, at the stake,
Could stand more steadfast for thy sake
Than I in Satan's cause.

But since thou hast thy love revealed,
And shown my soul a pardon sealed,
I can resist no more:
Couldst thou for such a sinner bleed?
Canst thou for such a rebel plead?
I wonder and adore!

If thou hadst bid thy thunders roll,
And lightnings flash to blast my soul,
I still had stubborn been:
But mercy has my heart subdued,
A bleeding Saviour I have viewed,
And now I hate my sin.

Now, Lord, I would be thine alone;
Come take possession of thine own,
For thou hast set me free;
Released from Satan's hard command,
See all my powers waiting stand,
To be employed by thee.

My will conformed to thine would move;
On thee my hope, desire, and love,
In fixed attention join;
My hands, my eyes, my ears, my tongue,
Have Satan's servants been too long,
But now they shall be thine.

And can I be the very same
Who lately durst blaspheme thy name,
And on thy gospel tread?
Surely each one who hears my case
Will praise thee, and confess thy grace
Invincible indeed!

The Change.

I WAS a grovelling creature once,
And basely cleaved to earth;
I wanted spirit to renounce
The clod that gave me birth.

But God has breathed upon a worm,
And sent me from above
Wings such as clothe an angel's form,
The wings of joy and love.

With these to Pisgah's top I fly,
And there delighted stand,
To view beneath a shining sky
The spacious promised land.

The Lord of all the vast domain
Has promised it to me:
The length and breadth of all the plain,
As far as faith can see.

How glorious is my privilege!
To thee for help I call;
I stand upon a mountain's edge,
O save me, lest I fall!

Though much exalted in the Lord,
My strength is not my own;
Then let me tremble at his word,
And none shall cast me down.

A Prayer, Living and Dying

Rock of ages, cleft for me,
Let me hide myself in thee;
Let the water and the blood
From thy riven side which flowed,
Be of sin the double cure,
Cleanse me from its guilt and power.

Not the labours of my hands
Can fulfil thy law's demands:
Could my zeal no respite know,
Could my tears forever flow;
All for sin could not atone,
Thou must save, and thou alone.

Nothing in my hand I bring,
Simply to thy cross I cling;
Naked come to thee for dress,
Helpless look to thee for grace:
Foul I to the fountain fly,
Wash me, Saviour, or I die.

While I draw this fleeting breath,
When my eye-strings break in death;
When I soar to worlds unknown,
See thee on the judgment throne;
Rock of ages, cleft for me,
Let me hide myself in thee.

Peace after a Storm.

WHEN darkness long has veiled my mind,
 And smiling day once more appears;
Then, my Redeemer, then I find
 The folly of my doubts and fears.

Straight I upbraid my wandering heart,
 And blush that I should ever be
Thus prone to act so base a part,
 Or harbour one hard thought of thee!

Oh! let me then at length be taught,
 What I am still so slow to learn:
That God is love, and changes not,
 Nor knows the shadow of a turn.

Sweet truth, and easy to repeat!
 But when my faith is sharply tried
I find myself a learner yet,
 Unskilful, weak, and apt to slide.

But O, my Lord, one look from thee
 Subdues my disobedient will;
Drives doubt and discontent away,
 And thy rebellious worm is still.

Thou art as ready to forgive
 As I am ready to repine;
Thou, therefore, all the praise receive;
 Be shame and self-abhorrence mine.

The Fountain Opened.

THERE is a fountain filled with blood
Drawn from Emmanuel's veins,
And sinners plunged beneath that flood,
Lose all their guilty stains.

The dying thief rejoiced to see
That fountain in his day,
And there have I, as vile as he,
Washed all my sins away.

Dear dying Lamb, thy precious blood
Shall never lose its power,
Till all the ransomed church of God
Be saved, to sin no more.

E'er since, by faith, I saw the stream
Thy flowing wounds supply,
Redeeming love has been my theme,
And shall be till I die.

Then in a nobler, sweeter song,
I'll sing thy power to save;
When this poor lisping stammering tongue
Lies silent in the grave.

Lord, I believe thou hast prepared,
(Unworthy though I be)
For me a blood-bought free reward,
A golden harp for me!

'Tis strung and tuned for endless years,
And formed by power divine,
To sound in God the Father's ears
No other name but thine.

My Lord and my God.

JOIN all the glorious names
Of wisdom, love, and power,
That ever mortals knew,
That angels ever bore:
All are too mean
To speak his worth;
Too mean to set
My Saviour forth.

But O, what gentle terms
What condescending ways
Does our Redeemer use,
To teach his heavenly grace!
Mine eyes with joy
And wonder see
What forms of love
He bears for me.

I love my Shepherd's voice;
His watchful eyes shall keep
My wandering soul among
The thousands of his sheep:

He feeds his flock,
He calls their names;
His bosom bears
The tender lambs.

Jesus, my great High Priest,
Offered his blood and died;
My guilty conscience seeks
No sacrifice beside:
His powerful blood
Did once atone,
And now it pleads
Before the throne.

My Advocate appears
For my defence on high;
The Father bows his ears,
And lays his thunder by.
Not all that hell
Or sin can say,
Shall turn his heart,
His love away.

My dear Almighty Lord,
My Conqueror and my King,
Thy sceptre and thy sword,
Thy reigning grace I sing.
Thine is the power;
Behold I sit
In willing bonds
Beneath thy feet.

Now let my soul arise
And tread the Tempter down;
My Captain leads me forth
To conquest and a crown.
A feeble saint
Shall win the day,
Though death and hell
Obstruct the way.

Should all the hosts of death,
And powers of hell unknown,
Put their most dreadful forms
Of rage and mischief on;
I shall be safe—
For Christ displays
Superior power,
And guardian grace.

Remember all the Way.

THUS far my God hath led me on,
And made his truth and mercy known;
My hopes and fears alternate rise,
And comforts mingle with my sighs.

Through this wide wilderness I roam,
Far distant from my blissful home;
Lord, let thy presence be my stay,
And guard me in this dangerous way.

Temptations everywhere annoy;
And sins and snares my peace destroy;
My earthly joys are from me torn,
And oft an absent God I mourn.

My soul with various tempests tossed,
Her hopes o'erturned, her projects crossed,
Sees every day new straits attend,
And wonders where the scene will end.

Is this, dear Lord, that thorny road
Which leads us to the mount of God?
Are these the toils thy people know,
While in the wilderness below?

'Tis even so—thy faithful love
Doth all thy children's graces prove;
'Tis thus our pride and self must fall,
That Jesus may be All in All.

The Morning Star.

O JESUS, life-light of my way,
In this poor stormy mortal day!
On earth I'm but a weary guest,
The load of sin leaves me no rest.

The way to endless life is hard,
And fainting feet my steps retard;
Ah Jesus! carry with thy hand
Me to my heavenly Fatherland!

Heavy lieth the sore complaint;
The flesh is weak, the heart is faint,
And my whole being cries in me,
Lord! never there, never with thee!

I'll bring my sorrow and my care
Unto thy cross, and leave them there;
O what can death-pains do to me?
Thy suffering my strength shall be.

Now I despise my faithless fear!
My voice may fail, yet thou wilt hear;
Thy Spirit shall my helper be,
And, Father! Father! cry in me.

And when the grave shall open stand,
When sinks my head and fails my hand—
My Light in yonder night of death,
Thy will be done—then take my breath.

My walking-staff I'll gladly lay
Upon my grave, and go my way
As it shall please thee to command,
Over into the better land.

Lord, in thy death my faith doth rest,
O help thou me, in death opprest;
Finish the sorrow and the strife,
Receive me to thy heavenly life.

Then when the last great day shall break,
Lord, bid my sleeping dust awake;
And in the judgment let me stand
In thy white robe, at thy right hand.

Immortal, glorious, shall I rise,
And see my God with changéd eyes;
And by thy grace made like to thee,
Forever in thy kingdom be.

A Better Country

O TELL me no more of this world's vain store,
The time for such trifles with me now is o'er;
A country I've found where true joys abound,
To dwell I'm determined on that happy ground.

The souls that believe, in Paradise live,
And me in that number will Jesus receive:
My soul, don't delay—he calls thee away,
Rise, follow thy Saviour, and bless the glad day.

No mortal doth know what he can bestow,
What light, strength, and comfort—go after him, go;
Lo, onward I move to a city above,
None guesses how wondrous my journey will prove.

Great spoils I shall win from death, hell, and sin,
'Midst outward afflictions shall feel Christ within:
And when I'm to die, Receive me, I'll cry,
For Jesus hath loved me, I cannot tell why.

But this I do find, we two are so joined,
He'll not live in glory and leave me behind:
So this is the race I am running, through grace,
Henceforth—till admitted to see my Lord's face.

And now I'm in care my neighbours may share
These blessings: to seek them will none of you dare?
In bondage, O why, and death will you lie,
When one here assures you free grace is so nigh?

I'm Going Home.

My heavenly home is bright and fair;
Nor pain nor death can enter there:
Its glittering towers the sun outshine,
That heavenly mansion shall be mine.
I'm going home, I'm going home,
I'm going home, to die no more!

My Father's house is built on high,
Far, far above the starry sky:
When from this earthly prison free,
That heavenly mansion mine shall be.

While here, a stranger far from home,
Affliction's waves may round me foam;
And though like Lazarus, sick and poor,
My heavenly mansion is secure.

Let others seek a home below,
Which flames devour, or waves o'erflow;
Be mine the happier lot to own
A heavenly mansion near the throne.

Then fail this earth, let stars decline,
And sun and moon refuse to shine;
All nature sink and cease to be,
This heavenly mansion stands for me.
I'm going home, I'm going home,
I'm going home, to die no more!

The House of God.

LORD of the worlds above,
  How pleasant and how fair
The dwellings of thy love,
  Thine earthly temples, are!
    To thine abode
      My heart aspires,
      With warm desires
    To see my God.

The sparrow for her young
  With pleasure seeks a nest,
And wandering swallows long
  To find their wonted rest!
    My spirit faints
      With equal zeal,
      To rise and dwell
    Among thy saints.

O happy souls, who pray
  Where God appoints to hear!
O happy men, who pay
  Their constant service there!
    They praise thee still;
      And happy they,
      Who love the way
    To Zion's hill.

They go from strength to strength,
  Through this dark vale of tears;

Till each arrives at length,
Till each in heaven appears.
O glorious seat,
When God, our King,
Shall thither bring
Our willing feet!

To spend one sacred day
Where God and saints abide,
Affords diviner joy
Than thousand days beside:
Where God resorts,
I love it more
To keep the door,
Than shine in courts.

God is our Sun and Shield,
Our light and our defence;
With gifts his hands are filled,
We draw our blessings thence.
He shall bestow,
On Jacob's race,
Peculiar grace,
And glory too.

The Lord his people loves;
His hand no good withholds
From those his heart approves,
From pure and pious souls.
Thrice happy he,
O God of hosts,
Whose spirit trusts
Alone in thee.

Looking Upward in a Storm.

God of my life, to thee I call,
Afflicted at thy feet I fall;
When the great water-floods prevail,
Leave not my trembling heart to fail!

Friend of the friendless and the faint!
Where should I lodge my deep complaint?
Where but with thee, whose open door
Invites the helpless and the poor?

Did ever mourner plead with thee,
And thou refuse that mourner's plea?
Does not the word still fixed remain,
That none shall seek thy name in vain?

That were a grief I could not bear,
Didst thou not hear and answer prayer;
But a prayer-hearing, answering God,
Supports me under every load.

Fair is the lot that's cast for me,
I have an Advocate with thee:
They whom the world caresses most,
Have no such privilege to boast.

Poor though I am, despised, forgot,
Yet God, my God, forgets me not;
And he is safe, and must succeed,
For whom the Lord vouchsafes to plead.

I will Fear no Evil.

Away, my unbelieving fear!
  Fear shall in me no more have place;
My Saviour doth not yet appear—
  He hides the brightness of his face;
But shall I therefore let him go,
  And basely to the tempter yield?
No, in the strength of Jesus, no,
  I never will give up my shield.

Although the vine its fruit deny,
  Although the olive yield no oil,
The withering fig-trees droop and die,
  The fields elude the tiller's toil,
The empty stalls no herd afford,
  And perish all the bleating race,
Yet will I triumph in the Lord—
  The God of my salvation praise.

In hope believing against hope,
  Jesus my Lord, my God, I claim;
Jesus, my strength, shall lift me up;
  Salvation is in Jesus' name.
To me he soon shall bring it nigh;
  My soul shall then outstrip the wind;
On wings of love mount up on high,
  And leave the world and sin behind.

The Child.

QUIET, Lord, my froward heart,
  Make me teachable and mild,
Upright, simple, free from art,
  Make me as a weanèd child.
From distrust and envy free,
Pleased with all that pleases thee.

What thou shalt to-day provide,
  Let me as a child receive;
What to-morrow may betide,
  Calmly to thy wisdom leave:
'Tis enough that thou wilt care;
Why should I the burden bear?

As a little child relies
  On a care beyond his own,
Knows he's neither strong nor wise,
  Fears to stir a step alone;
Let me thus with thee abide,
As my Father, Guard, and Guide.

Thus preserved from Satan's wiles,
  Safe from dangers, free from fears,
May I live upon thy smiles,
  Till the promised hour appears
When the sons of God shall prove
All their Father's boundless love.

The House of Prayer.

Thy mansion is the Christian's heart,
O Lord, thy dwelling-place secure!
Bid the unruly throng depart,
And leave the consecrated door.

Devoted as it is to thee,
A thievish swarm frequents the place;
They steal away my joys from me,
And rob my Saviour of his praise.

There, too, a sharp designing trade
Sin, Satan, and the World maintain;
Nor cease to press me, and persuade
To part with ease and purchase pain.

I know them, and I hate their din;
Am weary of the bustling crowd;
But while their voice is heard within,
I cannot serve thee as I would.

Oh! for the joy thy presence gives,
What peace shall reign when thou art there!
Thy presence makes this den of thieves
A calm delightful house of prayer.

And if thou make thy temple shine,
Yet, self-abased, will I adore;
The gold and silver are not mine;
I give thee what was thine before.

Let Him do what Seemeth Him Good.

LEAVE all to God,
Forsaken one, and still thy tears,
For the Highest knows thy pain,
Sees thy suffering and thy fears;
Thou shalt not wait his help in vain:
Leave all to God.

Be still and trust!
For his strokes are strokes of love
Thou must for thy profit bear;
He thy filial fear would move;
Trust thy Father's loving care:
Be still and trust!

Know, God is near!
Though thou think him far away,
Though his mercy long have slept,
He will come and not delay,
When his child enough hath wept;
For God is near.

O teach him not
When and how to hear thy prayers;
Never doth our God forget;
He the cross who longest bears
Finds his sorrows' bounds are set;
Then teach him not.

If thou love him,
Walking truly in his ways,
Then no trouble, cross, or death,
Shakes thy heart or quells thy praise:
All things serve thee here beneath,
If thou love God!

The Trial of Faith.

JEHOVAH hath said,
'Tis left on record,
"The righteous are one
With Jesus the Lord;"
At all times he loves them,
'Twas for them he died,
Yet oft times he proves them,
For grace must be tried.

Temptations and sins
In legions shall rise,
As goads in thy side
Or thorns in thine eyes;
And oft, to thy sorrow,
His face he will hide;
For God hath determined
Thy grace shall be tried.

With him on the mount
To-day thou shalt be,
Indulged by thy Lord
His glory to see;

There he may caress thee
  And call thee his bride,
Yet grace, though he bless thee,
  Shall surely be tried.

As gold from the flame
  He'll bring thee at last,
To praise him for all
  Through which thou hast past;
Then love everlasting
  Thy griefs shall repay,
And God from thine eyes
  Wipe all sorrows away.

Deliverance.

THE tempter to my soul hath said,
  "There is no help in God for thee:"
Lord, lift thou up thy servant's head;
  My glory, shield, and solace be.

Thus to the Lord I raised my cry—
  He heard me from his holy hill;
At his command the waves rolled by;
  He beckoned, and the winds were still.

I laid me down and slept—I woke;
  Thou, Lord, my spirit didst sustain;
Bright from the east the morning broke—
  Thy comforts rose on me again.

I will not fear, though armėd throngs
Surround my steps in all their wrath;
Salvation to the Lord belongs;
His presence guards his people's path.

Jesus All-sufficient.

If only he is mine—
If but this poor heart
Never more, in grief or joy,
May from him depart,
Then farewell to sadness,
All I feel is love, and hope, and gladness.

If only he is mine,
Then from all below,
Leaning on my pilgrim-staff,
Gladly forth I go
From the crowd who follow
In the broad, bright, road, their pleasures false and hollow.

If only he is mine,
Then all else is given;
Every blessing lifts my eyes
And my heart to heaven.
Filled with heavenly love,
Earthly hopes and fears no longer tempt to move.

There, when he is mine,
Is my Fatherland,

And my heritage of bliss
Daily cometh from his hand.
Now I find again,
In his people, love long lost, and mourned in vain.

Coronation.

All hail the power of Jesus' name!
Let angels prostrate fall;
Bring forth the royal diadem,
And crown him Lord of all.

Let high-born seraphs tune the lyre,
And as they tune it, fall
Before his face who tunes their choir,
And crown him Lord of all.

Crown him, ye morning stars of light,
He fixed this floating ball;
Now hail the strength of Israel's might,
And crown him Lord of all.

Crown him, ye martyrs of our God,
Who from his altar call;
Extol the stem of Jesse's rod,
And crown him Lord of all.

Ye seed of Israel's chosen race,
Ye ransomed from the fall,
Hail him who saves you by his grace,
And crown him Lord of all.

Hail him, ye heirs of David's line,
  Whom David Lord did call;
The God incarnate, Man divine—
  And crown him Lord of all.

Sinners! whose love can ne'er forget
  The wormwood and the gall,
Go, spread your trophies at his feet,
  And crown him Lord of all.

Let every tribe and every tongue
  That hear the Saviour's call,
Now shout in universal song,
  And crown him Lord of all.

Seeking after Christ.

JESUS, if still the same thou art,
  If all thy promises are sure,
Set up thy kingdom in my heart,
  And make me rich, for I am poor:
To me be all thy treasures given,
The kingdom of an inward heaven.

Thou hast pronounced the mourners blest,
  And lo! for thee I ever mourn:
I cannot, no, I will not rest,
  Till thou, my only rest, return;
Till thou, the Prince of peace, appear,
And I receive the Comforter.

Where is the blessedness bestowed
  On all that hunger after thee?

I hunger now, I thirst for God,
See, the poor fainting sinner see:
And satisfy with endless peace,
And fill me with thy righteousness.

Ah, Lord, if thou art in that sigh,
Then hear thyself within me pray;
Hear in my heart thy Spirit's cry,
Mark what my labouring soul would say;
Answer the deep unuttered groan,
And show that thou and I are one.

Shine on thy work, disperse the gloom;
Light in thy light I then shall see;
Say to my soul, "Thy light is come,
Glory divine is risen on thee:
Thy warfare's past, thy mourning 's o'er;
Look up, for thou shalt weep no more."

Lord, I believe thy promise sure,
And trust thou wilt not long delay;
Hungry and sorrowful and poor,
Upon thy word myself I stay:
Into thy hands my all resign,
And wait till all thou art is mine.

The Day of Rest.

WHEN the worn spirit wants repose,
And sighs her God to seek,
How sweet to hail the evening's close
That ends the weary week!

How sweet to hail the early dawn
   That opens on the sight,
When first the soul-reviving morn
   Sheds forth new rays of light.

Sweet day! thine hours too soon will cease:
   Yet while they gently roll,
Breathe, heavenly Spirit, source of peace,
   A Sabbath o'er my soul.

When will my pilgrimage be done,
   The world's long week be o'er,
That Sabbath dawn, which needs no sun,
   That day which fades no more?

Pleading the Promise.

O THOU that hearest prayer,
   Attend our humble cry;
And let thy servants share
   Thy blessing from on high:
We plead the promise of thy word;
Grant us thy Holy Spirit, Lord!

If earthly parents hear
   Their children when they cry;
If they, with love sincere,
   Their children's wants supply;
Much more wilt thou thy love display,
And answer when thy children pray.

Our heavenly Father, thou;
  We, children of thy grace;
O let thy Spirit now
  Descend and fill the place;
That all may feel the heavenly flame,
And all unite to praise thy name.

The Hour of Prayer.

My God! is any hour so sweet,
  From blush of morn to evening star,
As that which calls me to thy feet,
      The hour of prayer?

Blest is the tranquil hour of morn,
  And blest that hour of solemn eve,
When, on the wings of prayer up-borne,
      The world I leave.

Then is my strength by thee renewed;
  Then are my sins by thee forgiven;
Then dost thou cheer my solitude
      With hopes of heaven.

No words can tell what sweet relief
  There for my every want I find;
What strength for warfare, balm for grief,
      What peace of mind.

Hushed is each doubt, gone every fear;
  My spirit seems in heaven to stay;
And e'en the penitential tear
      Is wiped away.

Lord! till I reach that blissful shore,
No privilege so dear shall be,
As thus my inmost soul to pour
In prayer to thee.

Manna.

MANNA to Israel well supplied
The want of other bread;
While God is able to provide,
His people shall be fed.

(Thus, though the corn and wine should fail,
And creature-streams be dry,
The prayer of faith will still prevail,
For blessings from on high.)

Of his kind care how sweet a proof;
It suited every taste:
Who gathered most had just enough,
Enough, who gathered least.

'Tis thus our gracious Lord provides
Our comforts and our cares;
His own unerring hand divides,
And gives us each our shares.

He knows how much the weak can bear,
And helps them when they cry;
The strongest have no strength to spare,
For such he'll strongly try.

Daily they saw the manna come,
   And cover all the ground;
But what they tried to keep at home
   Corrupted soon was found.

Vain their attempts to store it up,
   This was to tempt the Lord:
Israel must live by faith and hope,
   And not upon a hoard.

My Heart is Fixed.

WHAT within me and without
   Hourly on my spirit weighs,
Burdening heart and soul with doubt,
   Darkening all my weary days:
In it I behold thy will,
   God, who giveth rest and peace,
And my heart is calm and still,
   Waiting till thou send release.

God! thou art my rock of strength,
   And my home is in thine arms,
Thou wilt send me help at length,
   And I feel no wild alarms.
Sin nor death can pierce the shield
   Thy defence has o'er me thrown,
Up to thee myself I yield,
   And my sorrows are thine own.

When my trials tarry long,
   Unto thee I look and wait,

Knowing none, though keen and strong,
  Can my trust in thee abate.
And this faith I long have nurst
  Comes alone, O God, from thee;
Thou my heart didst open first,
  Thou didst set this hope in me.

Christians! cast on him your load,
  To your tower of refuge fly;
Know he is the living God,
  Ever to his creatures nigh.
Seek his ever-open door
  In your hours of utmost need;
All your hearts before him pour,
  He will send you help with speed.

But hast thou some darling plan
  Cleaving to the things of earth?
Leanest thou for aid on man?
  Thou wilt find him nothing worth.
Rather trust the One alone,
  Whose is endless power and love,
And the help he gives his own
  Thou in very deed shalt prove.

On thee, O my God, I rest,
  Letting life float calmly on,
For I know the last is best,
  When the crown of joy is won.
In thy might all things I bear,
  In thy love find bitters sweet,
And, with all my grief and care,
  Sit in patience at thy feet.

O my soul, why art thou vexed?
  Let things go e'en as they will;
Though to thee they seem perplexed,
  Yet his order they fulfil.
Here he is thy strength and guard,
  Power to harm thee here has none;
Yonder will he each reward
  For the works he here has done.

Let thy mercy's wings be spread
  O'er me—keep me close to thee;
In the peace thy love doth shed
  Let me dwell eternally.
Be my All; in all I do
  Let me only seek thy will;
Where the heart to thee is true,
  All is peaceful, calm, and still.

Thanksgiving.

STAND up and bless the Lord,
  Ye people of his choice:
Stand up and bless the Lord your God,
  With heart and soul and voice.

Though high above all praise,
  Above all blessing high,
Who would not fear his holy name,
  And laud and magnify?

O for the living flame
  From his own altar brought,
To touch our lips, our minds inspire,
  And wing to heaven our thought!

There, with benign regard,
  Our hymns he deigns to hear;
Though unrevealed to mortal sense,
  The spirit feels him near.

God is our strength and song,
  And his salvation ours;
Then be his love in Christ proclaimed
  With all our ransomed powers.

Stand up and bless the Lord,
  The Lord your God adore;
Stand up and bless his glorious name
  Henceforth for evermore.

The Heavenly Way.

OH! for a closer walk with God,
  A calm and heavenly frame;
A light to shine upon the road
  That leads me to the Lamb!

Where is the blessedness I knew
  When first I saw the Lord?
Where is the soul-refreshing view
  Of Jesus and his word?

What peaceful hours I once enjoyed!
How sweet their memory still!
But they have left an aching void
The world can never fill.

Return, O holy Dove, return,
Sweet messenger of rest;
I hate the sins that made thee mourn,
And drove thee from my breast.

The dearest idol I have known,
Whate'er that idol be,
Help me to tear it from thy throne,
And worship only thee.

So shall my walk be close with God,
Calm and serene my frame;
So purer light shall mark the road
That leads me to the Lamb.

Looking Up.

MY God, my prayer attend!
Oh bow thine ear to me,
Without a hope—without a friend,
Without a help—but thee!

Oh guard my soul around,
Which loves and trusts thy grace;
Nor let the powers of hell confound
The hopes on thee I place!

Thy mercy I entreat—
  Let mercy hear my cries,
While humbly waiting at thy seat,
  My daily prayers arise.

Oh bid my heart rejoice,
  And every fear control;
Since at thy throne, with suppliant voice,
  To thee I lift my soul!

Valiant for the Truth.

Fight the good fight; lay hold
  Upon eternal life;
Keep but thy shield, be bold,
  Stand through the hottest strife;
Invincible while in the field,
Thou canst not fail, unless thou yield.

No force of earth or hell,
  Though fiends with men unite,
Truth's champion can compel,
  However prest, to flight;
Invincible upon the field,
He cannot fall, unless he yield.

Apollyon's arm may shower
  Darts thick as hail, and hide
Heaven's face, as in the hour
  When Christ on Calvary died;
No powers of darkness in the field
Can tread thee down, unless thou yield.

Trust in thy Saviour's might;
  Yea, till thy latest breath,
Fight, and like him in fight,
  By dying conquer death;
And all-victorious in the field,
Then with thy sword, thy spirit yield.

Great words are these, and strong;
  Yet Lord, I look to thee,
To whom alone belong
  Valour and victory;
With thee, my Captain, in the field,
I must prevail, I cannot yield.

Freedom.

SHALL we go on to sin
  Because thy grace abounds,
Or crucify the Lord again,
  And open all his wounds?

Forbid it, mighty God!
  Nor let it e'er be said,
That we, whose sins are crucified,
  Should raise them from the dead.

We will be slaves no more,
  Since Christ has made us free,
Has nailed our tyrants to his cross,
  And bought our liberty.

Lovest Thou Me?

HARK, my soul! it is the Lord;
'Tis thy Saviour, hear his word;
Jesus speaks, and speaks to thee:
"Say, poor sinner, lov'st thou me?

"I delivered thee when bound,
And when bleeding, healed thy wound:
Sought thee wandering, set thee right,
Turned thy darkness into light.

"Can a woman's tender care
Cease toward the child she bare?
Yes, she may forgetful be,
Yet will I remember thee.

"Mine is an unchanging love,
Higher than the heights above;
Deeper than the depths beneath,
Free and faithful, strong as death.

"Thou shalt see my glory soon,
When the work of grace is done;
Partner of my throne shalt be;—
Say, poor sinner, lov'st thou me?"

Lord, it is my chief complaint,
That my love is weak and faint;
Yet I love thee and adore,—
Oh for grace to love thee more!

None but Christ.

WHEN I survey the wondrous cross
On which the Prince of glory died,
My richest gain I count but loss,
And pour contempt on all my pride.

Forbid it, Lord, that I should boast,
Save in the death of Christ, my God;
All the vain things that charm me most,
I sacrifice them to his blood.

See, from his head, his hands, his feet,
Sorrow and love flow mingled down!
Did e'er such love and sorrow meet?
Or thorns compose so rich a crown?

Were the whole realm of nature mine,
That were a present far too small;
Love so amazing, so divine,
Demands my soul, my life, my all.

The Lord that Healeth Thee.

HEAL us, Emmanuel! here we are,
Waiting to feel thy touch:
Deep-wounded souls to thee repair,
And, Saviour, we are such.

Our faith is feeble, we confess,
  We faintly trust thy word;
But wilt thou pity us the less?
  Be that far from thee, Lord!

Remember him who once applied,
  With trembling, for relief;
"Lord, I believe," with tears he cried,
  "Oh help my unbelief!"

She too, who touched thee in the press,
  And healing virtue stole,
Was answered, "Daughter, go in peace,
  Thy faith hath made thee whole."

Concealed amid the gathering throng,
  She would have shunned thy view;
And if her faith was firm and strong,
  Had strong misgivings too.

Like her, with hopes and fears we come,
  To touch thee, if we may;
Oh! send us not despairing home!
  Send none unhealed away!

Our Refuge.

God of love, who hearest prayer,
Kindly for thy people care,
Who on thee alone depend:
Love us, save us to the end.

Save us, in the prosperous hour,
From the flattering tempter's power;
From his unsuspected wiles,
From the world's pernicious smiles.

Save us from the great and wise,
Till they sink in their own eyes,
Sweetly to thy yoke submit,
Lay their honour at thy feet.

Never let the world break in;
Fix a mighty gulf between;
Keep us little and unknown,
Prized and loved by God alone.

Let us still to thee look up—
Thee, thy Israel's strength and hope;
Nothing know, or seek, beside
Jesus, and him crucified.

He Careth for You.

SHALL I not trust my God,
Who doth so well love me?
Who as a Father cares so tenderly?
Shall I not lay the load
Which would my weakness break,
On his strong hand, who never doth forsake?

He doth know all my grief,
And all my heart's desire;
He'll stand by me till death, through flood and fire.
And he can send relief:

My Father's love, so free,
Till the new morning shall remain to me.

Who doth the birds supply,
Who grass, and trees, and flowers,
Doth beautifully clothe, through ceaseless hours;
Who hears us ere we cry;
Can he my need forget?
Nay, though he slay me, I will trust him yet.

When I his yoke do bear,
And seek my chiefest joy
But in his righteousness and sweet employ.
He makes my soul his care;
Early and late doth bless,
And crowneth work and purpose with success.

O blessèd be his name!
My Father cares for me!
I can no longer unbelieving be.
All praise to him proclaim;
I know he is my Friend—
I know the Lord will love me to the end!

Precious Promises.

How firm a foundation, ye saints of the Lord,
Is laid for your faith in his excellent word!
What more can he say than to you he hath said?
You, who unto Jesus for refuge have fled.

In every condition—in sickness, in health,
In poverty's vale, or abounding in wealth,
At home and abroad, on the land, on the sea,
As thy days may demand so thy succour shall be.

"Fear not, I am with thee; O be not dismayed!
I, I am thy God, and will still give thee aid;
I'll strengthen thee, help thee, and cause thee to stand,
Upheld by my righteous, omnipotent hand.

"When through the deep waters I call thee to go,
The rivers of sorrow shall not overflow;
For I will be with thee, thy troubles to bless,
And sanctify to thee thy deepest distress.

"When through fiery trials thy pathway shall lie,
My grace, all-sufficient, shall be thy supply;
The flame shall not hurt thee; I only design
Thy dross to consume and thy gold to refine.

"E'en down to old age, all my people shall prove
My sovereign, eternal, unchangeable love;
And when hoary hairs shall their temples adorn,
Like lambs they shall still in my bosom be borne.

"The soul that to Jesus hath fled for repose,
I will not, I will not desert to his foes;
That soul, though all hell should endeavour to shake,
I'll never—no, never—no, never forsake!"

Yet there is Room.

COME sinner, to the gospel feast,
 Oh come without delay;
For there is room in Jesus' breast
 For all who will obey.

There's room in God's eternal love
 To save thy precious soul;
Room in the Spirit's grace above
 To heal and make thee whole.

There's room within the church, redeemed
 With blood of Christ divine;
Room in the white-robed throng convened,
 For that dear soul of thine.

There's room in heaven among the choir,
 And harps, and crowns of gold,
And glorious palms of victory there,
 And joys that ne'er were told.

There's room around thy Father's board
 For thee and thousands more:
O come and welcome to the Lord;
 Yea, come this very hour.

I Come.

HERE am I, Lord! thou callest me:
Thou drawest me; I follow thee.
Soul and heart are thine alone;
O my Shepherd, take thine own!

I have oft thy call disdained;
I am late—my day has waned!
Yet it is my joy, that thou
Callest me, poor sinner! now.

Yes, I dare no more delay,
I will follow thee to-day.
To thy glorious mercy-seat
Now I come with trembling feet.

Lord, the case is now with me
As with Peter on the sea.
Ah reach out thy mighty hand;
Hold me up, and bring to land.

Thou didst call me: now call I,—
O my Saviour, come thou nigh!
Sin doth bind me, fear distress;
Save me with thy righteousness.

Make my weakness strong in thee,
Let thy strength my power be;
I'll follow, till my latest breath,
Through flood and fire, grief and death.

Retirement and Meditation.

My God, permit me not to be
A stranger to myself and thee;
Amidst a thousand thoughts I rove,
Forgetful of my highest love.

Why should my passions mix with earth,
And thus debase my heavenly birth?
Why should I cleave to things below,
And let my God, my Saviour, go?

Call me away from flesh and sense,
One sovereign word can draw me thence;
I would obey the voice divine,
And all inferior joys resign.

Be earth with all her scenes withdrawn;
Let noise and vanity be gone:
In secret silence of the mind
My heaven, and there my God, I find.

My Lot.

WHAT have I in this barren land?
My Jesus is not here;
Mine eyes will ne'er be blest until
My Jesus doth appear.

My Jesus is gone up to heaven,
And has a place for me;
For 'tis his will that where he is
His followers should be.

Canaan I view from Pisgah's top,
Of Canaan's grapes I taste;
My Lord, who sends them to me here,
Will send for me at last.

I have a God that changeth not;
  Why should I be perplexed?
My God, who owns me in this world,
  Will own me in the next.

My dearest friends they dwell above,
  Them will I go to see;
And all my friends in Christ below
  Will soon come after me.

Our only Rest.

VAIN are all terrestrial pleasures;
  Mixed with dross the purest gold;
Seek we then for heavenly treasures,
  Treasures never waxing old.
Let our best affections centre
  On the things around the throne;
There no thief can ever enter;
  Moth and rust are there unknown.

Earthly joys no longer please us;
  Here would we renounce them all;
Seek our only rest in Jesus—
  Him our Lord and Master call.
Faith, our languid spirits cheering,
  Points to brighter worlds above;
Bids us look for his appearing;
  Bids us triumph in his love.

May our lights be always burning,
And our loins be girded round,
Waiting for our Lord's returning,—
Longing for the welcome sound.
Thus the Christian life adorning,
Never need we be afraid,
Should he come at night or morning,
Early dawn or evening shade.

Eternity Near.

COME, let us anew our journey pursue,
With vigour arise,
And press to our permanent place in the skies.
Of heavenly birth, though wandering on earth,
This is not our place,
But strangers and pilgrims ourselves we confess.

At Jesus's call we gave up our all;
And still we forego,
For Jesus's sake, our enjoyments below.
No longing we find for the country behind;
But onward we move,
And still we are seeking a country above:—

A country of joy without any alloy;
We thither repair;
Our hearts and our treasure already are there.
We march hand in hand to Immanuel's land;
No matter what cheer
We meet with on earth, for eternity's here!

The rougher the way, the shorter our stay;
The tempests that rise
Shall gloriously hurry our souls to the skies:
The fiercer the blast, the sooner 'tis past;
The troubles that come
Shall come to our rescue, and hasten us home.

Here and There.

WHAT no human eye hath seen,
What no mortal ear hath heard,
What on thought hath never been,
In its noblest flights, conferred—
This hath God prepared in store
For his people evermore!

When the shaded pilgrim-land
Fades before my closing eye,
Then revealed on either hand,
Heaven's own scenery shall lie;
Then the veil of flesh shall fall,
Now concealing, darkening all.

Heavenly landscapes, calmly bright,
Life's pure river murmuring low,
Forms of loveliness and light
Lost to earth long time ago;
Yes, mine own, lamented long,
Shine amid the angel throng!

Many a joyful sight was given,
  Many a joyful vision here—
Hill, and vale, and starry even,
  Friendship's smile, affection's tear;
These were shadows, sent in love,
Of realities above!

When upon my wearied ear
  Earth's last echoes faintly die,
Then shall angel-harps draw near—
  All the chorus of the sky;
Long-hushed voices blend again,
Sweetly, in that welcome strain.

Here were sweet and varied tones,
  Bird, and breeze, and fountain's fall,
Yet creation's travail-groans
  Ever sadly sighed through all.
There no discord jars the air—
Harmony is perfect there!

When this aching heart shall rest,
  All its busy pulses o'er,
From her mortal robes undrest
  Shall my spirit upward soar.
Then shall unimagined joy
All my thoughts and powers employ.

Here devotion's healing balm
  Often came to soothe my breast—
Hours of deep and holy calm,
  Earnests of eternal rest;
But the bliss was here unknown
Which shall there be all my own!

Jesus reigns, the Life, the Sun
  Of that wondrous world above;
All the clouds and storms are gone,
  All is bright, and all is love.
All the shadows melt away
In the blaze of perfect day!

Be not Weary.

THEN, fainting soul, arise and sing;
Mount, but be sober on the wing;
Mount up, for heaven is won by prayer,
Be sober, for thou art not there;
Till death the weary spirit free,
Thy God hath said, 'Tis good for thee
To walk by faith, and not by sight:
  Take it on trust a little while;
Soon shalt thou read the mystery right
  In the full sunshine of his smile.

Jesus, Still Lead on.

JESUS, still lead on,
Till our rest be won!
And although the way be cheerless,
We will follow, calm and fearless.
Guide us by thy hand
To our Fatherland.

If the way be drear,
If the foe be near,
Let not faithless fears o'ertake us,
Let not faith and hope forsake us:
For, through many a foe,
To our home we go!

When we seek relief
From a long-felt grief—
When oppressed by new temptations,
Lord, increase and perfect patience.
Show us that bright shore
Where we weep no more!

Jesus, still lead on,
Till our rest be won!
Heavenly Leader, still direct us,
Still support, console, protect us,
Till we safely stand
In our Fatherland!

Light Shining out of Darkness.

God moves in a mysterious way
His wonders to perform;
He plants his footsteps in the sea,
And rides upon the storm.

Deep in unfathomable mines
Of never-failing skill,
He treasures up his deep designs,
And works his sovereign will.

Ye fearful saints, fresh courage take,
  The clouds ye so much dread
Are big with mercy, and shall break
  In blessings on your head.

Judge not the Lord by feeble sense,
  But trust him for his grace:
Behind a frowning providence
  He hides a smiling face.

His purposes will ripen fast,
  Unfolding every hour;
The bud may have a bitter taste,
  But sweet will be the flower.

Blind unbelief is sure to err,
  And scan his work in vain;
God is his own interpreter,
  And he will make it plain.

A Midnight Hymn.

IN the mid silence of the voiceless night,
When, chased by airy dreams, the slumbers flee,
Whom in the darkness doth my spirit seek,
      O God, but thee?

And if there be a weight upon my breast,
Some vague impression of the day foregone;
Scarce knowing what it is, I fly to thee,
      And lay it down.

Or if it be the heaviness that comes
In token of anticipated ill—
My bosom takes no heed of what it is,
Since 'tis thy will.

For O, in spite of past and present care,
Or anything beside—how joyfully
Passes that almost solitary hour,
My God, with thee!

More tranquil than the stillness of the night,
More peaceful than the silence of that hour,
More blest than anything, my bosom lies
Beneath thy power.

For what is there on earth that I desire,
Of all that it can give or take from me?
Or whom in heaven doth my spirit seek,
O God, but thee?

The High Way to Zion.

SING, ye redeemed of the Lord,
Your great Deliverer sing:
Pilgrims for Zion's city bound,
Be joyful in your King.

See the fair way his hand has raised;
How holy, and how plain!
Nor shall the simplest traveller err,
Nor ask the track in vain.

No ravening lion shall destroy,
  Nor lurking serpent wound;
Pleasure and safety, peace and praise,
  Through all the path are found.

A hand divine shall lead you on
  Through all the blissful road;
Till to the sacred mount you rise,
  And see your gracious God.

There garlands of immortal joy
  Shall bloom on every head;
While sorrow, sighing, and distress,
  Like shadows all are fled.

March on in your Redeemer's strength;
  Pursue his footsteps still;
And let the prospect cheer your eye
  While labouring up the hill.

Religion.

RELIGION is a glorious treasure,
  The purchase of a Saviour's love;
It fills the mind with consolation,
  It lifts the heart to things above;
It calms our fears, it soothes our sorrows,
  It smooths our way o'er life's rough sea;
'Tis mixed with goodness, meek, humble, patient,
  This heavenly portion mine shall be.

How vain, how fleeting, how transitory!
  This world with all its pomp and show;
Its vain delights and delusive pleasures,
  I gladly leave them all below;
But grace and glory shall be my story,
  While I in Jesus such beauties see;
While endless ages are onward rolling,
  This heavenly portion mine shall be.

This earthly house shall be dissolved,
  And mortal life shall soon be o'er—
All earthly cares and earthly sorrows
  Shall pain my eyes and heart no more;
Yet "pure religion" remains forever,
  And strengthened my glad heart shall be;
While endless ages are onward rolling
  This heavenly portion mine shall be.

Mystery.

GREAT mystery, I do behold,
That God should ever save a soul;
But here's a greater mystery,
That he bestowed his grace on me.

Great mystery, I can't tell why,
That Christ for sinners e'er should die;
But here's a greater mystery,
That he should ever die for me.

Great mystery, that Christ should place
His love on those of Adam's race;
But here's a greater mystery,
That he should set his love on me.

Why was I not still left behind,
With thousand others of mankind
Who run the dangerous, sinful race,
And die, and never taste his grace.

No mortal can a reason find;
'Tis mercy free, and grace divine:
O 'tis a glorious mystery,
And will be to eternity.

Invitation.

GRACE, how exceeding sweet to those
Who feel they sinners are!
Sunk and distrest, they taste and know
Their heaven is only there.

Rich grace, free grace, most sweetly calls,
Directly come who will,
Just as you are, for Christ receives
Poor helpless sinners still.

'Tis grace each day that feeds our souls,
Grace keeps us inly poor;
And O that nothing else but grace
May rule for evermore!

The Saint's Hope.

LORD, I am thine, but thou wilt prove
My faith, my patience, and my love:
When men of spite against me join,
They are the sword, the hand is thine.

Their hope and portion lie below;
'Tis all the happiness they know;
'Tis all they seek; they take their shares,
And leave the rest among their heirs.

What sinners value, I resign;
Lord, 'tis enough that thou art mine:
I shall behold thy blissful face,
And stand complete in righteousness.

This life's a dream, an empty show;
But the bright world to which I go
Hath joys substantial and sincere;
When shall I wake and find me there?

O glorious hour! O blest abode!
I shall be near, and like my God!
And flesh and sin no more control
The sacred pleasures of the soul.

My flesh shall slumber in the ground,
Till the last trumpet's joyful sound;
Then burst the chains with sweet surprise,
And in my Saviour's image rise.

Sojourners.

COME, children! on; this way
Will lead us home!
Like some poor wandering guest,
On earth I roam,
And seek eternal rest—
Come, children, come!
With God our business lies from day to day,
In heaven should be our hearts while here we stay.

Come, children, let us go,
But not alone;
Our Father goeth too,
And by his own
Will stand to help them through:
He from his throne
Sweet beams of sunlight on our path will throw;
O see what joy we have while here below.

Let each now make good speed,
The goal is near.
The fire-column see,
Our God is here.
Joined hand in hand are we:
With earnest fear
Let each the other strengthen in his need;
In this strange land we brothers are indeed.

It will not always last,
Therefore be brave!
And soon we all shall be
Across the wave:

There find, from sorrow free,
The rest we crave.
Then, when the saints from earth to heaven have past,
How well, how well, will heaven with earth contrast!

The End of that Man is Peace.

How blest the righteous when he dies!
When sinks a weary soul to rest!
How mildly beam the closing eyes!
How gently heaves th' expiring breast!

So fades a summer cloud away;
So sinks the gale when storms are o'er;
So gently shuts the eye of day;
So dies a wave along the shore.

A holy quiet reigns around—
A calm which life nor death destroys;
And nought disturbs the peace profound
Which his unfettered soul enjoys.

Farewell, conflicting hopes and fears,
Where lights and shades alternate dwell!
How bright the unchanging morn appears!
Farewell, inconstant world, farewell!

Triumphant smiles the victor's brow,
Fanned by some guardian angel's wing:
O grave! where is thy victory now?
And where, O death, is now thy sting?

Life's labour done, as sinks the clay,
  Light from its load the spirit flies,
While heaven and earth conspire to say,
  How blest the righteous when he dies!

Fear of Death.

WHY should we start, and fear to die?
  What timorous worms we mortals are!
Death is the gate of endless joy,
  And yet we dread to enter there.

The pains, the groans, the dying strife,
  Fright our approaching souls away;
Still we shrink back again to life,
  Fond of our prison and our clay.

O, if my Lord would come and meet,
  My soul should stretch her wings in haste;
Fly fearless through death's iron gate,
  Nor feel the terrors as she passed.

Jesus can make a dying bed
  Feel soft as downy pillows are;
While on his breast I lean my head,
  And breathe my life out sweetly there.

The Dying Believer to his Soul.

DEATHLESS principle, arise;
Soar, thou native of the skies.
Pearl of price, by Jesus bought,
To his glorious likeness wrought,
Go, to shine before the throne;
Deck his mediatorial crown:
Go, his triumphs to adorn;
Made for God, to God return.

Lo, he beckons from on high!
Fearless to his presence fly:
Thine the merit of his blood;
Thine the righteousness of God.

Angels, joyful to attend,
Hovering round thy pillow bend;
Wait to catch the signal given,
And escort thee quick to heaven.

Is thy earthly house distrest?
Willing to retain her guest?
'Tis not thou, but she, must die:
Fly, celestial tenant, fly.
Burst thy shackles, drop thy clay,
Sweetly breathe thyself away:
Singing, to thy crown remove,
Swift of wing, and fired with love.

Shudder not to pass the stream:
Venture all thy care on him;

Him, whose dying love and power
Stilled its tossing, hushed its roar.
Safe is the expanded wave;
Gentle as a summer's eve:
Not one object of his care
Ever suffered shipwreck there.
See the haven full in view!
Love divine shall bear thee through.
Trust to that propitious gale:
Weigh thy anchor, spread thy sail.

Saints, in glory perfect made,
Wait thy passage through the shade:
Ardent for thy coming o'er,
See, they throng the blissful shore.
Mount, their transports to improve:
Join the longing choir above:
Swiftly to their wish be given:
Kindle higher joy in heaven.
Such the prospects that arise
To the dying Christian's eyes!
Such the glorious vista Faith
Opens through the shades of death!

The Christian's Farewell.

YE golden lamps of heaven, farewell,
With all your feeble light;
Farewell, thou ever-changing moon,
Pale empress of the night.

And thou, refulgent orb of day,
In brighter flames arrayed;
My soul that springs beyond thy sphere,
No more demands thy aid.

Ye stars are but the shining dust
Of my divine abode;
The pavement of those heavenly courts,
Where I shall see my God.

The Father of eternal light
Shall there his beams display;
Nor shall one moment's darkness mix
With that unvaried day.

No more the drops of piercing grief
Shall swell into my eyes;
Nor the meridian sun decline
Amidst those brighter skies.

There all the millions of his saints
Shall in one song unite;
And each the bliss of all shall view,
With infinite delight.

Let us Run our Race with Patience.

Lord, can a helpless worm like me
Attempt to make her way to thee?
Yes, let me raise thy praises high,
In weakness thou canst strength supply.

'Twas by thy grace that I begun,
Resolved the heavenly race to run:
'Tis grace corrects me when I stray,
'Tis grace upholds me in the way.

Run on, my soul, and still adore,
Receiving still, still asking more;
In Christ thy strength and wisdom lies,
O look to him with steadfast eyes.

Look to that blood thy Saviour shed;
Thy Daysman dying in thy stead;
Behold him on the accursèd tree!
Great was the love he bore to thee.

He who thus loved thee unto death
Will love thee to thy latest breath;
Keep sight of him, my soul, and run—
He'll crown thee when thy race is done.

Work.

LORD, thou hast bid us labour,
Bid us toil;
And take up with our might and bear away
The load that thou dost give from day to day.
The slothful idler is to thee
Hateful to see!
Doth himself spoil,
And loads his neighbour.

With a true heart upheaving
My small load,
As thou appointest, Lord, so let me bear
The duty-burden trusted to my care.
And though my face should all be wet
With toilsome sweat;
Show thou the road—
Enough! no grieving!

But now, my heart, be careful
Lest thou care!
The Lord doth give me daily bread for nought,
And for the morrow doth himself take thought.
Then let me serve him, on my part,
With all my heart,
And wait my share
With spirit prayerful.

Ah Lord! now add thy blessing
To all I do!
And let thy grace and help my work attend,
From the beginning even to the end.
Let each day's burden teach my eyes,
My heart, to rise—
Thy rest pursue—
Thy peace possessing!

Emmanuel's Land.

COME, we who love the Lord,
  And let our joys be known;
Join in a song of sweet accord,
  And thus surround the throne.

The sorrows of the mind
  Be banished from this place!
Religion never was designed
  To make our pleasures less.

Let those refuse to sing
  Who never knew our God;
But servants of the heavenly King
  Should speak their joys abroad.

The God that rules on high,
  And thunders when he please,
That rides upon the stormy sky,
  And manages the seas;

This awful God is ours,
  Our Father and our love;
He shall send down his heavenly powers,
  To carry us above.

There we shall see his face,
  And never, never sin;
And from the rivers of his grace
  Drink endless pleasures in.

Yea, and before we rise
 To that immortal state,
The thoughts of such amazing bliss
 Should constant joys create.

The men of grace have found
 Glory begun below;
Celestial fruits, on earthly ground,
 From Faith and Hope may grow.

The hill of Zion yields
 A thousand sacred sweets
Before we reach the heavenly fields,
 Or walk the golden streets.

Then let our songs abound,
 And every tear be dry;
We're marching through Emmanuel's ground
 To fairer worlds on high.

Far Better.

O BEAUTIFUL abode of earth,
  Fall when thou wilt!
  Thy gold is gilt,
And clouds of anguish veil thy mirth;
Who loves not heaven, may bestow
His love on earthly pomp and show.
But I alone desire with thee,
Jesus, all preciousness! to be.

One who is weary with his load,
Faint with the sun,
Would fain have done—
And craves long shadows on his road:
That after so much labour past,
He may sleep sweet and sound at last.
But all my longing is with thee,
Jesus, my only rest, to be!

Another doth pursue his trade
By wave and cliff;
Where his frail skiff
Is tempest-tossed, and he afraid:
But I will faith-wings spread, and fly
Up, past the star-hills of the sky!
For Jesus, thou alone shalt be
The end of pilgrimage to me.

Come, death, sleep's only brother, thou;
Come take the helm,
And through thy realm
To the sure harbour guide my prow.
He may repel thee who doth fear,
But I rejoice to see thee near:
For thou alone canst usher me
Where I shall with my Jesus be!

Retirement.

FAR from the world, O Lord, I flee,
From strife and tumult far;
From scenes where Satan wages still
His most successful war.

The calm retreat, the silent shade,
With prayer and praise agree;
And seem by thy sweet bounty made
For those who follow thee.

There, if thy Spirit touch the soul,
And grace her mean abode,
O with what peace, and joy, and love,
She communes with her God!

There, like the nightingale, she pours
Her solitary lays;
Nor asks a witness of her song,
Nor thirsts for human praise.

Author and Guardian of my life,
Sweet source of light divine,
And (all harmonious names in one)
My Saviour, thou art mine.

What thanks I owe thee, and what love—
A boundless, endless store—
Shall echo through the realms above,
When time shall be no more.

Miracles of Grace.

HAIL! my ever-blessèd Jesus,
Only thee I wish to sing;
To my soul thy name is precious,
Thou, my prophet, priest, and king;

O! what mercy flows from heaven,
O! what joy and happiness!
Love I much?—I've much forgiven,
I'm a miracle of grace.

Once with Adam's race in ruin,
Unconcerned in sin I lay;
Swift destruction still pursuing,
Till my Saviour passed that way:
Witness, all ye hosts of heaven,
My Redeemer's tenderness;
Love I much?—I've much forgiven,
I'm a miracle of grace.

Shout, ye bright angelic choir,
Praise the Lamb enthroned above;
Whilst astonished, I admire
God's free grace and boundless love.
That blessed moment I received him
Filled my soul with joy and peace;
Love I much?—I've much forgiven,
I'm a miracle of grace.

Sufficient for Thee.

WHY, O my soul, these gloomy fears?
Why all these sighs, and groans, and tears?
O why this God-dishonouring grief?
Why all this wretched unbelief?

Though helpless in myself I lie,
And lost to all eternity;
Yet I shall triumph o'er the grave,
Since Jesus came to seek and save.

To save poor sinners such as me,
To set the captive prisoners free,
To comfort those that mourn—to heal
The wounds of all that misery feel.

To save the ruined and undone,
To seek the lost—Lord, I am one!
I see, and mourn my guilt with shame:
To seek out such the Saviour came.

Then let my gratitude abound,
I once was lost, but now am found;
I once was dead, but now I live:
Praise, praise is all that I can give.

The Witnesses.

Give me the wings of faith, to rise
  Within the vail, and see
The saints above, how great their joys;
  How bright their glories be!

Once they were mourning here below,
  And wet their couch with tears:
They wrestled hard, as we do now,
  With sins, and doubts, and fears.

I ask them whence their victory came;
They, with united breath,
Ascribe their conquest to the Lamb—
Their triumph to his death.

They marked the footsteps he had trod,
(His zeal inspired their breast);
And following their incarnate God,
Possessed the promised rest.

Our glorious Leader claims our praise
For his own pattern given;
While the long cloud of witnesses
Show the same path to heaven.

The Cross.

THE more the cross the nearer heaven;
Where is no cross, there God is not;
The world's turmoil doth hide his face,
Hell, sense, and self, make him forgot:
O where God draws a blessèd lot,
His mercy some dark lines doth trace!

The more the cross, the better Christian;
God lays the touch-stone to each soul.
How many a garden must lie waste
Did not a tear-storm o'er it roll!
Refining grief, a living coal,
Upon the Christian's heart is placed.

The more the cross, the more believing;
In desert lands the palm-trees grow;
And when the grape is strongly pressed,
Then doth its sweetness overflow;
And strength lies hid in every woe
As pearls do in the salt wave rest.

The more the cross, the more the praying;
The bruiséd plants yield sweetest balms;
Man doth not seek to find the pole
In quiet seas and steady calms;
And how should we have David's psalms
Had he not had a troubled soul?

The more the cross, the more the longing;
Out of the vale man upward goes;
Whose pathway through the desert lies,
He craves the land where Jordan flows;
When here the dove finds no repose,
Straight to the ark with joy she flies.

The more the cross, the sweeter death,
For man rejoices then to die,
When as his body is laid down
Much pain and sorrow are laid by;
His cross there on his grave doth lie—
See, man doth wear the victor's crown.

O Jesus, Lord, the crucified!
Now let the cross more welcome be;
Nor let my soul complaining toss;
But plant thou such a heart in me,
As patiently shall look to thee
For gain up yonder, from my loss.

There the Weary are at Rest.

COURAGE, my soul! behold the prize
The Saviour's love provides:
Eternal life beyond the skies
For all whom here he guides.

The wicked cease from troubling there,
The weary are at rest;
Sorrow, and sin, and pain, and care,
No more approach the blest.

A wicked world, and wicked heart,
With Satan now are joined;
Each acts a too successful part
In harassing my mind.

In conflict with this threefold troop,
How weary, Lord, am I!
Did not thy promise bear me up,
My soul must faint and die.

But fighting in my Saviour's strength,
Though many are my foes,
I shall a conqueror be, at length,
O'er all that can oppose.

Then why, my soul, complain or fear?
The crown of glory see!
The more I toil and suffer here,
The sweeter rest will be.

Yonder.

No shadows yonder!
  All light and song;
Each day I wonder,
  And say, How long
Shall time me sunder
  From that dear throng?

No weeping yonder!
  All fled away;
While here I wander
  Each weary day,
And sigh as I ponder
  My long, long stay.

No partings yonder!
  Time and space never
Again shall sunder;
  Hearts cannot sever;
Dearer and fonder
  Hands clasp for ever.

None wanting yonder,
  Bought by the Lamb!
All gathered under
  The evergreen palm;
Loud as night's thunder
  Ascends the glad psalm.

The Death and Burial of a Saint.

WHY do we mourn departing friends,
Or shake at death's alarms?
'Tis but the voice that Jesus sends
To call them to his arms.

Are we not tending upward too,
As fast as time can move?
Nor would we wish the hours more slow,
To keep us from our Love.

Why should we tremble to convey
Their bodies to the tomb?
There the dear flesh of Jesus lay,
And left a long perfume.

The graves of all the saints he blessed,
And softened every bed;
Where should the dying members rest
But with the dying Head?

Thence he arose, ascended high,
And showed our feet the way:
Up to the Lord our flesh shall fly
At the great rising day.

Then let the last loud trumpet sound,
And bid our kindred rise;
Awake, ye nations under ground,
Ye saints, ascend the skies.

This is not your Rest.

My soul, go boldly forth,
Forsake this sinful earth;
What hath it been to thee
But pain and sorrow?
And think'st thou it will be
Better to-morrow?

Why art thou for delay?
Thou cam'st not here to stay;
What tak'st thou for thy part
But heavenly pleasure?
Where then should be thy heart,
But where's thy treasure?

Thy God, thy Head's above;
There is the world of love;
Mansions there purchased are,
By Christ's own merit;
For them he doth prepare
Thee by his Spirit.

God is essential love;
And all the saints above
Are like unto him made,
Each in his measure.
Love is their life and trade,
Their constant pleasure.

What joys must there needs be
Where all God's glory see!

Feeling God's vital love,
Which still is burning;
And flaming God-ward move,
Full love returning.

Lord Jesus, take my spirit,
I trust thy love and merit:
Take home thy wandering sheep,
For thou hast sought it.
My soul in safety keep,
For thou hast bought it.

That Day.

Lo! he comes, with clouds descending,
Once for favoured sinners slain;
Thousand thousand saints attending,
Swell the triumph of his train:
Hallelujah!
Jesus comes—he comes to reign.

Now the Saviour, long expected,
See in solemn pomp appear;
All his saints, by man rejected,
Now shall meet him in the air:
Hallelujah!
See the day of God appear.

All the tokens of his passion
Still his dazzling body bears;

Cause of endless exultation
 To his ransomed worshippers;
 With what rapture
 Gaze we on those glorious scars.

Every eye shall now behold him
 Robed in dreadful majesty;
Those who set at nought and sold him,
 Pierced and nailed him to the tree,
 Deeply wailing,
 Shall the true Messiah see.

Every island, sea, and mountain,
 Heaven and earth shall flee away:
All who hate him, must, confounded,
 Hear the trump proclaim the day;
 Come to judgment!
 Come to judgment! come away!

At his call the dead awaken,
 Rise to life from earth and sea:
All the powers of nature, shaken
 By his look, prepare to flee:
 Careless sinner,
 What will then become of thee?

Horrors past imagination
 Will surprise thy trembling heart;
When thou hear'st thy condemnation,
 "Hence, accursèd wretch, depart!
 Thou with Satan
 And his angels, have thy part!"

But to those who have confessèd,
 Loved and served the Lord below,

He will say, "Come near, ye blessèd,
  See the kingdom I bestow:
      You, forever,
  Shall my love and glory know."

Under sorrow and reproaches
  May this thought our courage raise!
Swiftly God's great day approaches,
  Sighs shall then be changed to praise;
      May we triumph,
  When the world is in a blaze!

Answer thine own bride and Spirit;
  Hasten Lord, and quickly come!
The new heaven and earth to inherit—
  Take thy weeping exiles home!
      All creation
  Travails, groans, and bids thee come!

Yea! amen! let all adore thee,
  High on thine eternal throne!
Saviour, take the power and glory:
  Claim the kingdoms for thine own!
      O come quickly,
  Hallelujah! come, Lord, come!

How Long?

YE visions bright, of heavenly birth,
  Ye glories of the latter day,
Descend upon the fallen earth,
  And chase the shades of night away.

Bid streams of love and mercy flow
Through every vale of human woe,
Till sin, and care, and sorrow cease,
And all the world is hushed to peace.

How long, amid this dying race,
  Shall desolation hold her reign?
How long shall men despise the grace
  And love of him who once was slain?
How long shall heathen bow the knee
To gods that neither hear nor see?
Ye scenes of bliss, so long foretold,
When will your radiant hues unfold?

The gospel of the living God
  Shall echo the wide earth around,
Till every place of man's abode
  Shall know the joy-inspiring sound.
Who can the heavenly scene portray?
Who can describe the glorious day?
We hail its glimmerings from afar,
We hail the bright, the morning star!

Let there be Light.

Thou, whose almighty word
Chaos and darkness heard,
  And took their flight;
Hear us, we humbly pray,
And where the Gospel day
Sheds not its glorious ray,
  Let there be light.

Thou, who didst come to bring,
On thy redeeming wing,
  Healing and sight—
Health to the sick in mind,
Sight to the inly blind—
O now, to all mankind,
  Let there be light.

Spirit of truth and love,
Life-giving, holy Dove,
  Speed forth thy flight;
Move on the waters' face,
Bearing the lamp of grace;
And in earth's darkest place
  Let there be light.

Blessèd and holy Three,
Glorious Trinity,
  Wisdom, Love, Might—
Boundless as ocean's tide,
Rolling in fullest pride,
Through the world far and wide,
  Let there be light.

The Labourers.

Sow in the morn thy seed,
  At eve hold not thy hand;
To doubt and fear give thou no heed,
  Broad-cast it round the land.

Beside all waters sow,
The highway furrows stock,
Drop it where thorns and thistles grow,
Scatter it on the rock.

The good, the fruitful ground,
Expect not here nor there;
O'er hill and dale by spots 'tis found:
Go forth then, everywhere.

Thou know'st not which may thrive,
The late or early sown;
Grace keeps the precious germ alive,
When and wherever sown.

And duly shall appear,
In verdure, beauty, strength,
The tender blade, the stalk, the ear,
And the full corn at length.

Thou canst not toil in vain:
Cold, heat, and moist, and dry,
Shall foster and mature the grain
For garners in the sky.

Then when the glorious end,
The day of God is come,
The angel-reapers shall descend,
And heaven sing "Harvest-home!"

The Right must Win.

O IT is hard to work for God,
To rise and take his part
Upon this battle-field of earth,
And not sometimes lose heart!

He hides himself so wondrously,
As though there was no God;
He is least seen when all the powers
Of ill are most abroad;

Or he deserts us in the hour
The fight is all but lost;
And seems to leave us to ourselves
Just when we need him most.

O there is less to try our faith
In our mysterious creed,
Than in the Godless look of earth
In these our hours of need.

Ill masters good; good seems to change
To ill with greatest ease;
And, worst of all, the good with good
Is at cross purposes.

The Church, the Sacraments, the Faith,
Their uphill journey take,
Lose here what there they gain, and if
We lean upon them, break.

It is not so, but so it looks;
  And we lose courage then;
And doubts will come if God hath kept
  His promises to men.

Ah! God is other than we think;
  His ways are far above,
Far beyond reason's height, and reached
  Only by childlike love.

The look, the fashion of God's ways
  Love's lifelong study are;
She can be bold, and guess, and act,
  Where reason would not dare.

She has a prudence of her own;
  Her step is firm and free;
Yet there is cautious science, too,
  In her simplicity.

Workman of God! O lose not heart,
  But learn what God is like;
And in the darkest battle-field
  Thou shalt know where to strike.

O blest is he to whom is given
  The instinct that can tell
That God is on the field, when he
  Is most invisible!

And blest is he who can divine
  Where real right doth lie,
And dares to take the side that seems
  Wrong to man's blindfold eye!

O learn to scorn the praise of men!
O learn to lose with God!
For Jesus won the world through shame,
And beckons thee his road.

God's glory is a wondrous thing,
Most strange in all its ways,
And, of all things on earth, least like
What men agree to praise.

As he can endless glory weave
From time's misjudging shame,
In his own world he is content
To play a losing game.

Muse on his justice, downcast soul!
Muse, and take better heart;
Back with thine angel to the field,
Good luck shall crown thy part!

God's justice is a bed where we
Our anxious hearts may lay,
And, weary with ourselves, may sleep
Our discontent away.

For right is right, since God is God;
And right the day must win;
To doubt would be disloyalty,
To falter would be sin!

Strength.

CAST thy burden on the Lord,
Only lean upon his word;
Thou wilt soon have cause to bless
His unchanging faithfulness.

He sustains thee by his hand,
He enables thee to stand;
Those whom Jesus once hath loved,
From his grace are never moved.

Heaven and earth may pass away,
God's free grace shall not decay;
He hath promised to fulfil
All the pleasure of his will.

Jesus! guardian of thy flock,
Be thyself our constant rock;
Make us by thy powerful hand,
Firm as Zion's mountain stand.

The Battle-song of Gustavus Adolphus.

FEAR not, O little flock, the foe
Who madly seeks your overthrow,
    Dread not his rage and power.
What though your courage sometimes faints,
His seeming triumph o'er God's saints
    Lasts but a little hour.

Be of good cheer; your cause belongs
To him who can avenge your wrongs,
    Leave it to him our Lord.
Though hidden yet from all our eyes,
He sees the Gideon who shall rise
    To save us, and his word.

As true as God's own word is true,
Not earth or hell with all their crew
    Against us shall prevail.
A jest and by-word are they grown;
God is with us, we are his own,
    Our victory cannot fail.

Amen, Lord Jesus, grant our prayer!
Great Captain, now thine arm make bare;
    Fight for us once again!
So shall the saints and martyrs raise
A mighty chorus to thy praise,
    World without end. Amen.

Twenty-third Psalm.

THE Lord's my Shepherd, I'll not want,
  He makes me down to lie
In pastures green: he leadeth me
  The quiet waters by.

My soul he doth restore again,
  And me to walk doth make
Within the paths of righteousness,
  Even for his own name's sake.

Yea, though I walk in death's dark vale,
  Yet will I fear none ill;
For thou art with me, and thy rod
  And staff me comfort still.

My table thou hast furnishèd
  In presence of my foes;
My head with oil thou dost anoint,
  And my cup overflows.

Goodness and mercy all my life
  Shall surely follow me;
And in God's house for evermore
  My dwelling-place shall be.

Thy Word is Good.

Whatever God does is well!
His children find it so.
Some he doth not with plenty bless,
Yet loves them not the less;
But draws their hearts unto himself away—
O hearts, obey!

Whatever God does is well,
Whether he gives or takes!
And what we from his hand receive
Suffices us to live.
He takes and gives, while yet he loves us still.
Then love his will.

Whatever God does is well!
And what can our will do?

We cannot reap from what we sow
But what his power makes grow.
Sometimes he doth all other good destroy,
To be thy joy.

Whatever God does is well!
And his will shall prevail.
Doth he refuse thy hands to fill?
He knows thy heart to still.
A Christian, from a very little gift,
Much joy can sift.

Whatever God does is well!
Although the field look dark:
Yet cheerful in his path we go;
And by our faith we know
That Christ for us hath heavenly riches bought.
Can we lack aught?

Whatever God does is well!
In patience let us wait:
He doth himself our burdens bear,
He doth for us take care.
And he, our God, knows all our weary days.
Come, give him praise!

Evening Song, after a Day of Difficulty.

LORD, a happy child of thine,
  Patient through the love of thee,
In the light, the life, divine,
  Lives and walks at liberty.

Leaning on thy tender care,
  Thou hast led my soul aright—
Fervent was my morning prayer,
  Joyful is my song to-night.

O my Saviour, Guardian true,
  All my life is thine to keep—
At thy feet my work I do,
  In thy arms I fall asleep.

Tender mercies, on my way
  Falling softly like the dew,
Sent me freshly every day,
  I will bless the Lord for you.

Though I have not all I would,
  Though to greater bliss I go,
Every present gift of good
  To eternal love I owe.

Source of all that comforts me,
  Well of joy for which I long,
Let the song I sing to thee
  Be an everlasting song.

A New Year.

COME, let us anew our journey pursue,
    Roll round with the year,
And never stand still till the Master appear.
His adorable will let us gladly fulfil,
    And our talents improve,
By the patience of hope and the labours of love.

Our life is a dream; our time, as a stream,
Glides swiftly away,
And the fugitive moment refuses to stay.
The arrow is flown—the moment is gone;
The millennial year
Rushes on to our view, and eternity's here.

O that each, in the day of his coming, may say,
I have fought my way through;
I have finished the work thou didst give me to do.
O that each from his Lord may receive the glad word,
Well and faithfully done!
Enter into my joy, and sit down on my throne.

Life.

At every motion of our breath
Life trembles on the brink of death,
A taper's flame that upward turns,
While downward to the dust it burns.

A moment ushered us to birth,
Heirs of the commonwealth of earth;
Moment by moment years are past,
And one ere long will be our last.

'Twixt that, long fled, which gave us light,
And that which soon shall end in night,
There is a point no eye can see,
Yet on it hangs eternity.

This is that moment—who can tell
Whether it lead to heaven or hell?
This is that moment—as we choose,
The immortal soul we save or lose.

Time past and time to come are not;
Time present is our only lot;
O God! henceforth our hearts incline
To seek no other love than thine.

What Shall it Profit a Man?

WHAT is the thing of greatest price
 The whole creation round?
That, which was lost in Paradise,
 That, which in Christ is found.

The soul of man—Jehovah's breath!
 That keeps two worlds at strife;
Hell moves beneath to work its death;
 Heaven stoops to give it life.

God, to reclaim it, did not spare
 His well-belovéd Son;
Jesus, to save it, deigned to bear
 The sins of all in One.

The Holy Spirit sealed the plan,
 And pledged the blood divine,
To ransom every soul of man;
 That blood was shed for mine.

And is this treasure borne below
  In earthly vessels frail?
Can none its utmost value know
  Till flesh and spirit fail?

Then let us gather round the Cross,
  This knowledge to obtain,
Not by the soul's eternal loss,
  But everlasting gain.

To-morrow.

To-day mine, to-morrow thine!
  So we hear the slow bell ringing,
When in God's Acre to recline
  We the dead are softly bringing;
And the grave calls out, Resign:
To-day mine, to-morrow thine!

To-day life, to-morrow death!
  Life speeds its wings and tarries never;
Is not that a wisdom-breath—
  Think of life which stays forever?
Need of thinking each one hath:
To-day life, to-morrow death!

One follows another now,
  As the ocean waves wind-driven;
For all with which Hope can endow,
  What security is given?
Each in his sleeping-room must bow;
One follows another now!

O man, it is the old law,
  How many years, death counteth not.
Is thy health without one flaw?
  Soon even thy name shall be forgot.
Earth to itself all earth will draw—
O man, it is the old law!

Ah to be wise, as near my end!
  I wish to die before I'm dying;
That shall my soul from death defend,
  When death's last strength my soul is trying.
Prepare me thereto, God, my Friend!
Ah to be wise, as near my end!

Blessed who in Christ shall die!
  Death is changed to life forever;
He has life when death is nigh,
  Life beyond, which endeth never!
Who hath it not, undone must cry!
Blessed who in Christ shall die!

Help.

O THOU that wouldst not have
  One wretched sinner die;
Who diedst thyself, my soul to save
  From endless misery:
Show me the way to shun
  Thy dreadful wrath severe;
That when thou comest on thy throne,
  I may with joy appear.

Thou art thyself the way;
  Thyself in me reveal;
So shall I spend my life's short day
  Obedient to thy will:
So shall I love my God,
  Because he first loved me;
And praise thee in thy bright abode
  To all eternity.

Christ is All.

CHRIST, of all my hopes the ground—
  Christ, the spring of all my joy!
Still in thee let me be found,
  Still for thee my powers employ.

Let thy love my heart inflame;
  Keep thy fear before my sight;
Be thy praise my highest aim;
  Be thy smile my chief delight.

Fountain of o'erflowing grace!
  Freely from thy fulness give:
Till I close my earthly race,
  Be it "Christ for me to live!"

Firmly trusting in thy blood,
  Nothing shall my heart confound;
Safely I shall pass the flood,
  Safely reach Immanuel's ground.

When I touch the blessed shore,
  Back the closing waves shall roll;
Death's dark stream shall never more
  Part from thee my ravished soul.

Thus, oh! thus an entrance give
  To the land of cloudless sky;
Having known it "Christ to live,"
  Let me know it "gain to die."

The Full Assurance of Hope.

How happy every child of grace
  Who knows his sins forgiven!
This earth, he cries, is not my place;
  I seek my place in heaven:
A country far from mortal sight,
  Yet O by faith I see,
The land of rest, the saint's delight—
  The heaven prepared for me.

A stranger in the world below,
  I calmly sojourn here;
Nor can its happiness or woe
  Provoke my hope or fear:
Its evils in a moment end;
  Its joys as soon are past:
But O, the bliss to which I tend,
  Eternally shall last.

To that Jerusalem above,
With singing I repair;
While in the flesh, my hope and love,
My heart and soul, are there.
There my exalted Saviour stands,
My merciful High Priest;
And still extends his wounded hands
To take me to his breast!

O what a blessed hope is ours!
While here on earth we stay,
We more than taste the heavenly powers,
And ante-date the day:
We feel the resurrection near,
Our life in Christ concealed,
And with his glorious presence here
Our earthen vessels filled.

O would he more of heaven bestow!
And when the vessels break,
Let our triumphant spirits go
Before the God we seek;
In rapturous awe on him to gaze,
Who bought the sight for me;
And shout and wonder at his grace
To all eternity.

Christ's Intercession.

HE lives—the great Redeemer lives;
What joy the blest assurance gives;
And now, before his Father God,
Pleads the full merit of his blood.

Repeated crimes awake our fears,
And justice, armed with frowns, appears;
But in the Saviour's lovely face
Sweet mercy smiles—and all is peace!

Hence then, ye black, despairing thoughts—
Above our fears, above our faults
His powerful intercessions rise;
And guilt recedes, and terror dies.

In every dark, distressful hour,
When sin and Satan join their power,
Let this dear hope repel the dart,
That Jesus bears us on his heart.

Great Advocate, almighty Friend!
On him our humble hopes depend;
Our cause can never, never fail,
For Jesus pleads, and must prevail.

The Creature.

LORD, what is man! that child of pride,
That boasts his high degree?
If left one moment to himself
He sinks, and where is he?

In thee I live, and move, and am,
Thou deal'st me out my days;
Lord, as thou dost renew my life,
Let me renew thy praise.

To thee I come, from thee I am,
  And for thee I must be;
'Tis better for me not to live
  Than not to live to thee.

Thou art my living fountain, Lord,
  On me thy streams still flow;
Myself I render up to thee,
  To whom myself I owe.

This noble and immortal soul
  Thou breathedst into me,
And this my soul shall still breathe forth
  Immortal praise to thee.

Our Guide.

COME, gracious Spirit, heavenly Dove,
With light and comfort from above;
Be thou our Guardian, thou our Guide,
O'er every thought and step preside.

The light of truth to us display,
And make us know and choose thy way:
Plant holy fear in every heart,
That we from God may not depart.

Lead us to holiness—the road
That we must take to dwell with God;
Lead us to Christ, the living way,
Nor let us from his precepts stray;

Lead us to God, our final rest,
In his enjoyment to be blest;
Lead us to heaven, the seat of bliss,
Where pleasure in perfection is.

At the Haven.

High in yonder realms of light
  Dwell the raptured saints above;
Far beyond our feeble sight,
  Happy in Immanuel's love:
Pilgrims in this vale of tears,
  Once they knew, like us below,
Gloomy doubts, distressing fears,
  Torturing pain and heavy woe.

Mid the chorus of the skies,
  Mid the angelic lyres above,
Hark! their songs melodious rise,
  Songs of praise to Jesus' love:
Happy spirits! ye are fled
  Where no grief can entrance find—
Lulled to rest the aching head,
  Soothed the anguish of the mind.

All is tranquil and serene,
  Calm and undisturbed repose;
There no cloud can intervene,
  There no angry tempest blows:

Every tear is wiped away,
   Sighs no more shall heave the breast;
Night is lost in endless day,
   Sorrow in eternal rest.

Art Thou also His Disciple?

'Tis a point I long to know,
   Oft it causes anxious thought;
Do I love the Lord or no?
   Am I his, or am I not?

If I love, why am I thus?
   Why this dull, this lifeless frame?
Hardly, sure, can they be worse
   Who have never heard his name!

Could my heart so hard remain,
   Prayer a task and burden prove,
Every trifle give me pain,
   If I knew a Saviour's love?

When I turn my eyes within
   All is dark, and vain, and wild:
Filled with unbelief and sin,
   Can I deem myself a child?

If I pray, or hear, or read,
   Sin is mixed with all I do;
You that love the Lord indeed,
   Tell me, is it thus with you?

Yet I mourn my stubborn will,
  Find my sin a grief and thrall;
Should I grieve for what I feel
  If I did not love at all?

Could I joy his saints to meet,
  Choose the ways I once abhorred,
Find at times the promise sweet,
  If I did not love the Lord?

Lord, decide the doubtful case!
  Thou who art thy people's sun,
Shine upon thy work of grace,
  If it be indeed begun.

Let me love thee more and more,
  If I love at all, I pray;
If I have not loved before,
  Help me to begin to-day.

Look not Behind Thee.

WHY haltest thus, deluded heart?
  Why waverest longer in thy choice?
Is it so hard to choose the part
  Offered by heaven's entreating voice?
Oh look with clearer eyes again,
Nor strive to enter in, in vain.
          Press on!

Remember, 'tis not Cæsar's throne,
  Nor earthly honour, wealth, or might,
Whereby God's favour shall be shown
  To him who conquers in this fight;
Himself, and an eternity
Of bliss and rest, he offers thee.
  Press on!

God crowneth no divided heart;
  Oh hallow to him all thy life!
Who loveth Jesus but in part,
  He works himself much pain and strife,
And gains what he deserveth well,
Here conflict, and hereafter hell.
  Press on!

Who wrestling long, with many a cry,
  Can bid farewell at last to all;
Yet loveth still the Lord most high,
  Loves him alone whate'er befall,
Is counted worthy of the crown,
And on a kingly throne set down.
  Press on!

Then break the rotten bonds away
  That hinder you your race to run,
That make you linger oft and stay;
  Oh be your course afresh begun!
Let no false rest your soul deceive,
Up! 'tis a heaven you must achieve!
  Press on!

Omnipotence is on your side,
And wisdom watches o'er your heads,
And God himself will be your guide
So ye but follow where he leads;
How many, guided by his hand,
Have reached ere now their native land.
Press on!

Let not the body dull the soul;
Its weakness, fears, and sloth despise;
Man toils and roams from pole to pole
To gain some earthly fleeting prize;
The Highest Good he little cares
To win, or, striving, soon despairs.
Press on!

Oh help each other, hasten on,
Behold the goal is nigh at hand;
Soon shall the battle-field be won,
Soon shall your King before you stand!
To calmest rest he leads you now,
And sets his crown upon your brow.
Press on!

The Open Door.

Thou seest my feebleness,
Jesus, be thou my power,
My help and refuge in distress,
My fortress and my tower.

Give me to trust in thee;
  Be thou my sure abode:
My horn, and rock, and buckler be,
  My Saviour and my God.

Myself I cannot save,
  Myself I cannot keep,
But strength in thee I surely have,
  Whose eyelids never sleep.

My soul to thee alone,
  Now therefore I commend:
Thou, Jesus, love me as thine own,
  And love me to the end.

Humble Trust.

LORD, didst thou die, but not for me?
  Am I forbid to trust thy blood?
Hast thou not pardons rich and free?
  And grace, an overwhelming flood?

Who then shall drive my trembling soul
  From thee, to regions of despair?
Who has surveyed the sacred roll,
  And found my name not written there?

Presumptuous thought! to fix the bound,
  To limit mercy's sovereign reign:
What other happy souls have found
  I'll seek, nor shall I seek in vain.

I own my guilt, my sins confess:
  Can men or devils make them more?
Of crimes already numberless,
  Vain the attempt to swell the score.

Were the black list before my sight,
  While I remember thou hast died,
'Twould only urge my speedier flight,
  To seek salvation at thy side.

Low at thy feet I'll cast me down,
  To thee reveal my guilt and fear;
And, if thou spurn me from thy throne,
  I'll be the first who perished there.

Sing.

SING, sing his lofty praise,
Whom angels cannot raise,
  But whom they sing;
Jesus, who reigns above,
Object of angels' love,
Jesus, whose grace we prove,
  Jesus, our King.

Jesus the curse sustained,
Bitter the cup he drained,
  Happy for us:
Angels were filled with awe,
When their own King they saw
Honour his holy law,
  Honour it thus.

Rich is the grace we sing,
Poor is the praise we bring,
Not as we ought:
But when we see his face
In yonder glorious place,
Then we shall sing his grace,
Sing without fault.

Yet we will sing of him,
Jesus our lofty theme,
Jesus we'll sing;
Glory and power are his,
His too the kingdom is;
Triumph, ye saints, in this,
Jesus is King.

Give us this Day our Daily Bread.

WHILE others pray for grace to die,
O Lord, I pray for grace to live!
For every hour a fresh supply—
O see my need, and freely give.

I do not dread the hour of death—
If I am thine, no fears remain,—
I know that with my parting breath
I leave for ever mortal pain.

And if it should be then thy will
A cloud should on the future be,
The bow of promise spans it still,
I will believe—I need not see!

E'en if the darkness should appear
  Too deep for faith as well as sight;
If I am thine, thou wilt be near,
  And take me to thy heavenly light.

But oh, my Lord! in life's highway
  I crave the sunshine of thy face!
And every moment of the day
  I need thy strong supporting grace.

My weary spirit cannot drink
  At springs which rise from earth alone;
When I can do no more, I think
  Of living waters from thy throne.

I dare not, will not, Lord, deny
  That heart and feet both go astray,
Therefore the more to thee I cry
  To keep me in thy chosen way.

The more, the more my unbelief
  Keeps me from walking near to thee;
The more, Lord Jesus, is my grief,
  The more I long thy face to see!

Yet not my sorrow nor my pain
  Can keep my heart to heaven and thee ·
Lord, could I ever stray again
  If thou wouldst always look on me?

Send Forth Thy Light and Thy Truth.

Come, Holy Spirit, come,
With energy divine,
And on this poor benighted soul,
With beams of mercy shine.

Melt, melt this frozen heart;
This stubborn will subdue;
Each evil passion overcome,
And form me all anew.

Mine will the profit be,
But thine shall be the praise;
And unto thee will I devote
The remnant of my days.

My Name is Jacob.

Nay, I cannot let thee go
Till a blessing thou bestow:
Do not turn away thy face,
Mine's an urgent, pressing case.

Dost thou ask me who I am?
Ah, my Lord, thou know'st my name!
Yet the question gives a plea
To support my suit with thee.

Thou didst once a wretch behold,
In rebellion blindly bold,
Scorn thy grace, thy power defy,
That poor rebel, Lord, was I.

Once a sinner, near despair,
Sought thy mercy-seat by prayer;
Mercy heard, and set him free—
Lord, that mercy came to me.

Many years have passed since then,
Many changes have I seen,
Yet have been upheld till now;
Who could hold me up but thou?

Thou hast helped in every need,
This emboldens me to plead;
After so much mercy past,
Canst thou let me sink at last?

No—I must maintain my hold,
'Tis thy goodness makes me bold;
I can no denial take
When I plead for Jesus' sake.

Fear Him.

THROUGH all the changing scenes of life,
In trouble and in joy,
The praises of my God shall still
My heart and tongue employ.

Of his deliverance I will boast,
  Till all who are distressed,
From my example comfort take,
  And charm their griefs to rest.

The hosts of God encamp around
  The dwellings of the just;
Protection he affords to all
  Who make his name their trust.

O make but trial of his love,
  Experience will decide
How blest are they, and only they,
  Who in his truth confide.

Fear him, ye saints, and you will then
  Have nothing else to fear;
Make you his service your delight,
  Your wants shall be his care.

While hungry lions lack their prey,
  The Lord will food provide
For such as put their trust in him,
  And see their needs supplied.

Waiting.

"JESUS' hour is not yet come;"
  Let this word thy answer be,
Pilgrim, asking for thy home,
  Longing to be blest and free.
Yet a season tarry on—
Nobly borne, is nobly done.

While oppressing cares and fears,
  Night and day no respite leave,
Still prolonged through many years,
  None to help thee, or relieve;
Hold the word of promise fast,
Till deliverance comes at last.

Every creature-hope and trust,
  Every earthly prop or stay,
May lie prostrate in the dust,
  May have failed or passed away;
Then, when darkest falls the night,
Jesus comes, and all is light.

Yes, the Comforter draws nigh
  To the breaking, bursting heart,
For, with tender sympathy,
  He has seen and felt its smart:
Through its darkest hours of ill
He is waiting, watching still.

Dost thou ask, *When* comes his hour?
  Then, when it shall aid thee best.
Trust his faithfulness and power,
  Trust in him and quiet rest.
Suffer on, and hope, and wait—
Jesus never comes too late.

Blessèd day, which hastens fast,
  End of conflict and of sin!
Death itself shall die at last,
  Heaven's eternal joys begin.
Then eternity shall prove
God is Light, and God is Love.

Praise to the Redeemer.

Mighty God, while angels bless thee,
May an infant lisp thy name?
Lord of man as well as angels,
Thou art every creature's theme.
Hallelujah,
Hallelujah, Hallelujah. Amen.

Lord of every land and nation,
Ancient of eternal days!
Sounded through the wide creation
Be thy just, exalted praise.

For the grandeur of thy nature—
Grand beyond a seraph's thought—
For created works of power,
Works with skill and kindness wrought;

For thy providence that governs
Through thine empire's wide domain—
Wings an angel, guides a sparrow—
Blessèd be thy gentle reign.

But thy rich, thy free redemption,
Dark through brightness, all along!
Thought is poor, and poor expression—
Who dare sing that awful song?

Brightness of thy Father's glory,
Shall thy praise unuttered lie?
Fly, my tongue, such guilty silence!
Sing the Lord who came to die.

Did archangels sing thy coming?
   Did the shepherds learn their lays?
Shame would cover me, ungrateful,
   Should my tongue refuse thy praise.

From the highest throne in glory,
   To the cross of deepest woe—
All to ransom guilty captives!
   Flow my praise, forever flow.

Go, return, immortal Saviour;
   Leave thy footstool, take thy throne:
Thence return, and reign forever;
   Be the kingdom all thine own.
      Hallelujah!

Looking at the Cross.

In evil long I took delight,
   Unawed by shame or fear,
Till a new object struck my sight,
   And stopped my wild career.

I saw one hanging on a tree,
   In agonies and blood,
Who fixed his languid eyes on me,
   As near his cross I stood.

Sure, never, till my latest breath,
   Can I forget that look;
It seemed to charge me with his death,
   Though not a word he spoke.

24*

My conscience felt, and owned the guilt,
And plunged me in despair;
I saw my sins his blood had spilt,
And helped to nail him there.

Alas, I knew not what I did:
But now my tears are vain;
Where shall my trembling soul be hid?
For I the Lord have slain.

A second look he gave, which said,
"I freely all forgive;
This blood is for thy ransom paid,
I die that thou may'st live."

Thus while his death my sin displays,
In all its blackest hue,
Such is the mystery of grace,
It seals my pardon too.

With pleasing grief and mournful joy
My spirit now is filled,
That I should such a life destroy,
Yet live by him I killed.

The End of the Law.

'TIS finished! the Messiah dies—
Cut off for sins, but not his own;
Accomplished is the sacrifice—
The great redeeming work is done.

'Tis finished! all the debt is paid;
   Justice divine is satisfied;
The grand and full atonement made;
   Christ for a guilty world hath died.

The veil is rent; in him alone
   The living way to heaven is seen;
The middle wall is broken down,
   And all mankind may enter in.

The types and figures are fulfilled;
   Exacted is the legal pain;
The precious promises are sealed;
   The spotless Lamb of God is slain.

Death, hell, and sin, are now subdued;
   All grace is now to sinners given;
And lo! I plead the atoning blood,
   And in thy right I claim my heaven.

Assurance of Faith.

A DEBTOR to mercy alone,
   Of covenant mercy I sing;
Nor fear, with thy righteousness on,
   My person and off'rings to bring:
The terrors of law and of God
   With me can have nothing to do;
My Saviour's obedience and blood,
   Hide all my transgressions from view.

The work which his goodness began,
  The arm of his strength will complete;
His promise is yea and amen,
  And never was forfeited yet:
Things future, nor things that are now,
  Not all things below nor above,
Can make him his purpose forego,
  Or sever my soul from his love.

My name from the palms of his hands,
  Eternity will not erase:
Imprest on his heart it remains,
  In marks of indelible grace:
Yes, I to the end shall endure,
  As sure as the earnest is given;
More happy, but not more secure,
  The glorified spirits in heaven.

The Friend.

ONE there is above all others,
  Well deserves the name of Friend!
His is love beyond a brother's,
  Costly, free, and knows no end:
They who once his kindness prove,
Find it everlasting love!

Which of all our friends to save us
  Could or would have shed their blood?
But our Jesus died to have us
  Reconciled in him to God.

This was boundless love indeed!
Jesus is a friend in need.

Men when raised to lofty stations,
  Often know their friends no more;
Slight and scorn their poor relations,
  Though they valued them before:
But our Saviour always owns
Those whom he redeemed with groans.

When he lived on earth abased,
  Friend of sinners was his name;
Now above all glory raised,
  He rejoices in the same:
Still he calls them brethren, friends,
And to all their wants attends.

Could we bear from one another
  What he daily bears from us?
Yet this glorious Friend and Brother
  Loves us though we treat him thus:
Though for good we render ill,
He accounts us brethren still.

Oh! for grace our hearts to soften;
  Teach us, Lord, at length to love;
We, alas! forget too often
  What a Friend we have above.
But when home our souls are brought,
We will love thee as we ought.

Israel Doth not Know.

THE kine unguided went,
By the directest road,
When the Philistines homeward sent
The ark of Israel's God.

Lowing they passed along,
And left their calves shut up;
They felt an instinct for their young,
But would not turn or stop.

Shall brutes, devoid of thought,
Their Maker's will obey;
And we who by his grace are taught,
More stubborn prove than they?

He shed his precious blood
To make us his alone;
If washed in that atoning flood,
We are no more our own.

If he his will reveal,
Let us obey his call;
And think, whate'er the flesh may feel,
His love deserves our all.

We should maintain in view
His glory, as our end;
Too much we cannot bear, or do,
For such a matchless friend.

His saints should stand prepared
  In duty's path to run;
Nor count their greatest trials hard,
  So that his will be done.

With Jesus for our guide,
  The path is safe, though rough;
The promise says, "I will provide;"
  And faith replies, "Enough!"

Weakness.

WHO seeks in weakness an excuse,
  His sins will vanquish never;
Unless he heart and mind renews,
  He is deceived for ever.
    The straight and narrow way,
    That shines to perfect day,
He hath not found, hath never trod;
    Little he knows, I ween,
    What prayer and conflict mean
To one who hath the light of God.

In what the world calls weakness, lurks
  The very strength of evil;
Full mightily it helps the works
  Of our great foe the devil.
    Awake, my soul, awake,
    Quickly thy refuge take

With him, the Almighty, who can save:
    One look from Christ, thy Lord,
    Can sever every cord
That binds thee now, a wretched slave.

Know, the first step in Christian lore
  Is to depart from sin;
True faith will leave the world no more
  A place thy heart within,—
    Thy Saviour's Spirit first
    The heavy bonds must burst,
Wherein death bound thee in thy need;
    Then the freed spirit knows
    What strength he gives to those
Who with their Lord are risen indeed.

And what thy Spirit, Lord, began,
  Help thou with inner might!
Earth has no better gift for man
  Than strength and love of right.
    Oh make thy followers just!
    Who look to thee in trust;
Thy strength and justice let us know;
    Our souls through thee would wear
    The power of grace, most fair
Of all the jewels faith can show.

Strong Son of God, break down thy foes,
  So shall we conquer ours;
Strong in the might from thee that flows,
  We mourn not lack of powers,
    E'er since that from above,
    The witness of thy love

Thy Spirit came, and doth abide
With us, dispelling fear
And falsehood, that we here
May fight and conquer on thy side.

Give strength whene'er our strength must fail;
Give strength the flesh to curb;
Give strength when craft and sin prevail
To weaken and disturb.
The world doth lay her snares
To catch us unawares
Give strength to sweep them all away;
So in our utmost need,
And when death comes indeed,
Thy strength shall be our perfect stay.

The Believer's Safety.

THAT man no guard nor weapon needs,
Whose heart the blood of Jesus knows;
But safe may pass, if duty leads,
Through burning sands and mountain snows.

Released from guilt, he feels no fear,
Redemption is his shield and tower;
He sees his Saviour always near
To help in every trying hour.

Though I am weak, and Satan strong,
And often to assault me tries;
When Jesus is my shield and song,
Abashed the wolf before me flies.

His love possessing, I am blest,
Secure whatever change may come:
Whether I go to east or west,
With him I still shall be at home.

If placed beneath the northern pole,
Though winter reigns with rigour there,
His gracious beams would cheer my soul,
And make a spring throughout the year.

Or if the desert's sunburnt soil
My lonely dwelling e'er should prove,
His presence would support my toil,
Whose smile is life, whose voice is love.

Resignation.

ONE prayer I have,—all prayers in one,
When I am wholly thine;
Thy will, my God, thy will be done,
And let that will be mine.

All-wise, all-mighty, and all-good,
In thee I firmly trust;
Thy ways, unknown or understood,
Are merciful and just.

Is life with many comforts crowned,
Upheld in peace and health,
With dear affections twined around,
Lord, in my time of wealth,—

May I remember, that to thee,
Whate'er I have I owe;
And back in gratitude from me,
May all thy bounties flow.

Thy gifts are only then enjoyed,
When used as talents lent;
Those talents only well employed,
When in thy service spent.

And though thy wisdom takes away,
Shall I arraign thy will?
No, let me bless thy name, and say,
"The Lord is gracious still."

A pilgrim through the earth I roam,
Of nothing long possessed,
And all must fail when I go home,
For this is not my rest.

Write but my name upon the roll
Of thy redeemed above,
Then heart, and mind, and strength, and soul,
I'll love thee for thy love.

Peace in Believing.

Rejoice evermore,
With angels above,
In Jesus's power,
In Jesus's love;

With glad exultation
  Your triumph proclaim,
Ascribing salvation
  To God and the Lamb.

Thou, Lord, our relief
  In trouble hast been,
Hast saved us from grief,
  Hast saved us from sin:
The power of thy Spirit
  Hath set our hearts free,
And now we inherit
  All fulness in thee.

All fulness of peace,
  All fulness of joy,
A spiritual bliss
  That never shall die;
To us it is given,
  In Jesus, to know
The kingdom of heaven
  Commencing below.

A Morning Hymn.

CHRIST, whose glory fills the skies,
  Christ the true, the only light,
Sun of righteousness, arise,
  Triumph o'er the shades of night;
Day spring from on high, be near,
Day star, in my heart appear.

Dark and cheerless is the morn,
   Unaccompanied by thee;
Joyless is the day's return,
   Till thy mercy's beams I see
Till they inward light impart,
Glad my eyes and warm my heart.

Visit then this soul of mine,
   Pierce the gloom of sin and grief,
Fill me, radiancy divine,
   Scatter all my unbelief;
More and more thyself display,
Shining to the perfect day.

Dryness in Prayer.

O for the happy days gone by,
   When love ran smooth and free,
Days when my spirit so enjoyed
   More than earth's liberty!

O for the times when on my heart
   Long prayer had never palled,
Times when the ready thought of God
   Would come when it was called!

Then, when I knelt to meditate,
   Sweet thoughts came o'er my soul,
Countless, and bright, and beautiful,
   Beyond my own control.

O who hath locked those fountains up?
Those visions who hath stayed?
What sudden act hath thus transformed
My sunshine into shade?

This freezing heart, O Lord! this will
Dry as the desert sand,
Good thoughts that will not come, bad thoughts
That come without command,—

A faith that seems not faith, a hope
That cares not for its aim,
A love that none the hotter grows
At Jesus' blessèd name,—

The weariness of prayer, the mist
O'er conscience overspread,
The chill repugnance to frequent
The feast of angels' bread:—

If this drear change be thine, O Lord!
If it be thy sweet will,
Spare not, but to the very brim
The bitter chalice fill.

But if it hath been sin of mine,
O show that sin to me,
Not to get back the sweetness lost,
But to make peace with thee.

One thing alone, dear Lord! I dread;—
To have a secret spot
That separates my soul from thee,
And yet to know it not.

O when the tide of graces set
So full upon my heart,
I know, dear Lord! how faithlessly
I did my little part.

I know how well my heart hath earned
A chastisement like this,
In trifling many a grace away
In self-complacent bliss.

But if this weariness hath come
A present from on high,
Teach me to find the hidden wealth
That in its depths may lie.

So in this darkness I can learn
To tremble and adore,
To sound my own vile nothingness,
And thus to love thee more,—

To love thee, and yet not to think
That I can love so much,—
To have thee with me, Lord! all day,
Yet not to feel thy touch.

If I have served thee, Lord! for hire,
Hire which thy beauty showed,
Ah! I can serve thee now for nought,
And only as my God.

O blesséd be this darkness then,
This deep in which I lie,
And blesséd be all things that teach
God's dread supremacy!

Faint, yet Pursuing.

SOLDIERS of Christ, arise,
And put your armour on;
Engage your enemies;
Let every fear be gone:
Now take the field, the fight renew,
And never yield—"though faint, pursue."

Come feed on heavenly bread,
'Twill make you strong to fight;
God will supply your need,
And put your foes to flight:
His arm is strong, his word is true,
Ye saints, go on, "though faint, pursue."

Wage war with every foe,
For God is on your side,
Let all the nations know
That you in God confide:
Gird on your sword, the fight renew,
Look to the Lord, "though faint, pursue."

Though sin, and death, and hell,
Your heavenly march oppose;
Fear not, it shall be well,
God will confound your foes:
Go on, ye saints, the fight renew,
And Gideon like, "though faint, pursue."

Ne'er lay your weapons down,
Till death shall close the strife;
Till you receive a crown
Of everlasting life:
On God depend, the fight renew,
As Gideon conquered, so shall you.

With You Alway.

Why pour'st thou forth thine anxious plaint,
Despairing of relief,
As if the Lord o'erlooked thy cause,
And did not heed thy grief?

Hast thou not known, hast thou not heard
That firm remains, on high,
The everlasting throne of him
Who formed the earth and sky?

Art thou afraid his power shall fail
When comes thy evil day?
And can an all-creating arm
Grow weary, or decay?

Supreme in wisdom as in power,
The Rock of ages stands;
Though him thou canst not see, nor trace
The working of his hands.

He gives the conquest to the weak,
Supports the fainting heart:
And courage, in the evil hour,
His heavenly aids impart.

Mere human power shall fast decay,
And youthful vigour cease;
But they who wait upon the Lord
In strength shall still increase.

They with unwearied feet shall tread
The path of life divine;
With growing ardour onward move,
With growing brightness shine.

On eagles' wings they mount, they soar,
Their wings are faith and love,
Till past the cloudy regions here,
They rise to heaven above.

We Desire a Better Country.

I'M on my way to Canaan,
I bid this world farewell,
Come on, my fellow-travellers,
In spite of earth and hell:
Though Satan's army rages hard,
And all his hosts combine,
The Scripture doth engage the sword
And strength of love divine.

I'll blow the gospel trumpet loud,
And on the nations call,
For Christ hath me commission'd
To say he died for all:

Come try his grace, come prove him now,
 You shall the gift obtain;
He will not send you empty away,
 Nor let you come in vain.

And if you want more witnesses,
 We have some just at hand,
Who lately have experiencèd
 The glory of that land.
It comes in copious showers down—
 Our souls can scarce contain;
It fills our ransomed powers now,
 And yet we drink again.

The glories of that heavenly land
 I've ofttimes felt before,
And what I feel is but a taste
 Which makes me long for more.
Had I the pinions of a dove
 I'd fly and be at rest,
Then would I soar to worlds above,
 And dwell among the blest.

O could I reach that heavenly throng
 I'd ne'er return again,
Nor would I think the season long
 That I had suffered pain.
The sons of Zion marching home,
 Along the heavenly street,
There would I hail them as they come,
 And fall at Jesus' feet.

My soul looks up and sees him smile
  While he the blessing sends,
And I am thinking all the while—
  "When will this journey end?"
I contemplate it can't be long
  Till he will come again—
Then I shall join the heavenly throng,
  And in his kingdom reign.

The Narrow Way.

WHAT thousands never knew the road!
  What thousands hate it when 'tis known!
None but the chosen tribes of God
  Will seek or choose it for their own.

A thousand ways in ruin end,
  One only leads to joys on high;
By that my willing steps ascend,
  Pleased with a journey to the sky.

No more I ask or hope to find
  Delight or happiness below;
Sorrow may well possess the mind
  That feeds where thorns and thistles grow.

The joy that fades is not for me,
  I seek immortal joys above;
There glory without end shall be
  The bright reward of faith and love.

Cleave to the world, ye sordid worms,
  Contented lick your native dust!
But God shall fight with all his storms,
  Against the idol of your trust.

Come with Us.

SINNER go, will you go,
  To the high lands of heaven?
Where the storms never blow,
  And the long summer's given:
Where the bright blooming flowers
  Are their odours emitting;
And the leaves of the bowers
  In the breezes are flitting.

Where the saints robed in white—
  Cleansed in life's flowing fountain,
Shining beauteous and bright,
  They inhabit the mountain;
Where no sin, nor dismay,
  Neither trouble or sorrow,
Will be felt for to-day,
  Nor be feared for the morrow.

He's prepared thee a home—
  Sinner, canst thou believe it
And invites thee to come,
  Sinner, wilt thou receive it?

O come, sinner, come,
For the tide is receding,
And the Saviour will soon,
And forever, cease pleading.

Prayer for the Reign of Christ.

JESUS, immortal King, arise!
Rise and assert thy sway;
Till earth, subdued, its tribute brings,
And distant lands obey.

Ride forth, victorious conqueror, ride,
Till all thy foes submit,
And all the powers of hell resign
Their trophies at thy feet!

Send forth thy word, and let it fly
This spacious earth around;
Till every soul beneath the sun
Shall hear the joyful sound.

Oh may the great Redeemer's name
Through every clime be known!
And heathen gods, like Dagon, fall,
And Jesus reign alone.

From sea to sea, from shore to shore,
May Jesus be adored!
And earth, with all her millions, shout
Hosannas to the Lord.

Free Grace.

THE voice of free grace
 Cries, escape to the mountain;
For Adam's lost race
 Christ hath opened a fountain
For sin and transgression,
 And every pollution,
His blood it flows freely,
 As streams from the ocean.
  Hallelujah to the Lamb,
 By whom we find pardon,
  We will perfectly praise him
 When we've passed over Jordan.

That fountain so clear
 By which we find favour,
From Jesus' side flows,
 And proves him the Saviour.
Though your sins were increased
 As high as a mountain,
His blood it flows freely,
 As streams from a fountain.

O Jesus! ride on,
 Thy kingdom is glorious,
O'er sin, death, and hell,
 Thou wilt make us victorious;
Thy name shall be praised
 In the great congregation,
And saints shall delight
 In ascribing salvation.

When with Zion we stand,
  Having gained the blest shore,
With our harps in our hands
  We'll praise him evermore.
We will range the blest fields
  On the banks of the river,
And sing hallelujah
  For ever and ever.
    Hallelujah to the Lamb,
  By whom we find pardon,
    We will perfectly praise him
  When we've passed over Jordan.

The Goodly Land.

FAR from these scenes of night
  Unbounded glories rise,
And realms of joy and pure delight
  Unknown to mortal eyes.

Fair land!—could mortal eyes
  But half its charms explore,
How would our spirits long to rise,
  And dwell on earth no more!

No cloud those regions know—
  Realms ever bright and fair;
For sin, the source of mortal woe,
  Can never enter there.

O may the prospect fire
Our hearts w th ardent love,
Till wings of faith, and strong desire,
Bear every thought above.

Prepared, by grace divine,
For thy bright courts on high,
Lord, bid our spirits rise and join
The chorus of the sky.

Now.

Now I live;
But if to-night? to-morrow? know I not.
O well for me, when I can leave my lot
All unto God!
To him my faithful service give,
And through his Spirit's strength
Prepare for my account at length.

See the flower
Which full of brightness in the morning shone:
It doth no longer wave the stalk upon
When evening comes.
So lasts man's glory but an hour.
And canst thou, soul, thus waste
A life that flieth in such haste?

Stand thou clear
From earth. Here is thy struggle—yonder, rest.
Up, up, my soul! press forward, heaven is best!
Now hasten home!

Let earth seem distant—heaven more near.
How soon this life doth fly!
How soon comes that which shall not die!

Never delay
To do the duty which the hour brings,
Whether it be in great or smaller things;
For who doth know
What he shall do the coming day?
This moment is for thee;
The next, perhaps, thou wilt not see.

Father of all!
So let thy warning, 'watch!' be not in vain,—
Let my soul hear,
And daily answer to the call.
Then sudden death shall be
But a quick step to life and thee!

For the Saviour's Guidance.

My faith looks up to thee,
Thou Lamb of Calvary;
Saviour divine!
Now hear me while I pray;
Take all my guilt away;
O let me, from this day,
Be wholly thine.

May thy rich grace impart
Strength to my fainting heart;
My zeal inspire;

As thou hast died for me,
Oh may my love to thee,
Pure, warm, and changeless be—
A living fire.

While life's dark maze I tread,
And griefs around me spread,
Be thou my guide;
Bid darkness turn to day,
Wipe sorrow's tears away,
Nor let me ever stray
From thee aside.

When ends life's transient dream;
When death's cold, sullen stream
Shall o'er me roll;
Blest Saviour, then, in love,
Fear and distrust remove;
O bear me safe above—
A ransomed soul!

Safety.

How are thy servants blessed, O Lord,
How sure is their defence!
Eternal wisdom is their guide,
Their help, Omnipotence.

In foreign realms and lands remote,
Supported by thy care,
Through burning climes they pass unhurt,
And breathe in tainted air.

When by the dreadful tempest borne,
  High on the broken wave,
They know thou art not slow to hear,
  Nor impotent to save.

The storm is laid—the winds retire,
  Obedient to thy will:
The sea that roars at thy command,
  At thy command is still.

In midst of dangers, fears, and deaths,
  Thy goodness we'll adore;
We'll praise thee for thy mercies past,
  And humbly hope for more.

Our life, while thou preserv'st that life,
  Thy sacrifice shall be;
And death, when death shall be our lot,
  Shall join our souls to thee.

Jehovah-Jireh.

THOUGH troubles assail,
  And dangers affright,
Though friends should all fail,
  And foes all unite:
Yet one thing secures us,
  Whatever betide,
The Scripture assures us,
  The Lord will provide.

The birds without barn
  Or storehouse are fed;
From them let us learn
  To trust for our bread:
His saints what is fitting
  Shall ne'er be denied,
So long as 'tis written,
  The Lord will provide.

We may, like the ships,
  By tempests be tossed
On perilous deeps,
  But cannot be lost:
Though Satan enrages
  The wind and the tide,
The promise engages
  The Lord will provide.

His call we obey,
  Like Abra'm of old,
Not knowing our way,
  But faith makes us bold;
For though we are strangers,
  We have a good guide,
And trust, in all dangers,
  The Lord will provide.

When Satan appears
  To stop up our path,
And fill us with fears,
  We triumph by faith;

He cannot take from us,
  Though oft he has tried,
This heart-cheering promise,
  The Lord will provide.

He tells us we're weak,
  Our hope is in vain,
The good that we seek
  We ne'er shall obtain;
But when such suggestions
  Our spirits have plied,
This answers all questions—
  The Lord will provide.

No strength of our own
  Or goodness we claim,
Yet since we have known
  The Saviour's great name,
In this our strong tower
  For safety we hide:
The Lord is our power,
  The Lord will provide.

When life sinks apace,
  And death is in view,
This word of his grace
  Shall comfort us through:
No fearing or doubting,
  With Christ on our side,
We hope to die shouting,
  The Lord will provide.

Let there be Light.

O Spirit of the living God!
  In all thy plenitude of grace,
Where'er the foot of man hath trod,
  Descend on our apostate race.

Give tongues of fire and hearts of love,
  To preach the reconciling word;
Give power and unction from above,
  Where'er the joyful sound is heard.

Be darkness, at thy coming, light;
  Confusion, order in thy path;
Souls without strength inspire with might,
  Bid mercy triumph over wrath.

O Spirit of the Lord! prepare
  All the round earth her God to meet
Breathe thou abroad like morning air,
  Till hearts of stone begin to beat.

Baptize the nations; far and nigh
  The triumphs of the cross record;
The name of Jesus glorify,
  Till every kindred call him Lord.

God from eternity hath willed
  All flesh shall his salvation see;
So be the Father's love fulfilled,
  The Saviour's sufferings crowned through thee.

The Reign of Christ.

HAIL to the Lord's Anointed!
  Great David's greater Son;
Hail, in the time appointed,
  His reign on earth begun!
He comes to break oppression,
  To set the captive free,
To take away transgression,
  And rule in equity.

He comes with succour speedy
  To those who suffer wrong;
To help the poor and needy,
  And bid the weak be strong;
To give them songs for sighing,
  Their darkness turn to light,
Whose souls, condemned and dying,
  Were precious in his sight.

By such shall he be feared
  While sun and moon endure,
Beloved, obeyed, revered;
  For he shall judge the poor
Through changing generations,
  With justice, mercy, truth,
While stars maintain their stations,
  Or moons renew their youth.

He shall come down like showers,
  Upon the fruitful earth,
And love, joy, hope, like flowers,
  Spring in his path to birth:

Before him, on the mountains,
  Shall Peace, the herald, go;
And righteousness, in fountains,
  From hill to valley flow.

Arabia's desert ranger
  To him shall bow the knee,
The Ethiopian stranger
  His glory come to see:
With offerings of devotion,
  Ships from the Isles shall meet,
To pour the wealth of ocean
  In tribute at his feet.

Kings shall fall down before him,
  And gold and incense bring;
All nations shall adore him,
  His praise all people sing:
For he shall have dominion
  O'er river, sea, and shore,
Far as the eagle's pinion
  Or dove's light wing can soar.

For him shall prayer unceasing,
  And daily vows ascend;
His kingdom still increasing,
  A kingdom without end:
The mountain-dews shall nourish
  A seed in weakness sown,
Whose fruit shall spread and flourish,
  And shake like Lebanon.

O'er every foe victorious,
He on his throne shall rest,
From age to age more glorious,
All-blessing and all-blest;
The tide of time shall never
His covenant remove;
His name shall stand for ever,
That name to us is Love.

The Book of Nature and Scripture.

THE heavens declare thy glory, Lord;
In every star thy wisdom shines;
But when our eyes behold thy word,
We read thy name in fairer lines.

The rolling sun, the changing light,
And nights and days thy power confess;
But the blest volume thou hast writ,
Reveals thy justice and thy grace.

Sun, moon, and stars convey thy praise
Round the whole earth, and never stand;
So when thy truth began its race,
It touched and glanced on every land.

Nor shall thy spreading gospel rest
Till through the world thy truth has run,
Till Christ has all the nations blest
That see the light or feel the sun.

Great Sun of Righteousness, arise,
Bless the dark world with heavenly light;
Thy gospel makes the simple wise,
Thy laws are pure, thy judgments right.

Thy noblest wonders here we view,
In souls renewed and sins forgiven;
Lord, cleanse my sins, my soul renew,
And make thy word my guide to heaven.

Peace.

O HOW sweet it is to me
Before my gracious Lord to fall!
Talk with him continually,
Make my blessèd Jesus all.

Other pleasures I have sought,
Tried the world, a thousand times,
Peace pursued, but found it not,
For I still retained my crimes.

Never could my heart be blessed
Till from guilt I found it freed;
Jesus, now, has me released,
I, in him, am free indeed.

Saviour, bind me to thy cross,
Let thy love possess my heart;
All besides I count but dross;
Christ and I will never part.

In his blood such peace I find,
  In his love such joy is given;
He who is to Jesus joined
  Finds on earth a little heaven.

I Laid me Down and Slept.

WHAT though my frail eyelids refuse
  Continual watching to keep,
And punctual as midnight renews,
  Demand the refreshment of sleep;
A sovereign protector I have,
  Unseen, yet for ever at hand,
Unchangeably faithful to save,
  Almighty to rule and command.

From evil secure and its dread,
  I rest if my Saviour is nigh,
And songs his kind presence, indeed,
  Shall in the night season supply;
He smiles, and my comforts abound,
  His grace as the dew shall descend,
And walls of salvation surround
  The soul he delights to defend.

Kind author and ground of my hope,
  Thee, thee, for my God I avow,
My glad Eben-ezer set up,
  And own thou hast helped me till now;

I muse on the years that are past,
  Wherein my defence thou hast proved,
Nor wilt thou relinquish at last
  A sinner so signally loved.

Inspirer and hearer of prayer,
  Thou feeder and guardian of mine,
My all to thy covenant care
  I sleeping and waking resign;
If thou art my shield and my sun
  The night is no darkness to me,
And fast as my moments roll on,
  They bring me but nearer to thee.

Thy minist'ring spirits descend,
  To watch while thy saints are asleep,
By day and by night they attend,
  The heirs of salvation to keep;
Bright seraphs, despatched from thy throne,
  Repair to the stations assigned,
And angels elect are sent down
  To guard the elect of mankind.

Thy worship no interval knows,
  Their fervour is still on the wing;
And while they protect my repose,
  They chaunt to the praise of my King;
I, too, at the season ordained,
  Their chorus for ever shall join,
And love and adore, without end,
  Their faithful Creator, and mine.

Service.

WHAT shall I render to my God
  For all his kindness shown?
My feet shall visit thine abode,
  My songs address thy throne.

Among the saints that fill thine house
  My offering shall be paid;
There shall my zeal perform the vows
  My soul in anguish made.

How much is mercy thy delight,
  Thou ever blessèd God!
How dear thy servants in thy sight!
  How precious is their blood!

How happy all thy servants are!
  How great thy grace to me!
My life, which thou hast made thy care,
  Lord, I devote to thee.

Now I am thine, for ever thine,
  Nor shall my purpose move;
Thy hand has loosed my bonds of pain,
  And bound me with thy love.

Here in thy courts I leave my vow,
  And thy rich grace record;
Witness, ye saints, who hear me now,
  If I forsake the Lord.

The Elixir.

TEACH me, my God and King,
  In all things thee to see,
And what I do in any thing,
  To do it as for thee:

Not rudely, as a beast,
  To runne into an action;
But still to make thee prepossest,
  And give it his perfection.

A man that looks on glasse,
  On it may stay his eye;
Or if he pleaseth, through it passe,
  And then the heaven espie.

All may of thee partake:
  Nothing can be so mean,
Which with this tincture (for thy sake)
  Will not grow bright and clean.

A servant with this clause
  Makes drudgerie divine:
Who sweeps a room as for thy laws,
  Makes that and the action fine.

This is the famous stone
  That turneth all to gold
For that which God doth touch and own
  Cannot for less be told.

Harvest Hymn.

THE God of harvest praise ;
In loud thanksgivings raise
Hand, heart, and voice;
The valleys laugh and sing,
Forests and mountains ring,
The plains their tribute bring,
The streams rejoice.

Of food for man and beast,
Jehovah spreads a feast,
Above, beneath:
Ye herds and flocks draw near,
Fowls, ye are welcome here;
His goodness crowns the year
For all that breathe.

Garden and orchard ground
Autumnal fruits have crowned—
The vintage glows:
Here plenty pours her horn;
There the full tide of corn,
Swayed by the breath of morn,
The land o'erflows.

The wind, the rain, the sun,
Their genial work have done.
Wouldst thou be fed?
Man, to thy labour bow,
Thrust in the sickle now,
Reap where thou once didst plough—
God sends thee bread.

Thy few seeds scattered wide
His hand hath multiplied;
  Here thou may'st find
Christ's miracle renewed;
With self-producing food,
He feeds a multitude—
  He feeds mankind.

The God of harvest praise;
Hands, hearts, and voices raise
  With one accord;
From field to garner throng,
Bearing your sheaves along
And in your harvest song,
  Bless ye the Lord.

Yea, bless his holy name,
And your souls' thanks proclaim
  Through all the earth:
To glory in your lot
Is comely; but be not
His benefits forgot,
  Amidst your mirth.

Auspicious Morn.

AWAKE, ye saints, awake!
  And hail this sacred day:
In loftiest songs of praise
  Your joyful homage pay;
Come bless the day that God hath blest,
The type of heaven's eternal rest.

On this auspicious morn
  The Lord of life arose;
He burst the bars of death,
  And vanquished all our foes;
And now he pleads our cause above,
And reaps the fruit of all his love.

All hail, triumphant Lord!
  Heaven with hosannas rings,
And earth, in humbler strains,
  Thy praise responsive sings:
Worthy the Lamb, that once was slain,
Through endless years to live and reign.

Having Nothing

SOURCE of all good to which I aspire,
    Saviour most kind,
This is my hope and only desire,
    Thy favour to find.

My weakness and sin, my weariness, Lord,
    Are known unto thee;
From heaven whence all thy bounties are poured,
    My want thou dost see.

Thou knowest what good my spirit doth need,
    All others above,
And how I am poor in all things indeed,
    But most in thy love.

Poor, wretched, and needy, I lie at thy feet,
Beseeching thy grace;
And wait, though unworthy, for what I entreat,
A sight of thy face.

Look down on a heart which only doth seek
By thee to be fed,—
Which weary, and hungry, and guilty, and weak,
Asks heavenly bread.

These icicles melt by the light of thy face,
Which hang in my heart,
And fill my whole soul with the shining of grace,
Till darkness depart.

Be thou the sole glory and thou the chief good
My heart to control;
And be thou the daily and hourly food
To nourish my soul.

Become its rejoicing, its stronghold of love,
Its aim and its end;
Its glory on earth, and its glory above,
O Jesus, my friend!

Pray Without Ceasing.

PRAYER was appointed to convey
The blessings God designs to give:
Long as they live should Christians pray,
For only while they pray they live.

The Christian's heart his prayer indites,
He speaks as prompted from within ;
The Spirit his petition writes,
And Christ receives, and gives it in.

And wilt thou in dead silence lie,
When Christ stands waiting for thy prayer ?
My soul, thou hast a friend on high,
Arise, and try thy interest there.

If pains afflict, or wrongs oppress,
If cares distract, or fears dismay,
If guilt deject, if sin distress,
The remedy's before thee—pray.

'Tis prayer supports the soul that's weak ;
Though thought be broken, language lame :
Pray, if thou canst or canst not speak ;
But pray with faith in Jesus' name.

Depend on him, thou canst not fail ;
Make all thy wants and wishes known ;
Fear not—his merits must prevail !
Ask what thou wilt, it shall be done,

Weak Believers Encouraged.

YOUR harps, ye trembling saints,
Down from the willows take :
Loud, to the praise of love divine,
Bid every string awake.

Though in a foreign land,
  We are not far from home,
And nearer to our house above,
  We every moment come.

His grace will to the end,
  Stronger and brighter shine;
Nor present things, nor things to come,
  Shall quench the spark divine.

Fastened within the vail,
  Hope be your anchor strong;
His loving spirit the sweet gale,
  That wafts you smooth along.

Or, should the surges rise,
  And peace delay to come;
Blest is the sorrow, kind the storm,
  That drives us nearer home.

The people of his choice,
  He will not cast away;
Yet do not always here expect
  On Tabor's mount to stay.

When we in darkness walk,
  Nor feel the heavenly flame;
Then is the time to trust our God,
  And rest upon his name.

Soon shall our doubts and fears
  Subside at his control;
His loving kindness shall break through
  The midnight of the soul.

No wonder, when God's love
  Pervades your kindling breast,
You wish for ever to retain
  The heart-transporting guest.

Yet learn in every state,
  To make his will your own;
And when the joys of sense depart,
  To walk by faith alone.

By anxious fear depressed,
  When, from the deep ye mourn,
"Lord, why so hasty to depart,
  So tedious in return!"

Still on his plighted love,
  At all events rely:
The very hidings of his face,
  Shall train thee up to joy.

Wait till the shadows flee;
  Wait thy appointed hour:
Wait, till the bridegroom of thy soul
  Reveals his love with power.

The time of love will come,
  When thou shalt clearly see,
Not only that he shed his blood,
  But that it flowed for thee.

Tarry his leisure then,
  Although he seem to stay:
A moment's intercourse with him,
  Thy grief will overpay.

Blest is the man, O God,
That stays himself on thee!
Who waits for thy salvation, Lord,
Shall thy salvation see.

In Extremity

When I can trust my all with God,
In trial's fearful hour,—
Bow all resigned beneath his rod,
And bless his sparing power;—
A joy springs up amid distress,—
A fountain in the wilderness.

O to be brought to Jesus' feet,
Though trials fix me there,
Is still a privilege most sweet;
For he will hear my prayer;
Though sighs and tears its language be,
The Lord is nigh to answer me.

Then blessed be the hand that gave,
Still blessed when it takes;
Blessed be he who smites to save,
Who heals the heart he breaks:
Perfect and true are all his ways,
Whom heaven adores and earth obeys.

Onward.

BREAST the wave, Christian,
When it is strongest;
Watch for day, Christian,
When the night's longest.
Onward and onward still
Be thine endeavour,
The rest that remaineth
Shall be for ever.

Fight the fight, Christian,
Jesus is o'er thee,—
Run the race, Christian,
Heaven is before thee.
He that hath promised
Faltereth never—
The love of eternity
Flows on for ever.

Lift the eye, Christian,
Just as it closeth;
Raise the heart, Christian,
Ere it reposeth.
Thee from the love of Christ
Nothing shall sever,
Mount when thy work is done—
Praise him for ever!

For Patience.

Sweet Patience, come!
With long distress my spirit faints,
And my heart breaks with its complaints;
And eager pain, to find relief,
Solicits even change of grief,—
And unbelief disturbs my trust,
And shakes my hopes—as with a gust
Spring blossoms flutter from the stalk,
And withering lie upon the walk;—
Sweet Patience, come!

Sweet Patience, come!
Not from a low and earthly source—
Waiting, till things shall have their course,—
Not as accepting present pain
In hope of some hereafter gain,—
Not in a dull and sullen calm,—
But as a breath of heavenly balm,
Bidding my weary heart submit
To bear whatever God sees fit,
Sweet Patience, come!

Sweet Patience, come!
Tell me my Father hath not shed
One grief too many on my head:
Tell me his love remembers still
His children, suffering at his will.—
How excellent a thought to me
His loving kindness then shall be!
Then in the shadow of his wings
I'll hide me, from all troublous things;
Sweet Patience, come!

The Ruler's Daughter.

COULD the creatures help or ease us,
  Seldom should we think of prayer:
Few, if any, come to Jesus,
  Till reduced to self-despair:
Long we either slight or doubt him,
  But when all the means we try,
Prove we can not do without him,
  Then at last to him we cry.

Thus the ruler, when his daughter
  Suffered much, though Christ was nigh,
Still deferred it, till he thought her
  At the very point to die:
Though he mourned for her condition,
  He did not entreat the Lord,
Till he found that no physician
  But himself could help afford.

Jesus did not once upbraid him,
  That he had no sooner come
But a gracious answer made him,
  And went straightway with him home.
Yet his faith was put to trial,
  When his servants came, and said,
"Though he gave thee no denial,
  'Tis too late, the child is dead."

Jesus to prevent his grieving,
  Kindly spoke and eased his pain;

"Be not fearful, but believing,
  Thou shalt see her live again."
When he found the people weeping,
  "Cease," he said, "no longer mourn;
For she is not dead, but sleeping;"
  Then they laughéd him to scorn.

O thou meek and lowly Saviour,
  How determined is thy love!
Not this rude, unkind behaviour,
  Could thy gracious purpose move.
Soon as he the room had entered,
  Spoke and took her by the hand,
Death at once his prey surrendered,
  And she lived at his command.

Fear not, then, distressed believer,
  Venture on his mighty Name:
He is able to deliver,
  And his love is still the same:
Can his pity or his power
  Suffer thee to pray in vain?
Wait but his appointed hour,
  And thy suit thou shalt obtain.

I Will Trust and Not be Afraid.

BEGONE, unbelief,
  My Saviour is near,
And for my relief
  Will surely appear;

By prayer let me wrestle,
  And he will perform;
With Christ in the vessel,
  I smile at the storm.

Though dark be my way,
  Since he is my guide
'Tis mine to obey,
  'Tis his to provide;
Though cisterns be broken,
  And creatures all fail,
The word he has spoken
  Will surely prevail.

His love in time past,
  Forbids me to think
He 'll leave me at last
  In trouble to sink;
Each sweet Eben-ezer
  I have in review,
Confirms his good pleasure
  To help me quite through.

Determined to save,
  He watched o'er my path,
When, Satan's blind slave,
  I sported with death;
And can he have taught me
  To trust in his name,
And thus far have brought me
  To put me to shame?

Why should I complain
  Of want or distress,
Temptation or pain?
  He told me no less:
The heirs of salvation,
  I know from his word,
Through much tribulation
  Must follow their Lord.

How bitter that cup,
  No heart can conceive,
Which he drank quite up,
  That sinners might live!
His way was much rougher,
  And darker than mine;
Did Jesus thus suffer,
  And shall I repine?

Since all that I meet
  Shall work for my good,
The bitter is sweet,
  The med'cine is food;
Though painful at present,
  'Twill cease before long,
And then, O how pleasant
  The conqueror's song!

What is Prayer?

PRAYER is the soul's sincere desire,
Uttered or unexpressed,
The motion of a hidden fire
That trembles in the breast.

Prayer is the burthen of a sigh,
The falling of a tear;
The upward glancing of an eye,
When none but God can hear.

Prayer is the simplest form of speech
That infant lips can try;
Prayer the sublimest strains that reach
The majesty on high.

Prayer is the contrite sinner's voice
Returning from his ways,
While angels in their songs rejoice,
And cry, "Behold he prays!"

Prayer is the Christian's vital breath,
The Christian's native air,
His watchword at the gates of death;
He enters heaven with prayer.

The saints in prayer appear as one
In word, and deed, and mind,
While with the Father and the Son
Sweet fellowship they find.

Nor prayer is made by man alone,
  The Holy Spirit pleads,
And Jesus, on the eternal throne,
  For sinners intercedes.

O thou by whom we come to God,
  The life, the truth, the way!
The path of prayer thyself hast trod;
  Lord, teach us how to pray.

Thy Word is Good.

O HOW I love thy holy word,
Thy gracious covenant, O Lord!
It guides me in the peaceful way,
I think upon it all the day.

What are the mines of shining wealth,
The strength of youth, the bloom of health?
What are all joys, compared with those
Thine everlasting word bestows?

Long unafflicted, undismayed,
In pleasure's path, secure I strayed:
Thou mad'st me feel thy chastening rod,
And straight I turned unto my God.

What though it pierced my fainting heart—
I bless thine hand that caused the smart;
It taught my tears awhile to flow,
But saved me from eternal wo.

Oh! hadst thou left me unchastised,
Thy precepts I had still despised;
And still the snare in secret laid,
Had my unwary feet betrayed.

I love thee, therefore, O my God,
And breathe towards thy dear abode;
Where, in thy presence, fully blest,
Thy chosen saints for ever rest.

The Joy of the Lord is your Strength.

JOY is a fruit that will not grow
In nature's barren soil:
All we can boast till Christ we know,
Is vanity and toil.

But where the Lord has planted grace,
And made his glories known;
There fruits of heavenly joy and peace
Are found, and there alone.

A bleeding Saviour seen by faith,
A sense of pardoning love,
A hope that triumphs over death,
Give joys like those above.

To take a glimpse within the veil,
To know that God is mine,
Are springs of joy that never fail,
Unspeakable! divine!

These are the joys which satisfy,
And sanctify the mind;
Which make the spirit mount on high,
And leave the world behind.

No more, believers, mourn your lot,
But if you are the Lord's,
Resign to them that know him not,
Such joys as earth affords.

The God of Abraham.

The God of Abrah'm praise,
Who reigns enthroned above:
Ancient of everlasting days,
And God of love:
JEHOVAH, GREAT I AM!
By earth and heaven confessed;
I bow and bless the sacred Name,
Forever blest.

The God of Abrah'm praise,
At whose supreme command
From earth I rise, and seek the joys
At his right hand:
I all on earth forsake,
Its wisdom, fame, and power;
And him my only portion make,
My shield and tower.

He by himself hath sworn:
  I on his oath depend;
I shall, on eagles' wings upborne,
  To heaven ascend:
I shall behold his face,
  I shall his power adore,
And sing the wonders of his grace
  Forever more.

Though nature's strength decay,
  And earth and hell withstand,
To Canaan's bounds I urge my way,
  At his command;
The wat'ry deep I pass,
  With Jesus in my view;
And through the howling wilderness
  My way pursue.

The goodly land I see,
  With peace and plenty blest;
A land of sacred liberty,
  And endless rest.
There milk and honey flow,
  And oil and wine abonnd;
And trees of life forever grow,
  With mercy crowned.

There dwells the Lord our king,
  The Lord our Righteousness,
Triumphant o'er the world and sin,
  The Prince of peace;

On Zion's sacred height,
His kingdom still maintains;
And glorious, with his saints in light
Forever reigns.

He keeps his own secure;
He guards them by his side;
Arrays in garments white and pure,
His spotless bride;
With groves of living joys,
With streams of sacred bliss,
With all the fruits of paradise,
He still supplies.

The whole triumphant host
Give thanks to God on high;
Hail, Father, Son, and Holy Ghost,
They ever cry:
Hail, Abraham's God and mine!
(I join the heavenly lays,)
All might and majesty are thine,
And endless praise.

The Request.

FATHER, whate'er of earthly bliss
Thy sovereign will denies,
Accepted at thy throne of grace,
Let this petition rise:—

"Give me a calm, a thankful heart,
From every murmur free;
The blessings of thy grace impart,
And make me live to thee.

"Let the sweet hope that I am thine,
My life and death attend;
Thy presence through my journey shine,
And crown my journey's end."

The Heavens declare thy Glory.

THE spacious firmament on high,
With all the blue ethereal sky,
And spangled heavens, a shining frame,
Their great Original proclaim:
Th' unwearied sun, from day to day,
Does his Creator's power display,
And publishes to every land
The work of an Almighty hand.

Soon as the evening shades prevail,
The moon takes up the wondrous tale,
And nightly to the listening earth
Repeats the story of her birth:
While all the stars that round her burn,
And all the planets in their turn,
Confirm the tidings as they roll,
And spread the truth from pole to pole.

What though in solemn silence all
Move round the dark terrestrial ball?
What though no real voice nor sound
Amid their radiant orbs be found?
In reason's ear they all rejoice,
And utter forth a glorious voice,
For ever singing, as they shine,
"The hand that made us is divine."

The Hidden Life.

O HAPPY soul that lives on high,
While men lie grovelling here!
His hopes are fixed above the sky,
And faith forbids his fear.

His conscience knows no secret stings,
While grace and joy combine
To form a life, whose holy springs
Are hidden and divine.

He waits in secret on his God,
His God in secret sees:
Let earth be all in arms abroad,
He dwells in heavenly peace.

His pleasures rise from things unseen,
Beyond this world of time,
Where neither eyes nor ears have been,
Nor thoughts of mortals climb.

29*

He wants no pomp nor royal throne,
  To raise his figure here,
Content and pleased to live alone,
  Till Christ his life appear.

He looks to heaven's eternal hills,
  To meet that glorious day:
But patient waits his Saviour's will
  To fetch his soul away.

Witness of Heaven.

And may I hope, that when no more
  My pulse shall beat with life below,
I shall the God of grace adore,
  And all the bliss of glory know?

I, who deserve no place but hell,
  No portion but devouring fire,
Shall I with Christ my Saviour dwell,
  Possessed of all I now desire?

Will Jesus own a wretch like me?
  And tell to saints and angels round,
That when he suffered on the tree,
  My sins augmented every wound?

Will he from life's eternal book
  To earth and heaven proclaim my name;
On me, as on his chosen look,
  And make my lot with theirs the same?

He will! I read it in his word,
And in my heart the witness feel:
I shall be with, and like my Lord,
Though sin oppose in league with hell!

I shall be with him, when he comes
Triumphant down the pathless skies;
And when his voice breaks up the tombs,
Among his children I shall rise:—

Among his chosen I shall stand,
When quick and dead his throne surround,
Blessed with a place at his right hand,
And with immortal glory crowned.

There.

WHO can the thoughts conceive—
The feelings of his breast,
Who shall himself perceive
In heaven—at rest!

When there the spirit wakes,—
And springing from the dust,
Its new position takes
Among the just;—

Methinks all other joy
Would scarce at first be felt!
This would the tongue employ,
The heart would melt.

"My trial then is done,—
Ended the weary strife:
I've kept the faith, I've won
Eternal life.

"I've drawn my last sad breath;
Tears, sighs, are all forgot:
I've passed the gates of Death,—
He harmed me not.

No doubtings now, nor sin,
Can dim my title clear!
By Christ I've entered in—
I'm saved—I'm here!"

Your Lamp Burning.

MY God! I know full well
That I must die!
I am a man—soon rings his knell;
And no inheritance I find below
Which doth unchangèd lie.
Therefore I pray thee let thy mercy show,
How I can happy be, when death is nigh.

My God! I know not now
When I shall die!
All-knowing! none can know but thou.
Therefore, that death have no destroying power,
Wilt thou thy grace supply,—
That I may be, in every day and hour,
Ready for death and for eternity.

My God! I know no more
How I shall die,—
Death opens many a different door.
One soul toils forth in bitterness of woe:
Others with soft wings fly.
But how thou wilt my Lord, I leave it so,
Only at last may I be blest thereby.

My God! now know I not
Where I shall die,—
What sand shall cover that small spot.
Yet if thou wilt but grant that thy life-call
Shall wake me where I lie,—
So will I take the room where I shall fall;
For anywhere the earth is thine, Most High!

Now God, for ever blest!
When I shall die
So take my spirit to thy rest!
With Jesus now have I become thine heir?
True faith in him have I?
Then is it one to me, I have no care,
When, where, and how, death comes—to thee I fly!

Accepted in the Beloved

All praise to the Lamb! accepted I am,
Through faith in the Saviour's adorable name:
In him I confide, his blood is applied;
For me he hath suffered, for me he hath died.

Not a doubt doth arise, to darken the skies,
Or hide for a moment my Lord from my eyes:
In him I am blest, I lean on his breast,
And lo! in his wounds I continue to rest.

The Prospect Joyous.

AND let this feeble body fail,
And let it faint or die:
My soul shall quit the mournful vale,
And soar to worlds on high:
Shall join the disembodied saints,
And find its long-sought rest,—
That only bliss for which it pants,
In the Redeemer's breast.

In hope of that immortal crown
I now the cross sustain,
And gladly wander up and down,
And smile at toil and pain:
I suffer on my threescore years,
Till my Deliverer come,
And wipe away his servant's tears,
And take his exile home.

O what hath Jesus bought for me!
Before my ravished eyes
Rivers of life divine I see,
And trees of Paradise:
I see a world of spirits bright,
Who taste the pleasures there;

They all are robed in spotless white,
  And conquering palms they bear.

O what are all my sufferings here,
  If, Lord, thou count me meet
With that enraptured host to appear,
  And worship at thy feet!
Give joy or grief, give ease or pain,
  Take life or friends away,
But let me find them all again
  In that eternal day.

Times.

SOVEREIGN Ruler of the skies,
Ever gracious, ever wise!
All my times are in thy hand,
All events at thy command.

His decree who formed the earth,
Fixed my first and second birth:
Parents, native-place, and time,
All appointed were by Him.

He that formed me in the womb,
He shall guide me to the tomb;
All my times shall ever be
Ordered by his wise decree,

Times of sickness, times of health;
Times of penury and wealth:
Times of trial and of grief;
Times of triumph and relief,

Times the tempter's power to prove;
Times to taste a Saviour's love;
All must come, and last, and end,
As shall please my heavenly Friend.

Plagues and deaths around me fly;
Till he bids, I cannot die:
Not a single shaft can hit
Till the God of love sees fit.

O thou gracious, wise, and just,
In thy hands my life I trust;
Have I somewhat dearer still?
I resign it to thy will.

May I always own thy hand—
Still to the surrender stand;
Know that thou art God alone,
I and mine are all thy own.

Thee at all times I will bless;
Having thee, I all possess:
How can I bereavèd be,
Since I cannot part with thee?

Jesus All and in All.

THOU hidden Source of calm repose,
Thou all-sufficient Love divine,
My help and refuge from my foes,
Secure I am while thou art mine:
And lo! from sin, and grief, and shame,
I hide me, Jesus, in thy name.

Thy mighty name salvation is,
  And keeps my happy soul above:
Comfort it brings, and power, and peace,
  And joy, and everlasting love:
To me, with thy great name, are given
  Pardon, and holiness, and heaven.

Jesus, my all in all thou art;
  My rest in toil, my ease in pain;
The med'cine of my broken heart;
  In war, my peace; in loss, my gain;
My smile beneath the tyrant's frown;
In shame, my glory and my crown.

In want, my plentiful supply;
  In weakness, my almighty power;
In bonds, my perfect liberty;
  My light, in Satan's darkest hour;
In grief, my joy unspeakable;
My life in death, my all in all.

It is Good for Me.

SAVIOUR! though my rebellious will
  Has been by thy blest power renewed,
Yet in its secret workings still
  How much remains to be subdued.

Oft I recall, with grief and shame,
  How many years their course had run,
Ere grace my murmuring heart o'ercame,
  Ere I could say, "Thy will be done."

I wished a flowery path to tread,
 And thought 'twould safely lead to heaven;
A lonely room, a suffering bed,
 These for my training place were given.

Long I resisted, mourned, complained,
 Wished any other lot my own;
Thy purpose, Lord, unchanged remained,
 What wisdom planned, love carried on.

Year after year I turned away,
 But marred was every scheme I planned;
Still the same lesson, day by day,
 Was placed before me by thy hand.

At length thy patient, wondrous love,
 Unchanging, tender, pitying, strong,
Availed that stubborn heart to move,
 Which had rebelled, alas! so long.

Then was I taught by thee to say,
 "Do with me what to thee seems best;
Give, take, whate'er thou wilt away,
 Health, comfort, usefulness, or rest;

"Be my whole life in suffering spent;
 But let me be in suffering thine,—
Still, O my Lord, I am content,
 Thou now hast made thy pleasure mine."

The Shepherd of Israel.

My shepherd's name is Love—
Jehovah, God above;
Where tender herbage grows,
And peaceful water flows,
He gently leads, he kindly feeds,
And lulls me then to sweet repose.

If e'er I heedless stray,
He shows my feet the way;
Yea, though through dreary glades
I walk in dismal shades,
No harm I fear, for thou art near;
Thy faithful staff my progress aids.

When raging foes surround,
My comforts still abound;
I breathe a fragrant air,
And feed on sweetest fare:
Thus in thy fold, when worn and old,
I dwell secure beneath thy care.

The Saviour's Merit.

Saviour, I do feel thy merit,
  Sprinkled with redeeming blood,
And my weary, troubled spirit,
  Now finds rest with thee, my God:

I am safe, and I am happy,
  While in thy dear arms I lie;
Sin and hell no more molest me,
  While I feel my Saviour nigh.

Glory, glory, glory, glory,
  Glory be to God on high,
Glory, glory, glory, glory,
  Sing his praises through the sky;
Glory, glory, glory, glory,
  Glory to the Father give;
Glory, glory, glory, glory,
  Sing his praises all that live!

Now I'll sing my Saviour's merit,
  Tell the world of his dear name,
That if any want his Spirit,
  He is still the very same.
He that asketh still receiveth,
  He that seeks is sure to find;
Whosoe'er on him believeth,
  He will never cast behind.

Glory, glory, glory, glory,
  Glorious Christ of heavenly birth;
Glory, glory, glory, glory,
  Sing his praises through the earth.
Glory, glory, glory, glory,
  Glory to the Spirit be;
Glory, glory, glory, glory,
  To the Sacred One in Three.

Now our Advocate is pleading,
With his Father and our God;
And for us is interceding,
As the purchase of his blood;
Now methinks I hear him praying,
Father! save them—I have died;
And the Father answers, saying,
They are freely justified.

Worthy, worthy, worthy, worthy,
Worthy is the Lamb of God;
Worthy, worthy, worthy, worthy,
Who hath washed us in his blood.
Holy, holy, holy, holy,
Holy is the Lord of Hosts,
Holy, holy, holy, holy,
Father, Son, and Holy Ghost.

The Temper.

How should I praise thee, Lord! how should my rymes
Gladly engrave thy love on steel,
If what my soul doth feel sometimes,
My soul might ever feel.

Although there were some fourtie heavens, or more,
Sometimes I peere above them all;
Sometimes I hardly reach a score,
Sometimes to hell I fall.

O rack me not to such a vast extent;
  Those distances belong to thee:
The world's too little for thy tent,
  A grave too big for me.

Wilt thou meet arms with man, that thou dost stretch
  A crumme of dust from heaven to hell?
Will great God measure such a wretch?
  Shall he thy stature spell?

O let me, when thy roof my soul hath hid,
  O let me roost and nestle there,
Then of a sinner thou art rid,
  And I of hope and fear.

Yet take thy way; for sure thy way is best:
  Stretch or contract me, thy poore debtor;
This is but tuning of my breast,
  To make the musick better.

Whether I flie with angels, fall with dust,
  Thy hands made both, and I am there,
Thy power and love, my love and trust,
  Make one place every where.

I am thy Servant.

God of my life, through all its days
My grateful powers shall sound thy praise;
The song shall wake with opening light,
And warble to the silent night.

When anxious cares would break my rest,
And griefs would tear my throbbing breast,
Thy tuneful praises raised on high,
Shall check the murmur and the sigh.

When death o'er nature shall prevail,
And all its powers of language fail,
Joy through my swimming eyes shall break,
And mean the thanks I cannot speak.

But O, when the last conflict's o'er,
And I am chained to flesh no more,
With what glad accents shall I rise,
To join the music of the skies!

Soon shall I learn the exalted strains
Which echo o'er the heavenly plains;
And emulate, with joy unknown,
The glowing seraphs round thy throne.

The cheerful tribute will I give,
Long as a deathless soul can live;
A work so sweet, a theme so high,
Demands and crowns eternity.

Another Day.

Now O my soul! the circling sun
Has all his beams withdrawn:
Once more his daily race is run,
And gloomy night comes on.

Thus one day more of life is gone,
  A doubtful few remain:
Come then, review what thou hast done
  Eternal life to gain.

Dost thou get forward in thy race,
  As time still posts away?
And die to sin, and grow in grace,
  With every passing day?

This day, what conquest hast thou gained?
  What sin is overcome?
What fresh degree of grace obtained,
  To bring thee nearer home?

Thus let us still our course review,
  Our real state to learn;
And with redoubled zeal, pursue
  Our great and chief concern.

Evening Hymn.

INTERVAL of grateful shade,
Welcome to my weary head!
Welcome slumbers to mine eyes,
Tired with glaring vanities!
My great Master still allows
Needful periods of repose:
By my Heavenly Father blest,
Thus I give my powers to rest;
Heavenly Father! gracious name!
Night and day his love the same;

Far be each suspicious thought,
Every anxious care forgot:
Thou, my ever bounteous God,
Crownest my days with various good:
Thy kind eye that cannot sleep,
These defenceless hours shall keep;
Blest vicissitude to me!
Day and night I'm still with thee.

What though downy slumbers flee,
Strangers to my couch and me?
Sleepless well I know to rest,
Lodged within my Father's breast.
While the empress of the night
Scatters mild her silver light;
While the vivid planets stray
Various through their mystic way;
While the stars unnumbered roll
Round the ever-constant pole;
Far above these spangled skies,
All my soul to God shall rise;
'Midst the silence of the night
Mingling with those angels bright,
Whose harmonious voices raise
Ceaseless love and ceaseless praise:
Through the throng his gentle ear
Shall my tuneless accents hear:
From on high doth he impart
Secret comfort to my heart.
He in these serenest hours
Guides my intellectual powers,

And his Spirit doth diffuse,
Sweeter far than midnight dews;
Lifting all my thoughts above,
On the wings of faith and love.
Blest alternative to me,
Thus to sleep, or wake, with thee!

What if death my sleep invade?
Should I be of death afraid?
Whilst encircled by thine arm,
Death may strike but cannot harm.
What if beams of opening day
Shine around my breathless clay?
Brighter visions from on high
Shall regale my mental eye,
Tender friends awhile may mourn
Me from their embraces torn;
Dearer, better friends I have
In the realms beyond the grave.
See the guardian angels nigh
Wait to waft my soul on high!
See the golden gates displayed!
See the crown to grace my head!
See a flood of sacred light,
Which no more shall yield to night.
Transitory world, farewell!
Jesus calls, with him to dwell.
With thy heavenly presence blest,
Death is life, and labour rest.
Welcome sleep or death to me,
Still secure, for still with thee.

Perfect Freedom.

If thou impart thyself to me,
No other good I need:
If thou, the Son, shalt make me free,
I shall be free indeed.

I cannot rest till in thy blood
I full redemption have;
But thou, through whom I come to God,
Canst to the utmost save.

From sin,—the guilt, the power, the pain,
Thou wilt redeem my soul:
Lord, I believe—and not in vain;
My faith shall make me whole.

I, too, with thee, shall walk in white;
With all thy saints shall prove
The length and depth, and breadth and height,
Of everlasting love.

The Dawn.

These years of life—what do they seem?—
A little dream
Of pain and pleasure, blent together,—
A time of sharply changing weather;

Where brilliant sunbeams gleam and die
On heavy storm clouds sailing by,—
Where falling tears
Are bright with hope and cold with fears.

The years, the clouds, have had their course,—
Their mingled force
Has bowed my heart and bent my head.
Sunshine and storm alike are fled.
And in their place a heavy gray
Dulls all the tinting of the day.
Shall growing light
Follow the gray?—or deepening night?

What shall the future progress be,
Of life with me?
God knows,—I roll on him my care,—
Night is not night if he be there.
When daylight is no longer mine,
And stars forbidden are, to shine,
I'll turn my eyes
To where eternal day shall rise.

That coming light no mortal cloud
Can quite enshroud!
Through all our doubts,—above the range
Of every fear, and every change,—
My faith can see with weary eye,
The dawn of heaven on earth's dim sky;
And from afar,
Shines on my soul the morning star.

For Heaven.

YE angels, who stand round the throne,
And view my Immanuel's face,
In rapturous songs make him known,
Tune, tune your soft harps to his praise:
He formed you the spirits you are,
So happy, so noble, so good;
When others sunk down in despair,
Confirmed by his power, ye stood.

Ye saints, who stand nearer than they,
And cast your bright crowns at his feet,
His grace and his glory display;
O tell of his love as is meet!
He saved you from hell and the grave—
He ransomed from death and despair;
For you he was mighty to save;
Almighty to bring you safe there.

Oh when will the period appear,
When I shall unite in your song,
I'm weary of lingering here;
And I to your Saviour belong;
I'm fettered and chained up in clay;
I struggle and pant to be free;
I long to be soaring away,
My God and my Saviour to see!

I want to put on my attire,
Washed white in the blood of the Lamb;
I want to be one of your choir,
And tune my sweet harp to his name;

I want—O I want to be there,
  Where sorrow and sin bid adieu —
Your joy and your friendship to share,
  To wonder and worship with you!

Until Death.

  Be faithful to the end,—
Let not danger nor distress
Make thy heart love Jesus less.
  Until death trust thou that Friend!
Ah! the suffering of this earth
All the glory is not worth,
Which thy Lord will give to thee
When up yonder thou shalt be.

  Be faithful in thy grief,—
Let not storms from Christ divide,
Let not weeping, Jesus hide!
  Murmur not, to get relief,—
For impatience makes thy care
Heavier much for thee to bear.
Happy he, whose child-like will
Lets God lead him up the hill.

  Be faithful in thy faith!
Let not any robber bold
Take it from thy heart's stronghold;
  Keep thy covenant till death.

Then in the o'erflowing wave
God is with thee, strong to save.
Ah, thou goest there forlorn,
When thou art to him forsworn!

Be faithful in thy love.
See the love God has for thee!
Love thy neighbour—even when he
Lays more care thy cares above:
Think how Jesus prayed for those
By whose hands his cross arose!
Even as God doth thee forgive,
So let mercy in thee live.

And in thy hope stand true!
Trust thou firmly in God's word!
Is thy cry in trouble heard,
Comes he not to help thee through?
Hope thou in him firmly yet!
For the Lord doth not forget,
Even now is help proclaimed;
Hope can never make ashamed.

Then forward! steadfast be
In faith, love, hope, for ever!
Lord, I hear, and I will never
Leave my God, who leaves not me.
He is my soul's rejoicing still,
Griefs no more my joy can kill.
Reach forth thy hand, O God, my Friend!
Make me faithful to the end!

Death and Life.

THROUGH sorrow's night, and danger's path,
Amidst the deepening gloom,
We, soldiers of an injured King,
Are marching to the tomb.

There, when the turmoil is no more,
And all our powers decay,
Our cold remains in solitude
Shall sleep the years away.

Our labours done, securely laid
In this our last retreat,
Unheeded o'er our silent dust
The storms of life shall beat.

Yet not thus lifeless, thus inane,
The vital spark shall lie;
For o'er life's wreck that spark shall rise
To seek its kindred sky.

These ashes too, this little dust,
Our Father's care shall keep,
Till the last angel rise and break
The long and dreary sleep.

Then love's soft dew o'er every eye
Shall shed its mildest rays,
And the long silent dust shall burst
With shouts of endless praise.

Our Abiding City.

"We've no abiding city here,"—
This may distress the worldly mind;
But should not cost the saint a tear,
Who hopes a better rest to find.

"We've no abiding city here,"—
Sad truth, were this to be our home;
But let this thought our spirits cheer,
"We seek a city yet to come."

"We've no abiding city here,"—
Then let us live as pilgrims do;
Let not the world our rest appear,
But let us haste from all below.

"We've no abiding city here,"
We seek a city out of sight:
Zion its name, the Lord is there,
It shines with everlasting light.

Zion!—Jehovah is her strength!
Secure she smiles at all her foes,
And weary travellers at length
Within her sacred walls repose.

O sweet abode of peace and love,
Where pilgrims freed from toil are blest,—
Had I the pinions of the dove,
I'd fly to thee and be at rest.

But hush, my soul, nor dare repine,
  The time thy God appoints is best;
While here to do his will be mine;
  And his to fix my time of rest.

Where neither Moth nor Rust doth Corrupt.

To thee, O dear, dear country,
  Mine eyes their vigils keep;
For very love, beholding
  Thy happy name, they weep:
The mention of thy glory
  Is unction to the breast,
And medicine in sickness,
  And love, and life, and rest.
O one, O only mansion,
  O Paradise of joy!
Where tears are ever banished
  And joys have no alloy:
Beside thy living waters
  All plants are, great and small—
The cedar of the forest,
  The hyssop on the wall.
Thy ageless walls are bounded
  With amethyst unpriced.
The saints build up its fabric,
  And the corner-stone is Christ.
Thou hast no shore, fair ocean,
  Thou hast no time, bright day,
Dear fountain of refreshment
  To pilgrims far away:

Upon the Rock of Ages
They raise the holy tower;
Thine is the victor's laurel,
And thine the golden dower.
They stand, those halls of Zion,
Conjubilant with song,
And bright with many an angel,
And many a martyr throng:
The Prince is ever in them,
The light is aye serene,
The pastures of the blessed
Are decked in glorious sheen.
There is the throne of David,
And there, from toil released,
The shout of them that triumph,
The song of them that feast:
And they, beneath their Leader
Who conquered in the fight,
For ever and for ever
Are clad in robes of white.

The Desired Haven.

"LORD, the waves are breaking o'er me and around;
Oft of coming tempest I hear the moaning sound:
Here there is no safety, rocks on either hand;
'Tis a foreign roadstead, a strange and hostile land.
Wherefore should I linger! others, gone before,
Long since safe are landed on a calm and friendly shore:

Now the sailing orders in mercy, Lord, bestow—
Loose the cable, let me go!

"Lord, the night is closing round my feeble bark;
How shall I encounter its watches long and dark?
Sorely worn and shattered by many a billow past,
Can I stand another rude and stormy blast?
Ah! the promised haven I never may attain,
Sinking and forgotten amid the lonely main;
Enemies around me, gloomy depths below.
Loose the cable, let me go!

"Lord, I would be near thee, with thee where thou art—
Thine own word hath said it, 'tis 'better to depart;'
There to serve thee better, there to love thee more,
With thy ransomed people to worship and adore.
Ever to thy presence thou dost call thine own—
Why am I remaining, helpless and alone?
Oh! to see thy glory, thy wondrous love to know!
Loose the cable, let me go!

"Lord, the lights are gleaming from the distant shore,
Where no billows threaten, where no tempests roar;
Long belovéd voices calling me I hear—
Oh! how I sweet *their* summons falls upon my ear!
Here are foes and strangers, faithless hearts and cold,
There is fond affection, fondly proved of old!
Let me haste to join them: may it not be so?
Loose the cable, let me go!"

Hark, the solemn answer! hark the promise sure!
"Blessed are the servants who to the end endure!
Yet a little longer hope and tarry on—
Yet a little longer, weak and weary one!
More to perfect patience, to grow in faith and love,
More *my* strength and wisdom, and faithfulness to prove:
Then the sailing orders the Captain *shall* bestow—
Loose the cable, let thee go!"

The Dying Christian.

Happy soul, thy days are ending,
All thy mourning days below;
Go,—the angel guards attending,
To the sight of Jesus go.
Waiting to receive thy spirit,
Lo! the Saviour stands above;
Shews the purchase of his merit,
Reaches out his arms of love.

Struggle through thy latest passion,
To thy great Redeemer's breast;
To his uttermost salvation,
To his everlasting rest.
For the joy he sets before thee,
Bear a momentary pain;
Die, to live a life of glory;
Suffer, with thy Lord to reign.

Our Inheritance.

How weak the thoughts and vain,
Of self-deluded men;
Men, who fixed to earth alone,
  Think their houses shall endure,
Fondly call their lands their own,
  To their distant heirs secure.

How happy, then, are we,
Who build, O Lord, on thee!
What can our foundation shock?
  Tho' the scattered earth remove,
Stands our city on a rock,
  On the rock of heavenly love.

A house we call our own,
Which cannot be o'erthrown;
In the general ruin sure,
  Storms and earthquakes it defies;
Built immovably secure;
  Built eternal in the skies.

High on Immanuel's land
We see the fabric stand;
From a tottering world remove
  To our steadfast mansion there:
Our inheritance above
  Cannot pass from heir to heir.

Jacob's Vow.

O God of Jacob, by whose hand
   Thine Israel still is fed,
Who through this weary pilgrimage
   Hast all our fathers led.

To thee our humble vows we raise,
   To thee address our prayer,
And in thy kind and faithful breast
   Deposit all our care.

If thou, through each perplexing path,
   Wilt be our constant guide;
If thou wilt daily bread supply,
   And raiment wilt provide;

If thou wilt spread thy shield around,
   Till these our wanderings cease,
And at our Father's loved abode
   Our souls arrive in peace:

To thee, as to our covenant God,
   We'll our whole selves resign;
And count, that not our tenth alone,
   But all we have is thine.

Rest for Weary Souls.

DOES the gospel word proclaim
Rest for those that weary be?
Then my soul put in thy claim,
Sure that promise speaks to thee;
Marks of grace I cannot show,
All polluted is my best;
Yet I weary am I know,
And the weary long for rest.

Burdened with a load of sin,
Harassed with tormenting doubt,
Hourly conflicts from within,
Hourly crosses from without:
All my little strength is gone,
Sink I must without supply;
Sure upon the earth is none
Can more weary be than I.

In the ark the weary dove
Found a welcome resting-place,
Thus my spirit longs to prove
Rest in Christ the ark of grace.
Tempest-tossed I long have been,
And the flood increases fast,
Open, Lord, and take me in,
Till the storm be overpast.

Safely lodged within thy breast,
What a wondrous change I find!
Now I know thy promised rest
Can compose a troubled mind.

You that weary are like me,
Hearken to the gospel call;
To the ark for refuge flee,
Jesus will receive you all!

To Whom shall we go.

COME, humble sinner, in whose breast
A thousand thoughts revolve;
Come with your guilt and fear oppressed
And make this last resolve:

"I'll go to Jesus, though my sin
Hath like a mountain rose;
I know his courts, I'll enter in,
Whatever may oppose.

"Prostrate I'll lie before his throne,
And there my guilt confess;
I'll tell him I'm a wretch undone,
Without his sovereign grace.

"I'll to the gracious king approach
Whose sceptre pardon gives;
Perhaps he may command my touch,
And then the suppliant lives.

"Perhaps he will admit my plea,
Perhaps will hear my prayer;
But if I perish, I will pray—
And perish only there.

"I can but perish, if I go,—
  I am resolved to try;
For if I stay away, I know
  I must for ever die."

The Woman of Canaan.

PRAYER an answer will obtain,
  Though the Lord awhile delay;
None shall seek his face in vain,
  None be empty sent away.

When the woman came from Tyre,
  And for help to Jesus sought;
Though he granted her desire,
  Yet at first he answered not.

Could she guess at his intent,
  When he to his followers said,
"I to Israel's sheep am sent;
  Dogs must not have children's bread."

She was not of Israel's seed,
  But of Canaan's wretched race;
Thought herself a dog indeed;
  Was not this a hopeless case?

Yet although from Canaan sprung,
  Though a dog herself she styled,
She had Israel's faith and tongue,
  And was owned for Abra'm's child.

From his word she draws a plea:
  "Though unworthy children's bread,
'Tis enough for one like me,
  If with crumbs I may be fed."

Jesus then his heart revealed:
  "Woman, canst thou thus believe?
I to thy petition yield,
  All that thou canst wish, receive."

'Tis a pattern set for us,
  How we ought to wait and pray;
None who plead and wrestle thus,
  Will be empty sent away.

Heavy Laden.

OH that my load of sin were gone!
  Oh that I could at last submit
At Jesus' feet to lay me down—
  To lay my soul at Jesus' feet.

When shall mine eyes behold the Lamb?
  The God of my salvation see?
Weary, O Lord, thou know'st I am,
  Yet still I cannot come to thee.

Rest for my soul I long to find:
  Saviour, if mine indeed thou art—
Give me thy meek and lowly mind,
  And stamp thine image on my heart.

Break off the yoke of inbred sin,
  And fully set my spirit free;
I cannot rest till pure within,
  Till I am wholly lost in thee.

Fain would I learn of thee, my God;
  Thy light and easy burden prove—
The cross, all stained with hallowed blood,
  The labour of thy dying love.

I would—but thou must give the power;
  My heart from every sin release;
Bring near, bring near the joyful hour,
  And fill me with thy perfect peace.

Come, Lord, the drooping sinner cheer,
  Let not my Jesus long delay;
Appear, in my poor heart appear;
  My God, my Saviour, come away.

All Things are Ready.

LET the beasts their breath resign,
Strangers to the life divine;
Who their God can never know,
Let their spirit downward go.
You for higher ends were born:
You may all to God return:
Dwell with him above the sky:
Why will ye for ever die?

What could your Redeemer do
More than he hath done for you?
To procure your peace with God,
Could he more than shed his blood?
After all his flow of love,
All his drawings from above,
Why will ye your Lord deny?
Why will ye for ever die?

The Prayer of the Church.

JESUS! thy church with longing eyes
For thine expected coming waits;
When will the promised light arise,
And glory beam on Zion's gates.

E'en now, when tempests round us fall,
And wintry clouds o'ercast the sky,
Thy words with pleasure we recall,
And deem that our redemption's nigh.

Oh! come and reign o'er every land;
Let Satan from his throne be hurled,
All nations bow to thy command,
And grace revive a dying world.

Teach us in watchfulness and prayer
To wait for thine appointed hour;
And fit us, by thy grace, to share
The triumphs of thy conquering hour.

The Glory of the Latter Day.

BEHOLD, the mountain of the Lord,
In latter days shall rise
Above the mountains and the hills,
And draw the wondering eyes.

To this the joyful nations round,
All tribes and tongues shall flow;
"Up to the hill of God," they say,
"And to his house, we'll go."

The beam that shines from Zion's hill
Shall lighten every land:
The king who reigns in Salem's towers
Shall all the world command.

Among the nations he shall judge,
His judgments truth shall guide
His sceptre shall protect the just,
And quell the sinner's pride.

No strife shall rage, nor hostile feuds
Disturb those peaceful years;
To ploughshares men shall beat their swords
To pruning hooks their spears.

No longer hosts encountering hosts,
Shall crowds of slain deplore;
They hang the trumpet in the hall,
And study war no more.

Come then, O house of Jacob, come,
To worship at his shrine;
And walking in the light of God,
With holy beauties shine.

The Martyrs' Hymn.

Flung to the heedless winds,
Or on the waters cast,
The martyrs' ashes, watched,
Shall gathered be at last;
And from that scattered dust,
Around us and abroad,
Shall spring a plenteous seed
Of witnesses for God.

The Father hath received
Their latest living breath;
And vain is Satan's boast
Of victory in their death;
Still, still, though dead, they speak,
And trumpet-tongued, proclaim
To many a wakening land,
The one availing Name.

They shall be Mine, saith the Lord.

Our souls by love together knit,
Cemented, mixed in one;
One hope, one heart, one mind, one voice,
'Tis heaven on earth begun.

Our hearts have burned while Jesus spake,
  And glowed with sacred fire;
He stopped and talked, and fed, and blessed,
  And filled the enlarged desire.
  "A Saviour!" let creation sing,
  "A Saviour!" let all heaven ring;
  He's God with us, we feel him ours,
  His fulness in our souls he pours;
  'Tis almost done, 'tis almost o'er,
  We're joining those who 've gone before;
  We soon shall reach the blissful shore,
  We soon shall meet to part no more.

We're soldiers fighting for our God,
  Let trembling cowards fly;
We'll stand unshaken, firm and fixed
  With Christ to live and die.
Let devils rage and men assail,
  We'll cut our passage through;
Let foes unite and friends desert,
  We'll seize the crown in view.

The little cloud increases still,
  The heavens are big with rain;
We haste to catch the teeming shower,
  And all its moisture drain;
A rill, a stream, a torrent flows,
  But pour the mighty flood;
O sweep the nations, shake the earth,
  Till all proclaim thee God.

And when thou mak'st thy jewels up,
  And sett'st thy starry crown;

When all thy sparkling gems shall shine,
  Proclaimed by thee thine own;
May we, a little band of love,
  We sinners, saved by grace,
From glory unto glory changed,
  Behold thee face to face.

The Heavenly Jerusalem.

HEAR what God the Lord hath spoken,
  "O my people, faint and few,
Comfortless, afflicted, broken,
  Fair abodes I build for you;
Thorns of heart-felt tribulation
  Shall no more perplex your ways:
You shall name your walls, Salvation,
  And your gates shall all be praise.

"There like streams that feed the garden,
  Pleasures without end shall flow;
For the Lord your faith rewarding,
  All his bounty shall bestow;
Still in undisturbed possession
  Peace and righteousness shall reign;
Never shall you feel oppression,
  Hear the voice of war again.

"Ye no more your suns descending,
  Waning moons no more shall see;
But, your griefs forever ending,
  Find eternal noon in me;

God shall rise, and shining o'er you
  Change to day the gloom of night;
He, the Lord, shall be your glory,
  God, your everlasting light.

Excellencies of Christ.

How shall I my Saviour set forth?
  How shall I his beauties declare?
O how shall I speak of his worth,
  Or what his chief dignities are?
His angels can never express,
  Nor saints who sit nearest his throne,
How rich are his treasures of grace:—
  No, this is a myst'ry unknown.

In him all the fulness of God
  For ever transcendently shines;
Though once like a mortal he stood,
  To finish his gracious designs:
Though once he was nailed to the cross,
  Vile rebels like me to set free;
His glory sustainèd no loss,
  Eternal his kingdom shall be.

His wisdom, his love, and his power,
  Seemed then with each other to vie;
When sinners he stooped to restore,
  Poor sinners condemnèd to die!

He laid all his grandeur aside,
And dwelt in a cottage of clay:
Poor sinners he loved, till he died
To wash their pollution away.

O sinner, believe and adore
The Saviour so rich to redeem;
No creature can ever explore
The treasures of goodness in him:
Come, all ye who see yourselves lost,
And feel yourselves burdened with sin,
Draw near while with terror you're tossed,
Believe—and your peace shall begin.

Now sinner, attend to his call,
"Whoso hath an ear let him hear!"
He promises mercy to all
Who feel their sad wants, far and near:
He riches has ever in store,
And treasures that never can waste:
Here's pardon, here's grâce, yea, and more—
Here's glory eternal at last.

Beyond Jordan.

THERE is a land of pure delight,
Where saints immortal reign:
Infinite day excludés the night,
And pleasures banish pain.

There everlasting spring abides,
  And never-withering flowers:
Death, like a narrow sea, divides
  This heavenly land from ours.

Sweet fields, beyond the swelling flood,
  Stand dressed in living green;
So to the Jews old Canaan stood,
  While Jordan rolled between.

But timorous mortals start and shrink,
  To cross this narrow sea;
And linger shivering on the brink,
  And fear to launch away.

Oh! could we make our doubts remove,
  Those gloomy doubts that rise,
And see the Canaan that we love,
  With unbeclouded eyes!

Could we but climb where Moses stood,
  And view the landscape o'er,
Not Jordan's stream, nor death's cold flood,
  Should fright us from the shore.

Lord, open his Eyes that He may See.

O WATCHMAN, will the night of sin
    Be never past?
O watchman, doth the day begin
To dawn upon thy straining sight at last?
    Will it dispel
Ere long the mists of sense wherein I dwell?

Now all the earth is bright and glad
With the fresh morn;
But all my heart is cold and dark and sad;
Sun of the soul, let me behold thy dawn!
Come Jesus, Lord!
Oh quickly come, according to thy word!

Do we not live in those blest days
So long foretold,
When thou shouldst come to bring us light and grace?
And yet I sit in darkness as of old,
Pining to see
Thy glory; but thou still art far from me.

Long since thou cam'st to be the light
Of all men here;
And yet in me is nought but blackest night.
Wilt thou not then to me, thine own, appear?
Shine forth and bless
My soul with vision of thy righteousness?

If thus in darkness ever left,
Can I fulfil
The works of light, while of all light bereft?
How shall I learn in love and meekness still
To follow thee,
And all the sinful works of darkness flee?

The light of reason cannot give
Life to my soul;
Jesus alone can make me truly live.

One glance of his can make my spirit whole.
Arise, and shine
On this poor longing, waiting heart of mine!

Single and clear, not weak or blind,
The eye must be,
To which thy glory shall an entrance find;
For if thy chosen ones would gaze on thee,
No earthly screen
Between their souls and thee must intervene.

Jesus, do thou mine eyes unseal,
And let them grow
Quick to discern whate'er thou dost reveal,
So shall I be delivered from that woe,
Blindly to stray
Through hopeless night, while all around is day.

Undertake for Me.

As those that watch for the day
Through the restless night of pain,
When the first faint streaks of grey
Bring rest and ease again,—
As they turn their sleepless eyes
The eastern sky to see,
Long hours before sunrise —
So waiteth my soul for thee!

As those that watch for the day
Through the long, long night of grief,
When the soul can only pray
That the day may bring relief,—

When the eyes with weeping spent,
  No dawn of hope can see,
But the heart keeps watch intent,—
  So waiteth my soul for thee!

As those that watch for the day
  Through that deepest night of all,
When trembling and sin have sway,
  And the shades of thy absence fall:
As they search through clouds of fear
  The Morning Star to see,
And the Light of Life appear—
  So waiteth my soul for thee!

As those that watch for the day
  And know that the day will rise!—
Though the weary hours delay,
  As they pass under midnight skies,—
Though the Sun of Righteousness
  Only faith's clear eye can see,
Because thou hast promised to bless,
  Lord Jesus, I wait for thee!

Mercy.

O LORD, turn not thy face away
  From him that lies prostrate;
Lamenting sore his sinful life,
  Before the Mercy-gate;

Which thou dost open wide for those
That do lament their sin:
O shut it not against me, Lord,
But let me enter in.

Call me not to a strict account,
How I have livèd here;
For then I know, right well, O Lord,
Most vile I shall appear.

I need not to confess my life,
For surely thou canst tell
What I have been; and what I am
Thou knowest very well.

So come I to the throne of grace,
Where mercy doth abound,
Desiring mercy for my sins,
To heal my deadly wound.

Mercy, O Lord! mercy I ask:
This is the total sum;
For mercy, Lord, is all my prayer:
Oh let thy mercy come!

Repentance.

WEARY of wandering from my God,
And now made willing to return,
I hear, and bow beneath the rod;
To him with penitence I mourn:
I have an advocate above,—
A friend before the throne of love.

O Jesus, full of truth and grace,—
  More full of grace than I of sin,—
Yet once again I seek thy face;
  Open thine arms and take me in!
And freely my backslidings heal,
And love the faithless sinner still.

Thou know'st the way to bring me back,—
  My fallen spirit to restore;
O! for thy truth and mercy's sake,
  Forgive, and bid me sin no more:
The ruins of my soul repair,
And make my heart a house of prayer.

Ah, give me, Lord, the tender heart,
  That trembles at the approach of sin;
A godly fear of sin impart;
  Implant and root it deep within,
That I may dread thy gracious power,
And never dare to offend thee more.

Bartimeus.

"Mercy, O thou son of David!"
  Thus blind Bartimeus prayed;
"Others by thy grace are savèd,
Now to me afford thine aid."
  Many for his crying chid him,
But he called the louder still;
  Till the gracious Saviour bid him
"Come and ask me what you will."

Money was not what he wanted,
  Though by begging used to live:
But he asked, and Jesus granted,
  Alms which none but he could give;
"Lord, remove this grievous blindness,
  Let my eyes behold the day;"
Straight he saw, and won by kindness
  Followed Jesus in the way.

O! methinks I hear I him praising,
  Publishing to all around,
"Friends, is not my case amazing!
  What a Saviour I have found.
Oh! that all the blind but knew him,
  And would be advised by me;
Surely they would hasten to him,
  He would cause them all to see."

In the Morning.

THERE is a heaven above the skies,
A heaven where pleasure never dies;
—We'll all rise together in the morning—
A heaven I sometimes hope to see,
But fear again 'tis not for me.
—We'll all rise together in the morning.
  In the morning, children, in the morning,
  We'll all rise together in the morning,

The way is difficult and strait,
And narrow is the gospel gate;

Ten thousand dangers are therein,
Ten thousand snares to take me in.

I travel through a world of foes,
Through conflicts sore my spirit goes:
The tempter cries I ne'er shall stand,
Nor reach fair Canaan's happy land.

The way of danger I am in,
Beset with devils, men, and sin,
But in this way thy track I see,
The track of him who died for me.

I trace the footsteps of my God,
Who on the cross sustained my load:
'Twas on that dark and doleful day,
In streaming blood he passed this way.

Come life, come death, come then what will,
His footsteps I will follow still;
Through dangers thick, and hell's alarms,
I shall be safe in his dear arms.

Then O my soul, arise and sing;
Behold thy Saviour, Friend and King!
With pleasing smiles he now looks down,
And cries, "Press on, and here's the crown.

"Prove faithful then a few more days,
Fight the good fight, and win the race,
And then thy soul with me shall reign,
Thy head a crown of glory gain."
In the morning, children, in the morning;
We'll all rise together in the morning.

Affliction Sweetened.

WHEN languor and disease invade
  This trembling house of clay,
'Tis sweet to look beyond our cage,
  And long to fly away.

Sweet to look inward, and attend
  The whispers of his love:
Sweet to look upward, to the place
  Where Jesus pleads above.

Sweet to look back, and see my name
  In life's fair book set down;
Sweet to look forward, and behold
  Eternal joys my own.

Sweet to reflect how grace divine
  My sins on Jesus laid;
Sweet to remember that his blood
  My debt of suffering paid.

Sweet in his righteousness to stand,
  Which saves from second death;
Sweet to experience, day by day,
  His Spirit's quickening breath.

Sweet on his faithfulness to rest,
  Whose love can never end;
Sweet on his covenant of grace
  For all things to depend.

Sweet in the confidence of faith
  To trust his firm decrees;
Sweet to lie passive in his hands,
  And know no will but his.

Sweet to rejoice in lively hope
  That when my change shall come,
Angels will hover round my bed,
  And waft my spirit home.

Then shall my dis-imprisoned soul
  Behold him and adore;
Be with his likeness satisfied,
  And grieve and sin no more.

Shall see him wear that very flesh
  On which my guilt was lain;
His love intense, his merit fresh,
  As though but newly slain.

Soon too my slumbering dust shall hear
  The trumpet's quickening sound;
And by my Saviour's power rebuilt,
  At his right hand be found.

These eyes shall see him in that day,
  The God that died for me;
And all my rising bones shall say,
  Lord, who is like to thee.

If such the views which grace unfolds,
  Weak as it is below;
What raptures must the Church above,
  In Jesus' presence know!

If such the sweetness of the stream,
What must the fountain be;
Where saints and angels draw their bliss
Immediately from thee!

O may the unction of these truths,
For ever with me stay;
Till from her sinful cage dismissed,
My spirit flies away.

Thy Will be Done.

THROUGH all the various shifting scenes
Of life's mistaken good or ill;
Thy hand, O God, conducts unseen
Our changes by thy sovereign will.

Thou givest with paternal care,
Howe'er unjustly we complain,
To each their necessary share
Of joy and sorrow, care and pain.

Trust we to youth, or friend, or power,
Fix we on this terrestrial ball?
When most secure, the coming hour
If thou see fit, may blast them all.

When lowest sunk with grief and shame,
Filled with affliction's bitter cup,
Lost to relations, friends, and fame,
Thy powerful hand can raise us up.

Thy gracious consolations cheer,
  Thy smiles suppress the deep-fetched sigh,
Thy hand can dry the trickling tear
  That secret wets the afflicted eye.

All things on earth, and all in heaven,
  On thy eternal will depend;
And all for greater good were given,
  And all shall in thy glory end.

This be my case; to all beside
  Indifferent let my wishes be;
Passion be calm, and dumb be pride,
  And fixed, O God, my soul on thee.

Morning, and Evening, and at Noon.

When morn awakes our hearts
  To form the early prayer;
When toil-worn day departs,
  And gives a pause to care;
When those our soul loves best
  Kneel with us in thy fear,
To ask thy peace and rest—
  Our God, our Father, hear!

When worldly snares without
  And evil thoughts within,
Of grace would raise a doubt,
  Or lure us back to sin;

When human strength proves frail,
 And will but half sincere,
When faith begins to fail—
 Our God, our Father, hear!

When in our cup of mirth
 The drop of trembling falls,
And the frail props of earth
 Are crumbling round our walls;
When back we gaze with grief,
 And forward glance with fear;
When faileth man's relief,
 Our God, our Father, hear!

And when death's awful hand
 Unbars the gates of time,
Eternity's dim land
 Disclosing, dread, sublime,
When flesh and spirit quake
 Before thee to appear—
O then, for Jesus' sake,
 Our God, our Father, hear!

Israel's Host.

COME, let us join our friends above,
 That have obtained the prize;
And on the eagle wings of love
 To joys celestial rise.

Let all the saints terrestrial sing,
  With those to glory gone;
For all the servants of our King,
  In earth and heaven, are one.

One family we dwell in him,
  One church above, beneath,
Though now divided by the stream,
  The narrow stream, of death.

One army of the living God,
  To his command we bow;
Part of his host have crossed the flood,
  And part are crossing now.

Ten thousand to their endless home
  This solemn moment fly;
And we are to the margin come,
  And we expect to die.

His militant embodied host,
  With wishful looks we stand,
And long to see that happy coast,
  And reach the heavenly land.

Our old companions in distress
  We haste again to see,
And eager long for our release,
  And full felicity.

E'en now, by faith, we join our hands
  With those that went before;
And greet the blood-besprinkled bands
  On the eternal shore.

Our spirits too shall quickly join,
  Like theirs with glory crowned,
And shout to see our Captain's sign,
  To hear his trumpet sound.

Lord Jesus, be our constant guide:
  And when the word is given,
Bid death's cold flood its waves divide,
  And land us safe in heaven.

Forsaking all to follow Christ.

JESUS, I my cross have taken,
  All to leave, and follow thee;
Naked, poor, despised, forsaken,
  Thou from hence my all shalt be,
Perish every fond ambition,
  All I've sought, or hoped, or known,
Yet how rich is my condition,
  God and heaven are still my own!

Let the world despise and leave me;
  They have left my Saviour too;
Human hearts and looks deceive me, —
  Thou art not, like them, untrue;
And whilst thou shalt smile upon me,
  God of wisdom, love, and might,
Foes may hate, and friends disown me:
  Show thy face, and all is bright.

Go, then, earthly fame and treasure,
  Come disaster, scorn, and pain,
In thy service pain is pleasure,
  With thy favour loss is gain.
I have called thee, Abba, Father,
  I have set my heart on thee;
Storms may howl, and clouds may gather,
  All must work for good to me.

Man may trouble and distress me,
  'Twill but drive me to thy breast;
Life with trials hard may press me,
  Heaven will bring me sweeter rest.
O 'tis not in grief to harm me,
  While thy love is left to me;
O 'twere not in joy to charm me,
  Were that joy unmixed with thee.

Soul, then know thy full salvation;
  Rise o'er sin and fear and care;
Joy to find in every station,
  Something still to do or bear.
Think what Spirit dwells within thee;
  Think what Father's smiles are thine;
Think that Jesus died to win thee,—
  Child of heaven, canst thou repine?

Haste thee on from grace to glory,
  Armed by faith and winged with prayer,
Heaven's eternal days before thee,
  God's own hand shall guide thee there.

Soon shall close thy earthly mission,
  Soon shall pass thy pilgrim days,
Hope shall change to glad fruition,
  Faith to sight, and prayer to praise.

Contentment.

FIERCE passions discompose the mind,
  As tempests vex the sea;
But calm content and peace we find,
  When, Lord, we turn to thee.

In vain by reason and by rule
  We try to bend the will;
For none but in the Saviour's school
  Can learn the heavenly skill.

Since at his feet my soul has sat,
  His gracious words to hear;
Contented with my present state,
  I cast on him my care.

"Art thou a sinner, soul?" he said,—
  "Then how canst thou complain?
How light thy troubles here, if weighed
  With everlasting pain!

"If thou of murmuring wouldst be cured,
  Compare thy griefs with mine;
Think what my love for thee endured,
  And thou wilt not repine.

"'Tis I appoint thy daily lot,
And I do all things well;
Thou soon shalt leave this wretched spot,
And rise with me to dwell.

"In life my grace shall strength supply,
Proportioned to thy day;
At death, thou still shalt find me nigh,
To wipe thy tears away."

Thus I, who once my wretched days
In vain repining spent,
Taught in my Saviour's school of grace,
Have learned to be content.

Jacob's Ladder.

If the Lord our leader be,
We may follow without fear;
East or west, by land or sea,
Home, with him, is everywhere:
When from Esau Jacob fled,
Though his pillow was a stone,
And the ground his humble bed,
Yet he was not left alone.

Kings are often waking kept,
Racked with cares on beds of state;
Never king like Jacob slept,
For he lay at heaven's gate:

Lo! he saw a ladder reared,
Reaching to the heavenly throne,
At the top the Lord appeared,
Spake, and claimed him for his own,

"Fear not, Jacob, thou art mine,
And my presence with thee goes;
On thy heart my love shall shine,
And my arm subdue thy foes:
From my promise comfort take,
For my help in trouble call;
Never will I thee forsake,
Till I have accomplished all."

Well does Jacob's ladder suit
To the gospel throne of grace;
We are at the ladder's foot,
Every hour, in every place:
By assuming flesh and blood,
Jesus heaven and earth unites;
We by faith ascend to God,
God to dwell with us delights.

They who know the Saviour's name,
Are for all events prepared;
What can changes do to them,
Who have such a guide and guard?
Should they traverse earth around,
To the ladder still they come:
Every spot is holy ground,
God is there—and he's their home.

The Good that I Would.

Fain would my thoughts fly up to thee,
  Thy peace, sweet Lord, to find;
But when I offer, still the world
  Lays clogs upon my mind.

Sometimes I climb a little way,
  And thence look down below;
How nothing then do all things seem,
  That here make such a show!

Then round about I turn my eyes,
  To feast my hungry sight;
I meet with heaven in everything,—
  In everything delight.

I see thy wisdom ruling all,
  And it with joy admire;
I see myself among such hopes
  As set my heart on fire.

When I have thus triumphed awhile.
  And think to build my nest,
Some cross conceit comes fluttering by,
  And interrupts my rest.

Then to the earth again I fall,
  And from my low dust cry,
"'Twas not in my wing, Lord, but thine
  That I got up so high."

And now my God, whether I rise,
   Or still lie down in dust,
Both I submit to thy blest will,
   In both on thee I trust.

Guide thou my way, who art thyself
   My everlasting end,
That every step, or swift or slow,
   Still to thyself may tend.

Amen!

YEA, my spirit fain would sink
   In thy heart and hands, my God,
Waiting till thou shew the end
   Of the ways that thou hast trod;
Stripped of self, how calm her rest
On her loving Father's breast!

And my soul repineth not,
   Well content whate'er befall;
Murmurs, wishes, of self-will,
   They are slain and vanquished all,
Restless thoughts, that fret and crave,
Slumber in her Saviour's grave.

And my soul is free from care,
   For her thoughts from all things cease
That can pierce like sharpest thorns,
   Wounding sore the inner peace,—
He who made her careth well,
She but seeks in peace to dwell.

And my soul despaireth not,
  Loving God amid her woe;
Grief that wrings and breaks the heart
  Only they who hate him know:
They who love him still possess
Comfort in their worst distress.

And my soul complaineth not,
  For she knows not pain or fear,
Clinging to her God in faith,
  Trusting though he slay her here.
'Tis when flesh and blood repine,
Sun of joy, thou canst not shine.

Thus my soul before her God
  Lieth still, nor speaketh more,
Conqueror thus o'er pain and wrong,
  That once smote her to the core;
Like a silent ocean, bright
With her God's great praise and light.

Loving Kindness.

Awake, my soul, to joyful lays,
And sing the great Redeemer's praise;
He justly claims a song from me,
His loving-kindness, O how free

He saw me ruined in the fall,
Yet loved me notwithstanding all;
He saved me from my lost estate,
His loving-kindness, O how great!

Though numerous hosts of mighty foes,
Though earth and hell my way oppose,
He safely leads my soul along,
His loving-kindness, O how strong!

When trouble, like a gloomy cloud,
Has gathered thick and thundered loud,
He near my soul has always stood,
His loving-kindness, O how good!

Often I feel my sinful heart
Prone from my Jesus to depart;
But though I have him oft forgot,
His loving-kindness changes not.

Soon shall I pass the gloomy vale,
Soon all my mortal powers must fail;
Oh! may my last expiring breath,
His loving-kindness sing in death.

Then let me mount and soar away
To the bright world of endless day,
And sing with rapture and surprise
His loving-kindness in the skies.

The Fountain of Life.

HAIL, everlasting spring!
  Celestial fountain, hail!
Thy streams salvation bring,
  The waters never fail;

Still they endure,
And still they flow,
For all our woe
A sovereign cure.

Blest be his wounded side,
And blest his bleeding heart,
Who all in anguish died
Such favours to impart.
His sacred blood
Shall make us clean
From every sin,
And fit for God

To that dear source of love
Our souls this day would come:
And thither from above,
Lord, call the nations home;
That Jew and Greek
With rapturous songs
On all their tongues
Thy praise may speak.

Missionary Hymn.

From Greenland's icy mountains,
From India's coral strand,
Where Afric's sunny fountains
Roll down their golden sand,

From many an ancient river,
  From many a palmy plain,
They call us to deliver
  Their land from error's chain.

What though the spicy breezes
  Blow soft o'er Ceylon's isle,
Though every prospect pleases,
  And only man is vile;
In vain with lavish kindness
  The gifts of God are strewn;
The heathen, in his blindness,
  Bows down to wood and stone.

Shall we, whose souls are lighted
  With wisdom from on high,
Shall we to men benighted
  The lamp of life deny?
Salvation! O Salvation!
  The joyful sound proclaim
Till earth's remotest nation
  Has learned Messiah's name.

Waft, waft, ye winds, his story,
  And you, ye waters, roll,
Till like a sea of glory
  It spreads from pole to pole;
Till o'er our ransomed nature,
  The Lamb for sinners slain,
Redeemer, King, Creator,
  In bliss returns to reign.

Prayer for Children.

GRACIOUS Lord, our children see,
By thy mercy we are free;
But shall these, alas! remain
Subjects still of Satan's reign?
Israel's young ones, when of old
Pharaoh threatened to withhold,
Then thy messenger said "No;
Let the children also go!"

When the angel of the Lord,
Drawing forth his dreadful sword,
Slew with an avenging hand,
All the first-born of the land;
Then thy people's doors he passed,
Where the bloody sign was placed:
Hear us, now, upon our knees,
Plead the blood of Christ for these!

Lord, we tremble, for we know
How the fierce malicious foe,
Wheeling round his watchful flight,
Keeps them ever in his sight:
Spread thy pinions, King of kings!
Hide them safe beneath thy wings;
Lest the ravenous bird of prey
Stoop, and bear the brood away.

Conquering, and to Conquer.

HE dies, the friend of sinners dies!
  Lo, Salem's daughters weep around;
A solemn darkness veils the skies!
  A sudden trembling shakes the ground!
Come saints, and drop a tear or two,
  For him who groaned beneath your load;
He shed a thousand drops for you,
  A thousand drops of richer blood.

Here's love and grief beyond degree:
  The Lord of Glory dies for men!
But lo! what sudden joys we see:
  Jesus, the dead, revives again!
The rising God forsakes the tomb,
  (In vain the tomb forbids his rise;)
Cherubic legions guard him home,
  And shout him welcome to the skies.

Break off your tears, ye saints, and tell
  How high your great Deliverer reigns;
Sing how he spoiled the hosts of hell,
  And led the monster Death in chains!
Say "Live forever, wondrous King!
  Born to redeem, and strong to save!"
Then ask the monster—"Where's thy sting?
  And where's thy victory, boasting grave?"

Looking Off.

O EYES that are weary,
  And hearts that are sore!
Look off unto Jesus,
  And sorrow no more!
The light of his countenance
  Shineth so bright,
That on earth, as in heaven,
  There need be no night.

"Looking off unto Jesus,"
  My eyes cannot see
The troubles and dangers
  That throng about me:
They cannot be blinded
  With sorrowful tears,
They cannot be shadowed
  With unbelief-fears.

Looking off unto Jesus,
  My spirit is blest,—
In the world I have turmoil—
  In him I have rest.
The sea of my life
  All about me may roar,—
When I look unto Jesus,
  I hear it no more.

Looking off unto Jesus,
  I go not astray;
My eyes are on him,
  And he shews me the way.

The path may seem dark
  As he leads me along,
But following Jesus
  I cannot go wrong.

Looking off unto Jesus,
  My heart cannot fear,—
Its trembling is still,
  When I see Jesus near:
I know that his power
  My safeguard will be,
For, "Why are ye troubled?"
  He saith unto me.

Looking off unto Jesus
  Oh may I be found,
When the waters of Jordan
  Encompass me round:
Let them bear me away
  In his presence to be!
'Tis but seeing him nearer
  Whom always I see.

Then, then I shall know
  The full beauty and grace
Of Jesus my Lord,
  When I stand face to face:
I shall know how his love
  Went before me each day,
And wonder that ever
  My eyes turned away.

Only Jesus.

When, gracious Lord, when shall it be
That I shall find my all in thee?
The fulness of thy promise prove,—
The seal of thine eternal love.

A poor blind child I wander here,
If haply I may feel thee near:
O dark! dark! dark! I still must say,
Amidst the blaze of gospel day.

Thee, only thee, I fain would find,
And cast the world and flesh behind;
Thou, only thou, to me be given,
Of all thou hast in earth or heaven.

When from the arm of flesh set free,
Jesus, my soul shall fly to thee;
Jesus, when I have lost my all,
I shall upon thy bosom fall.

Hitherto hath the Lord Helped us.

Come, thou Fount of every blessing,
  Tune my heart to sing thy grace:
Streams of mercy, never ceasing,
  Call for songs of loudest praise.
Teach me some melodious sonnet,
  Sung by flaming tongues above:
Praise the mount—I'm fixed upon it;
  Mount of God's unchanging love!

Here I raise my Eben-ezer;
  Hither by thy help I'm come;
And I hope, by thy good pleasure,
  Safely to arrive at home.
Jesus sought me when a stranger,
  Wandering from the fold of God:
He to save my soul from danger,
  Interposed his precious blood.

O, to grace how great a debtor
  Daily I'm constrained to be!
Let that grace, now, like a fetter,
  Bind my wandering heart to thee.
Prone to wander, Lord, I feel it—
  Prone to leave the God I love;
Here's my heart, Oh take and seal it
  Seal it for thy courts above.

Who shall Separate us?

REJOICE, ye saints, in every state,
  Divine decrees remain unmoved:
No turns of providence abate
  God's care for those he once hath loved.

Firmer than heaven his cov'nant stands,
  Though earth should shake and skies depart,
You're safe in your Redeemer's hands,
  Who bears your names upon his heart.

Our Surety knows for whom he stood,
And gave himself a sacrifice:
The souls once sprinkled with his blood,
Possess a life that never dies.

Though darkness spread around our tent,
Though fear prevail, and joy decline,
God will not of his oath repent;
Dear Lord, thy people still are thine.

Why take ye Thought.

O Lord, my best desire fulfil,
And help me to resign
Life, health, and comfort to thy will,
And make thy pleasure mine.

Why should I shrink at thy command,
Whose love forbids my fears?
Or tremble at the gracious hand
That wipes away my tears?

No, let me rather freely yield
What most I prize, to thee;
Who never hast a good withheld,
Or wilt withhold from me.

Thy favour, all my journey through
Thou art engaged to grant;
What else I want, or think I do,
'Tis better still to want.

Wisdom and mercy guide my way;
  Shall I resist them both?
A poor blind creature of a day,
  And crushed before the moth!

But ah! my inward spirit cries,
  Still bind me to thy sway;
Else the next cloud that veils the skies,
  Drives all these thoughts away.

This is the Way

How many and great are the foes which infest
The way through this world to the Canaan of rest!
The traveller ever his Lord would obey,
Yet oft is discouraged because of the way.

Though Satan, the world, and corruption combine,
And try to prevent the poor Pilgrim's design;
They cannot destroy, though they often betray,
And make him discouraged because of the way.

When good he would do, imperfections abound,
His graces are weak, and temptations surround;
For many turn back, and would lead him astray
Which makes him discouraged because of the way.

Yet why should the Christian, of Canaan despair,
Perplexed or alarmed with discouraging fear?
Let him but his map and his leader obey,
Nor more be discouraged becaues of the way.

In Christ inexhaustible treasures are stored.
And Jesus will suitable blessings afford;
Then why should the pilgrim be filled with dismay?
Or why be discouraged because of the way?

Unquenchable love and omnipotent power,
Will land him ere long on the heavenly shore;
There pleasure eternal will amply repay,
For all the discouragements found in the way.

Counting the Cost.

AM I a soldier of the cross,
A follower of the Lamb,
And shall I fear to own his cause,
Or blush to speak his name?

Must I be carried to the skies
On flowery beds of ease,
While others fought to win the prize,
And sailed through bloody seas?

Are there no foes for me to face?
Must I not stem the flood?
Is this vile world a friend to grace,
To help me on to God?

Sure I must fight if I would reign;
Increase my courage, Lord:
I'll bear the toil, endure the pain,
Supported by thy word.

Thy saints, in all this glorious war,
  Shall conquer, though they die;
They view the triumph from afar,
  And seize it with their eye.

When that illustrious day shall rise,
  And all thy armies shine
In robes of victory through the skies—
  The glory shall be thine.

Religion.

RELIGION bids all sin depart,
  And folly flies her chastening rod;
She makes the humble, contrite heart,
  A temple of the living God.

Beyond the narrow vale of time,
  Where bright celestial ages roll,
To scenes eternal, scenes sublime,
  She points the way, and leads the soul.

At her approach, the grave appears
  The gate of paradise restored;
Her voice the watching cherub hears,
  And drops his double flaming sword.

Baptized with her renewing fire,
  We shall the crown of glory gain;
Rise when the hosts of heaven expire,
  And reign with God, for ever reign.

My Times are in Thy Hand.

FATHER, I know that all my life
Is portioned out for me,
And the changes that are sure to come,
I do not fear to see;
But I ask thee for a present mind,
Intent on pleasing thee.

I ask thee for a thoughtful love,
Through constant watching, wise,
To meet the glad with joyful smiles,
And to wipe the weeping eyes;
And a heart at leisure from itself,
To soothe and sympathise.

I would not have the restless will
That hurries to and fro,
Seeking for some great thing to do,
Or secret thing to know;
I would be treated as a child,
And guided where I go.

Wherever in the world I am,
In whatsoe'er estate,
I have a fellowship with hearts
To keep and cultivate;
And a work of lowly love to do
For the Lord on whom I wait.

So I ask thee for the daily strength,
To none that ask denied,

And a mind to blend with outward life,
  While keeping at thy side;
Content to fill a little space,
  If thou be glorified.

And if some things I do not ask,
  In my cup of blessing be,
I would have my spirit filled the more
  With grateful love to thee—
More careful—not to serve thee *much*,
  But to please thee *perfectly*.

There are briars besetting every path,
  That call for patient care;
There is a cross in every lot,
  And an earnest need for prayer;
But a lowly heart that leans on thee,
  Is happy anywhere.

In a service which thy will appoints,
  There are no bonds for me;
For my inmost heart is taught "the truth,"
  That makes thy children "free;"
And a life of self-renouncing love
  Is a life of liberty.

All Things in Christ.

THOU very present aid
  In suffering and distress;
The mind which still on thee is stayed,
  Is kept in perfect peace.

The soul by faith reclined
  On the Redeemer's breast,
'Mid raging storms exults to find
  An everlasting rest.

Sorrow and fear are gone,
  Whene'er thy face appears;
It stills the sighing orphan's moan,
  And dries the widow's tears.

It hallows every cross;
  It sweetly comforts me;
Makes me forget my every loss,
  And find my all in thee.

Jesus, to whom I fly,
  Doth all my wishes fill;
What though created streams are dry?
  I have the fountain still.

Stripped of each earthly friend,
  I find them all in one:
And peace and joy which never end,
  And heaven, in Christ, begun.

The Waters Prevailed Greatly.

ONCE the dove, by Noah sent,
  Wandering from east to west,
  Finding not a spot of rest,
Back unto the ark she went.

Thus, my Lord! a weary soul
  Which hath sought for rest in vain,
  Now returns to thee again,—
Yields her to thy sweet control.

Lord, the world is cold and dark,
  And I miss the way to thee:
  O extend thy hand to me,
Take me back within the ark.

From the storm my shelter be,
  On the storm-cloud write thy sign:—
  When the world doth brightest shine,
Keep my eyes still fixed on thee.

Delight in God.

GREAT God, indulge my humble claim,
  Thou art my hope, my joy, my rest;
The glories that compose thy name,
  Stand all engaged to make me blest.

Thou great and good, thou just and wise,
  Thou art my Father and my God;
And I am thine, by sacred ties—
  Thy son, thy servant, bought with blood.

With heart and eyes and lifted hands
  For thee I long, to thee I look;
As travellers, in thirsty lands,
  Pant for the cooling water brook.

With early feet I love to appear
  Among thy saints, and seek thy face;
Oft have I seen thy glory there,
  And felt the power of sovereign grace.

My life itself, without thy love,
  No taste of pleasure could afford;
'Twould but a tiresome burden prove,
  If I were banished from the Lord.

I'll lift my hands, I'll raise my voice,
  While I have breath to pray or praise;
This work shall make my heart rejoice,
  And spend the remnant of my days.

Welcome Cross.

'Tis my happiness below
  Not to live without the cross,
But the Saviour's power to know,
  Sanctifying every loss:
Trials must and will befall;
  But with humble faith to see
Love inscribed upon them all,
  This is happiness to me.

God in Israel sows the seeds
  Of affliction, pain, and toil;
These spring up and choke the weeds
  Which would else o'erspread the soil;

Trials make the promise sweet;
  Trials give new life to prayer;
Trials bring me to his feet,
  Lay me low, and keep me there.

Did I meet no trials here,
  No chastisements by the way,
Might I not with reason fear
  I should prove a castaway?
Bastards may escape the rod,
  Sunk in earthly, vain delight:
But the true-born child of God
  Must not, would not if he might.

The End of the Day.

COME forth! come on, with solemn song!
The road is short, the rest is long!
The Lord brought here, he calls away:
    Make no delay,
This home was for a passing day.

Here in an inn a stranger dwelt,
Here joy and grief by turns he felt;
Poor dwelling, now we close thy door!
    The task is o'er,
The sojourner returns no more!

Now of a lasting home possest,
He goes to seek a deeper rest.
Good night! the day was sultry here,
    In toil and fear,
Good night! the night is cool and clear.

Chime on, ye bells! again begin,
And ring the Sabbath morning in;
The laborer's week-day work is done,
The rest begun,
Which Christ hath for his people won!

Jesus, thou reignest, Lord alone,
Thou wilt return and claim thine own.
Come quickly, Lord! return again!
Amen! Amen!
Thine seal us ever, now and then!

The Prepared City.

O MOTHER dear, Jerusalem,
When shall I come to thee?
When shall my sorrows have an end?
Thy joys when shall I see?

O happy harbour of God's saints!
O sweet and pleasant soil!
In thee no sorrows can be found,
No grief, no care, no toil.

In thee no sickness is at all,
Nor hurt nor any sore;
There is no death nor ugly sight,
But life for evermore.

No dimming cloud o'ershadows thee,
No cloud nor darksome night:
But every soul shines as the sun,
For God himself gives light.

Jerusalem! Jerusalem!
  Would God I were in thee!
O that my sorrows had an end,
  Thy joys that I might see.

Thy turrets and thy pinnacles
  With carbuncles do shine,
With jasper, pearl, and chrysolite,
  Surpassing pure and fine.

Thy houses are of ivory,
  Thy windows crystal clear,
Thy streets are laid with beaten gold,
  There angels do appear.

Thy walls are made of precious stone,
  Thy bulwarks diamond square,
Thy gates are made of orient pearl,—
  O God, if I were there!

Thy gardens and thy pleasant walks
  My study long have been;
Such dazzling views, by human sight
  Have never yet been seen.

If Heaven be thus so glorious, Lord,
  Why should I stay from thence?
What folly's this, that I should dread
  To die and go from hence!

Reach down, O Lord, thine arm of grace,
  And cause me to ascend
Where congregations ne'er break up,
  And Sabbaths never end.

Jesus, my Lord, to Glory's gone,
Him will I go and see;
And all my brethren here below,
Will soon come after me.

My friends, I bid you all adieu,
I leave you in God's care:
And if I never more see you,
Go on, I'll meet you there.

When we've been there ten thousand years,
Bright shining as the sun,
We've no less days to sing God's praise,
Than when we first begun.

Above All, the Shield.

Faith fails;
Then in the dust
Lie failing rest and light and trust.
So doth the troubled soul itself distress,
And choke the fountain in the wilderness.
I care not what your peace assails!
The deep root is: faith fails.

Faith fails,
When in the breast
The Lord's sweet presence doth not rest;
For who believes, clouds cannot make afraid;
He knows the sun doth shine behind the shade:
He rides at anchor through the gales.
Do you not so? faith fails.

Faith fails;
Its foes alarm,
And persecution's threats disarm;
False friends can scarcely wish it a good day,
Before it taketh fright, and shrinks away.
When God doth guard, what foe prevails?
Why then the fear? Faith fails.

Faith fails;
Else cares would die—
And we should on God's care rely.
Man for the coming day doth grieve and fret,
And all past days doth sinfully forget.
For every beast God's care avails,
Why not for us? Faith fails.

Faith fails;
Then cometh fear,
If sickness comes, if death is near.
O man, why is it when the times are bad,
And the days evil, that thy face is sad?
How is it that thy courage quails?
It must be this: faith fails.

My God!
Let my faith be
Living and working actively,
With hope and joy, that death may not surprise.
So let them sweetly close my eyes;
The Christian's *life* to death may yield,—
Hope stands—faith has the field.

Then thou Knewest my Path.

My God! lo here before thy face
 I cast me in the dust;
Where is the hope of happier days,
 Where is my wonted trust?
Where are the sunny hours I had
 Ere of thy light bereft?
Vanished is all that made me glad,
 My pain alone is left.

I shrink with fear and sore alarm
 When threatening ills I see,
As in mine hour of need thine arm
 No more could shelter me;
As though thou couldst not see the grief
 That makes my courage quail,
As though thou wouldst not send relief,
 When human helpers fail.

Cannot thy might avert e'en now
 What seems my certain doom,
And still with light and succour bow
 To him who weeps in gloom?
Art thou not evermore the same?
 Hast not thyself revealed
In Holy Writ, that we may claim
 Thee for our strength and shield?

O Father, compass me about
 With love, for I am weak;
Forgive, forgive my sinful doubt
 Thy pitying glance I seek;

For torn and anguished is my heart,
 Thou seest it, my God,
Oh soothe my conscience' bitter smart,
 Lift off my sorrows' load.

I know thy thoughts are peace toward me,
 Safe am I in thy hands,
Could I but firmly build on thee,
 For sure thy counsel stands!
Whate'er thy word hath promised, all
 Wilt thou full surely give;
Wherefore from thee I will not fall,
 Thy word doth make me live.

Though mountains crumble into dust,
 Thy covenant standeth fast;
Who follows thee in pious trust,
 Shall reach the goal at last.
Though strange and winding seem the way,
 While yet on earth I dwell,
In heaven my heart shall gladly say,
 Thou, God, dost all things well.

Take courage then, my soul, nor steep
 Thy days and nights in tears,
Soon shalt thou cease to mourn and weep,
 Though dark are now thy fears.
He comes, he comes, the Strong to save,
 He comes, nor tarries more,
His light is breaking o'er the wave,
 The clouds and storms are o'er.

Encouragement.

REJOICE, believer in the Lord,
Who makes your cause his own;
The hope that's built upon his word
Can ne'er be overthrown.

Though many foes beset your road,
And feeble is your arm,
Your life is hid with Christ in God,
Beyond the reach of harm.

Weak as you are, you shall not faint,
Or, fainting, shall not die!
Jesus, the strength of every saint,
Will aid you from on high.

Though now unseen by outward sense,
Faith sees him always near,
A guide, a glory, a defence;
Then what have you to fear?

As surely as he overcame,
And triumphed once for you;
So surely you that love his name
Shall triumph in him too.

Easter Day.

CHRIST, the Lord, in death-bonds lay,
Made a prisoner for our sin,
Thence uprising the third day,
Endless life for us did win.
Therefore will we joyful bring
Endless praises to our King;
Ever hallelujah! sing.

When no one could Death subdue,
When among the sons of earth
All were powerless to do,
All were guilty from their birth:
Then did Death lift up his head,
Walked the earth with mighty tread,
And all men in bondage led.

But the Lord, the Son of God,
Now has come to our relief,
He hath borne away the load
Of our sin and fear and grief.
Death no more can hold us bound—
Death is but an empty sound,—
Nothing of his sting is found.

O how wonderful to see
Death and Life in conflict meet!
Life hath won the victory,
Trodden Death beneath his feet.
Even as the Scripture shews,
He hath conquered all our foes:
Death was slain, but Jesus rose!

See the very Paschal Lamb,
  Who God's anger turned aside,—
He for love hath borne the shame,
  He upon the cross hath died.
    Let his blood be sprinkled o'er
    All the sideposts of the door;
    Death can strike at us no more.

So we keep the feast to-day
  With heart-joy and full delight,
Here his beams of mercy play,
  Christ hath risen upon our night.
    He his grace doth sweetly send,
    While our hearts before him bend,
    The long sin-night is at an end.

Now as Israelites we eat
  Paschal bread with love and joy,
Staff in hand, and shoes on feet,
  All old leaven would destroy.
    Christ will be that bread indeed,
    He our famished souls will feed:
    Faith can sing in every need,
      Hallelujah!

Unto You this Day.

JESUS is come, O joy heaven-lighted!
  He who was from the beginning is here:
Godhead and manhood in him are united;
  Creator, how com'st thou us creatures so near?

Angels and men, tell the heathen benighted,
  O joy heaven-lighted! that Jesus is come.

Jesus is come! Now fall off our fetters!
  The powers of hell are broken and flee.
Jesus redeems us, poor penniless debtors;
  He, the strong Son of God, maketh right free:
Takes us from shame, and in honour doth set us;
  Now fall off our fetters, for Jesus has come!

Jesus is come, the great King of glory;
  All heaven and earth, proclaim ye his might!
Master, all hearts must fly open before thee,—
  Ye heavenly portals, unfold at the sight!
Sinners, he setteth a kingdom before ye;
  The great King of glory, our Jesus is come!

Jesus is come, an offering for sinners:
  The sins of the whole world beareth this Lamb:
He is the sufferer, we are the winners—
  Our full redemption to purchase he came.
Love! in thy wonders we are but beginners!
  An offering for sinners, our Jesus is come!

Jesus is come, the fount of salvation:
  Come, who are thirsty, and drink ye who will!
Make to your fatal wounds sweet application,
  Brought from the source his atonement doth fill!
All who are needy have full invitation:
  A fount of salvation, our Jesus is come!

Jesus is come, tell earth's farthest section!
  Hasten ye, under his banner to be!
Swear to him truly, with deep heart-affection:
  Say: we will live and will die now with thee.
Amen, O Jesus, lead on to perfection!
  Tell earth's farthest section, that Jesus is come.

Good News.

THE gospel comes with welcome news
  To sinners lost like me:
Their various schemes let others choose;
  Saviour, I come to thee!

Of sinners sure I am the chief,
  But grace is rich and free,
This lovely truth affords relief
  To *sinners*, even to *me.*

Of merit now let others speak,
  But merit I have none;
I'm justified for Jesus' sake,
  I'm saved by grace alone.

'Twas grace my stubborn heart first won;
  'Tis grace that holds me fast:
Grace will complete the work begun,
  And save me at the last.

Then shall my soul with rapture trace
  What God hath done for me;
And celebrate redeeming grace,
  Throughout eternity.

One Fold.

THOU who in that bitter night
  Didst die for us, long years ago;
Thou who through thy love's strong might
  Hast made our hearts thy mercy know:
O remind thy little flock,
  Who so lightly disagree,
What thy last petition spoke—
  "Let them all be one in me."

God the Happiness of His People.

MY God, whose all-pervading eye
  Views earth beneath, and heaven above,
Witness, if here or there thou seest
  An object of mine equal love.

Not the gay scenes, where mortal men
  Pursue their bliss, and find their woe,
Detain my rising heart, which springs
  The nobler joys of heaven to view.

Not all the fairest sons of light,
  That lead the army round thy throne,
Can bound its flight: it presseth on,
  And seeks its rest in God alone.

Fixed near the immortal source of bliss,
  Dauntless and joyous it surveys
Each form of horror and distress,
  That earth, combined with hell, can raise.

This feeble flesh shall faint and die;
  This heart renew its pulse no more;
Even now it views the moment nigh,
  When life's last movements all are o'er.

But come, thou vanquished King of dread,
  With thy own hand thy power destroy;
'Tis thine to bear my soul to God,
  My portion, and eternal joy.

Sanctification of Believers.

YE who know your sins forgiven,
  And are happy in the Lord;
Have you read that gracious promise,
  Which is left upon record;
"I will sprinkle you with water,
  I will cleanse you from all sin;
Sanctify and make you holy,
  I will dwell and reign within."

Though you have much peace and comfort,
  Greater things you yet may find!
Freedom from unholy tempers;
  Freedom from the carnal mind;

To procure your perfect freedom,
  Jesus suffered, groaned, and died;
On the cross the healing fountain
  Gushèd from his wounded side.

O ye tender babes in Jesus,
  Hear your heavenly Father's will;
Claim your portion, plead his promise,
  And he quickly will fulfil:
Pray, and the refining fire
  Will come streaming from above!
Now believe and gain the blessing,
  Nothing less than perfect love.

If you have obtained this treasure,
  Search, and you shall surely find
All the christian marks and graces,
  Planted, growing in your mind:
Perfect faith, and perfect patience,
  Perfect lowliness, and then!
Perfect hope, and perfect meekness,
  Perfect love for God and men.

Be as holy and as happy,
  And as useful here below,
As it is your Father's pleasure;
  Jesus only, Jesus know:
Spread, O spread the holy fire,
  Tell, O tell what God has done!
Till the nations are conformèd
  To the image of his Son.

Sin Confessed.

LORD, I am vile, conceived in sin,
And born unholy and unclean;
Sprung from the man whose guilty fall
Corrupts the race, and taints us all.

Soon as we draw our infant breath,
The seeds of sin grow up for death:
Thy law demands a perfect heart;
But we're defiled in every part.

Great God, create my heart anew,
And form my spirit pure and true;
O make me wise betimes to spy
My danger and my remedy.

Behold, I fall before thy face;
My only refuge is thy grace:
No outward forms can make me clean;
The leprosy lies deep within.

No bleeding bird, nor bleeding beast,
Nor hyssop branch, nor sprinkling priest,
Nor running brook, nor flood, nor sea,
Can wash the dismal stain away.

Jesus, my God, thy blood alone
Hath power sufficient to atone:
Thy blood can make me white as snow,
No Jewish types can cleanse me so.

The Fountain of Living Waters.

A FOUNTAIN of life and of grace
 In Christ, our Redeemer we see:
For us, who his offers embrace,
 For all, it is open and free:
Jehovah, himself, doth invite
 To drink of his pleasures unknown:
The streams of immortal delight
 That flow from his heavenly throne.

As soon as in him we believe,
 By faith of his Spirit we take,
And, freely forgiven, receive
 The mercy for Jesus's sake!
We gain a pure drop of his love;
 The life of eternity know;
Angelical happiness prove,
 And witness a heaven below.

Distractions in Prayer.

AH! dearest Lord, I cannot pray,
 My fancy is not free;
Unmannerly distractions come,
 And force my thoughts from thee.

The world that looks so dull all day,
 Grows bright on me at prayer,
And plans that ask no thought but then,
 Wake up and meet me there.

All nature one full fountain seems
  Of dreamy sight and sound,
Which, when I kneel, breaks up its deeps,
  And makes a deluge round.

Old voices murmur in my ear,
  New hopes start into life,
And past and future gayly blend
  In one bewitching strife.

My very flesh has restless fits;
  My changeful limbs conspire
With all these phantoms of the mind
  My inner self to tire.

I cannot pray; yet Lord! thou know'st
  The pain it is to me
To have my vainly-struggling thoughts
  Thus torn away from thee.

Ah! Jesus! teach me how to prize
  These tedious hours when I,
Foolish and mute before thy face,
  In helpless worship lie.

Prayer was not meant for luxury,
  Or selfish pastime sweet;
It is the prostrate creature's place
  At his Creator's feet.

Had I kept stricter watch each hour
  O'er tongue and eye and ear,
Had I but mortified all day
  Each joy as it came near,—

Had I, dear Lord! no pleasure found
But in the thought of thee,
Prayer would have come unsought, and been
A truer liberty.

Yet thou art oft most present, Lord!
In weak distracted prayer;
A sinner out of heart with self
Most often finds thee there.

And prayer that humbles, sets the soul
From all illusions free,
And teaches it how utterly,
Dear Lord! it hangs on thee.

The soul, that on self-sacrifice
Is covetously bent,
Will bless thy chastening hand that makes
Its prayer its punishment.

Ah, Jesus! why should I complain?
And why fear aught but sin?
Distractions are but outward things;
Thy peace dwells far within!

These surface-troubles come and go,
Like rufflings of the sea;
The deeper depth is out of reach
To all, my God, but Thee!

Church-Lock and Key.

I know it is my sinne which locks thine eares,
  And bindes thy hands!
Out-crying my requests, drowning my tears;
Or else the chilnesse of my faint demands.

But as cold hands are angrie with the fire,
  And mend it still:
So I do lay the want of my desire,
Not on my sinnes, or coldnesse, but thy will.

Yet heare, O God, onely for his bloud's sake,
  Which pleads for me:
For though sinnes plead too, yet like stones they
    make
His bloud's sweet current much more loud to be.

Take away all Iniquity

Come, Holy Spirit, heavenly Dove,
  With all thy quickening powers,
Kindle a flame of sacred love
  In these cold hearts of ours.

Look how we grovel here below,
  Fond of these trifling toys:
Our souls can neither fly nor go
  To reach eternal joys.

In vain we tune our formal songs,
  In vain we strive to rise,
Hosannas languish on our tongues,
  And our devotion dies.

Dear Lord! and shall we ever live
  At this poor dying rate,
Our love so faint, so cold to thee,
  And thine to us so great?

Come, Holy Spirit, heavenly Dove,
  With all thy quickening powers,
Come shed abroad a Saviour's love,
  And that shall kindle ours.

The Midnight Cry.

THOU Judge of quick and dead,
  Before whose bar severe,
With holy joy or guilty dread
  We all shall soon appear;
Our cautioned souls prepare
  For that tremendous day,
And fill us now with watchful care,
  And stir us up to pray.

To pray, and wait the hour,
  That awful hour unknown,
When robed in majesty and power,
  Thou shalt from heaven come down,

The immortal Son of man,
  To judge the human race,
With all thy Father's dazzling train,
  With all thy glorious grace!

To guide our earthly joys,
  To increase our gracious fears,
Forever let the archangel's voice
  Be sounding in our ears
The solemn midnight cry,—
  Ye dead, the Judge is come;
Arise, and meet him in the sky,
  And meet your instant doom.

O may we all be found
  Obedient to thy word,
Attentive to the trumpet's sound,
  And looking for the Lord.
O may we thus ensure
  A lot among the blest;
And watch a moment, to secure
  An everlasting rest.

Choose.

O HOW narrow is the way
  That leads the sinner day by day
To where the heavenly mansions be!
  O how many men desire
  Those halls of joy, yet faint and tire,
And never come the joy to see;

Because the wordly-minded heart
In God's pure kingdom hath no part.

Here the cross and pain they shun,
Earth is sought, and earth is won;
And pride and envy rule alone:
Love of self grows strong and deep:
Ah, the narrow way is steep,
And leadeth where sharp thorns are strewn,
And every hour it brings to light
Some foe that we must flee or fight.

Then heaven's gate is narrow too;
And whosoever will pass through
Must make himself a little child;
No human greatness enters there:
Each one a borrowed robe must wear,
Or be for ever heaven-exiled.
Think ye much, and strive and pray,—
The course of sin leads far away.

Ah, where shall I find strength to win?
And who will set me free from sin?
I, without one good work or thought,
How shall I find and keep the way?
How can I life and service lay
At Jesus' feet, and keep back nought?
Jesus, my soul's sweet heavenly guest,
How can a sinner love him best?

Saviour, thy Spirit give to me;
Let all my life transformèd be;
This grief and burden of my sin
The heavenly Comforter can cure:

New-make my heart, and make it pure;
And give me a strong faith within.
O Grace-of-souls, let not the foe
Pluck me from thee, to endless woe.

Stamp thine own image, bright and clear,
Deep in my soul; O God, be near,
Give the strong faith-shield unto me,
And when I fail, forgive and spare.
Let thy sweet grace within me bear
Fruits of the Spirit, unto thee,—
Courage and peace none can destroy,
And meekness, patience, and pure joy.

E'en now O Lord, thy Spirit send,
And let his presence o'er us bend
And ever in our hearts abide;
Come, O thou Spirit of all grace,
That we may one day have a place
Whither thy love our steps shall guide.—
There, in the kingdom of the just,—
There, where our treasure cannot rust.

Celestial Prospects.

SWEET glories rush upon my sight,
And charm my wondering eyes;
The regions of immortal light;
The beauties of the skies.

All hail! ye fair celestial shores!
Ye lands of endless day!
Swift on my view your prospect pours,
And drives my griefs away.

There's a delightful clearness now,
My clouds of doubt are gone,
Fled is my former darkness too,
My fears are all withdrawn.

Short is the passage—short the space
Between my home and me;
There! there behold the radiant place!
How near the mansions be!

Immortal wonders! boundless things!
In those dear worlds appear:
Prepare me, Lord, to stretch my wings,
And in those glories share.

Here Am I

My will would like a life of ease,—
And power to do, and time to rest,—
And health and strength my will would please,
But Lord I know thy will is best.

If I have strength to do thy will,
That should be power enough for me:
Whether to work or to sit still
The appointment of the day may be.

And if by sickness I may grow
  More patient, holy, and resigned;
Strong health I need not wish to know,
  And greater ease I cannot find.

And rest—I need not seek it here,
  For perfect rest *remaineth* still:
When in thy presence we appear,
  Rest shall be given by thy will.

Lord, I have given my life to thee,
  And every day and hour is thine,—
What thou appointest let them be:
  Thy will is better, Lord, than mine.

Soon and for Ever.

Soon—and for ever!
  Such promise our trust,
Though ashes to ashes,
  And dust unto dust;
Soon—and for ever
  Our union shall be
Made perfect, our glorious
  Redeemer, in thee.
When the sins and the sorrows
  Of time shall be o'er;
Its pangs and its partings
  Remembered no more;

When life cannot fail,
  And when death cannot sever,
Christians with Christ shall be
  Soon—and for ever.

Soon, and for ever,
  The breaking of day
Shall drive all the night-clouds
  Of sorrow away,—
Soon, and for ever,
  We'll see as we're seen,
And learn the deep meaning
  Of things that have been.
When fightings without us,
  And fears from within,
Shall weary no more
  In the warfare of sin;
Where tears and where fears
  And where death shall be—never,
Christians with Christ shall be,
  Soon, and for ever.

Soon, and for ever,
  The work shall be done,
The warfare accomplished,
  The victory won;
Soon, and for ever,
  The soldier lay down
His sword for a harp,
  And his cross for a crown.
Then droop not in sorrow,
  Despond not in fear,

A glorious to-morrow
  Is brightening and near:
When,—blessèd reward
  Of each faithful endeavour,—
Christians with Christ shall be
  Soon, and for ever.

By Faith.

'Tis by the faith of joys to come
  We walk through deserts dark as night;
Till we arrive at heaven our home,
  Faith is our guide, and faith our light.

The want of sight she well supplies,
  She makes the pearly gates appear;
Far into distant worlds she pries,
  And brings eternal glories near.

Cheerful we tread the desert through,
  When faith inspires a heavenly ray,
Though lions roar, and tempests blow,
  And rocks and dangers fill the way.

So Abrah'm, by divine command,
  Left his own house to walk with God;
His faith beheld the promised land,
  And fired his zeal along the road.

All is Yours.

O foolish heart, be still!
  And vex thyself no more!
Wait thou for God, until
  He open pleasure's door.
Thou knowst not what is good for thee,
    But God doth know,—
Let him thy strong reliance be,
    And rest thee so.

He counted all my days,
  And every joy and tear,
Ere I knew how to praise,
  Or even had learned to fear.
Before I him my Father knew,
    He called me child;
His help has guarded me all through
    This weary wild.

The least of all my cares
  Is not to him unknown,—
He sees and he prepares
  The pathway for his own;
And what his hand assigns to me,
    That serves my peace,—
The greatest burden it might be,
    Yet joy's increase!

I live no more for earth;
  Nor seek my full joy here;
The world seems little worth
  When heaven is shining clear.

Yet joyfully I go my way,
So free, so blest!
Sweetening my toil from day to day,
With thoughts of rest.

Give me, my Lord, whate'er
Will bind my heart to thee;
For that I make my prayer,
And know thou hearest me!
But all that might keep back my soul—
Make thee forgot,—
Though of earth-good it were the whole,
O give it not!

When sickness-pains distress,
And want doth follow fear,
And men their hate express,
My sky shall still be clear.
Then wait I, Lord, and wait for thee;
And I am still,—
Though mine should unaccomplished be,
Do thou thy will!

Thou art the strength and stay
Of every weary soul;
Thy wisdom rules the way,
Thy pity does control.
What ill can happen unto me
When thou art near?
Thou wilt, O God, my keeper be,
I will not fear!

Canaan.

TOGETHER let us sweetly live;
  I am bound for the land of Canaan;
Together let us sweetly die;
  I am bound for the land of Canaan.
O Canaan! bright Canaan!
  I am bound for the land of Canaan.
O Canaan, it is my happy home;
  I am bound for the land of Canaan.

If you get there before I do,
Look out for me, I'm coming too.
  I am bound for the land of Canaan.

I have some friends before me gone,
And I'm resolved to travel on.
  I am bound for the land of Canaan.

Our songs of praise shall fill the skies,
While higher still our joys shall rise.
  I am bound for the land of Canaan.

Then come with me, beloved friend,
The joys of heaven shall never end.
  I am bound for the land of Canaan.

Happiness Found.

HAPPINESS, thou lovely name,
  Where's thy seat, O tell me where?
Learning, pleasure, wealth, and fame,
  All cry out, "It is not here":

Not the wisdom of the wise
Can inform me where it lies,
Not the grandeur of the great
Can the bliss, I seek, create.

Object of my first desire,
Jesus, crucified for me!
All to happiness aspire,
Only to be found in thee:
Thee to praise, and thee to know,
Constitute our bliss below;
Thee to see, and thee to love,
Constitute our bliss above.

Lord, it is not life to live,
If thy presence thou deny;
Lord, if thou thy presence give,
'Tis no longer death to die:
Source and giver of repose,
Singly from thy smile it flows;
Peace and happiness are thine;
Mine they are, if thou art mine.

Whilst I feel thy love to me,
Every object teems with joy;
Here O may I walk with thee,
Then into thy presence die!
Let me but thyself possess,
Total sum of happiness!
Real bliss I then shall prove,
Heaven below and heaven above.

The Sabbath of the Soul.

O FATHER, though the anxious fear
May cloud tomorrow's way,
Nor fear nor doubt shall enter here;
All shall be thine today.

We will not bring divided hearts
To worship at thy shrine;
But each unholy thought departs,
And leaves the temple thine.

Sleep, sleep today, tormenting cares,
Of earth and folly born!
Ye shall not dim the light that streams
From this celestial morn.

Tomorrow will be time enough
To feel your harsh control;
Ye shall not violate this day,
The Sabbath of my soul.

Sleep, sleep forever, guilty thoughts;
Let fires of vengeance die;
And purged from sin, may I behold
A God of purity.

Neither Pain nor Sorrow.

HERE the Christian meets with trials,
Oft immersed in human woe ;
Fierce temptations, various sorrows,
Are his portion here below.

But the world to which he's travelling
Hath no evil to annoy;
There is nothing to molest him,
Nothing to disturb his joy.

There he'll see the unfading beauties
Of the dear Immanuel's face ;
There behold the streaming glory,
All the rising heights of grace.

Burst in everlasting praises,
Chant in most melodious strains ;
Traverse the celestial country,
Ride in triumph o'er the plains.

Hark, my soul, they're sweetly singing!
What a wondrous happy throng !
O what sounds of Hallelujahs
Echo in the noble song!

Come, Lord Jesus, O come quickly,
Let me to thy throne arise ;
Bear a part in that grand music,
Join the chorus of the skies.

To Will, is Present with Me.

I WOULD, but cannot sing,
  Guilt has untuned my voice,
The serpent's sin-envenomed sting,
  Has poisoned all my joys.

I know the Lord is nigh,
  And would, but cannot pray;
For Satan meets me when I try,
  And frights my soul away.

I would, but can't repent,
  Though I endeavour oft;
This stony heart can ne'er relent,
  Till Jesus makes it soft.

I would, but cannot love,
  Though wooed by love divine;
No arguments have power to move
  A soul so base as mine.

I would, but cannot rest
  In God's most holy will;
I know what he appoints is best,
  Yet murmur at it still.

O could I but believe!
  Then all would easy be;
I would, but cannot—Lord, relieve;
  My help must come from thee!

But if indeed I would,
  Though I can nothing do;
Yet the desire is something good,
  For which my praise is due.

By nature prone to ill,
  'Till thine appointed hour
I was as destitute of will,
  As now I am of power.

Wilt thou not crown at length,
  The work thou hast begun?
And with a will, afford me strength,
  In all thy ways to run.

The Propitiation.

O THOU that hear'st the prayer of faith,
Wilt thou not save a soul from death
  That casts itself on thee?
I have no refuge of my own,
But fly to what my Lord hath done
  And suffered once for me.

Slain in the guilty sinner's stead,
His spotless righteousness I plead,
  And his availing blood:
Thy merit, Lord, my robe shall be,
Thy merit shall atone for me,
  And bring me near to God.

Then snatch me from eternal death,
The Spirit of adoption breathe,
His consolations send;
By him some word of life impart,
And sweetly whisper to my heart,
"Thy Maker is thy friend."

The King of terrors then would be,
A welcome messenger to me,
That bids me come away;
Unclogged by earth or earthly things,
I'd mount upon his sable wings
To everlasting day.

Depth of Mercy.

DEPTH of mercy! can there be
Mercy still reserved for me?
Can my God his wrath forbear?
Me, the chief of sinners, spare?

I have long withstood his grace,
Long provoked him to his face;
Would not hearken to his calls,
Grieved him by a thousand falls.

Kindled his relentings are,
Me he now delights to spare;
Cries, "How shall I give thee up?"
Lets the lifted thunder drop.

There for me the Saviour stands,
Shews his wounds, and spreads his hands!
God is love! I know, I feel;
Jesus weeps and loves me still.

Jesus, answer from above,
Is not all thy nature love!
Wilt thou not the wrong forget?
Suffer me to kiss thy feet?

Now incline me to repent!
Let me now my fall lament!
Now my soul's revolt deplore!
Weep, believe, and sin no more.

If any Man will hear My Voice.

BEHOLD the Saviour at thy door,
He gently knocks, has knocked before;
Has waited long, is waiting still,
You treat no other friend so ill.

O lovely attitude!—he stands
With melting heart, and outstretched hands!
O matchless kindness! and he shows
This matchless kindness to his foes.

Admit him;—for the human breast
Ne'er entertained so kind a guest;
Admit him;—or the hour's at hand,
When at his door denied you'll stand.

Open my heart, Lord, enter in,
Slay every foe, and conquer sin:
Here then to thee I all resign,
My body, soul, and all are thine.

Here is My Heart.

HERE is my heart!—my God, I give it thee;
I heard thee call and say,
"Not to the world, my child, but unto me,"—
I heard, and will obey.
Here is love's offering to my King,
Which in glad sacrifice I bring.
Here is my heart.

Here is my heart!—surely the gift, though poor,
My God will not despise;
Vainly and long I sought to make it pure;
To meet thy searching eyes;
Corrupted first in Adam's fall,
The stains of sin pollute it all.
My guilty heart!

Here is my heart!—my heart so hard before,
Now by thy grace made meet;
Yet bruised and wearied, it can only pour
Its anguish at thy feet;
It groans beneath the weight of sin,
It sighs salvation's joy to win.
My mourning heart!

Here is my heart!—in Christ its longings end,
Near to his cross it draws;
It says "Thou art my portion, O my friend!
Thy blood my ransom was."
And in the Saviour it has found
What blessedness and peace abound.
My trusting heart!

Here is my heart!—ah! Holy Spirit, come,
Its nature to renew,
And consecrate it wholly as thy home,
A temple fair and true.
Teach it to love and serve thee more,
To fear thee, trust thee, and adore.
My cleansèd heart!

Here is my heart!—it trembles to draw near
The glory of thy throne;
Give it the shining robe thy servants wear,
Of righteousness thine own:
Its pride and folly chase away,
And all its vanity, I pray.
My humble heart.

Here is my heart!—teach it, O Lord, to cling
In gladness unto thee;
And in the day of sorrow still to sing,
"Welcome my God's decree."
Believing, all its journey through,
That thou art wise, and just, and true,
My waiting heart!

Here is my heart!—O Friend of friends, be near
To make each tempter fly;
And when my latest foe I wait with fear,
Give me the victory!
Gladly on thy love reposing,
Let me say, when life is closing,
"Here is my heart!"

The Highway of Holiness.

JESUS, my all, to heaven is gone:
He whom I fix my hopes upon:
His track I see, and I'll pursue
The narrow way, till him I view.
Happy day, happy day,
When Jesus washed my sins away;
He taught me how to watch and pray,
And live rejoicing every day.

The way the holy prophets went,
The road that leads from banishment;
The King's highway of holiness
I'll go, for all his paths are peace.

No stranger shall proceed therein,
No lover of the world and sin,
No lion, no devouring care,
No sin nor sorrow shall be there.

No,—nothing shall go up thereon,
But travelling souls, and I am one;

Wayfaring men to Canaan bound,
Shall only in the way be found.

This is the way I long have sought,
And mourned because I found it not;
My grief a burden long has been,
Because I was not saved from sin.

The more I strove against its power,
I felt its weight and guilt the more;
Till late I heard my Saviour say,—
Come hither, soul, I am the way.

Lo! glad I come; and thou, blest Lamb,
Shalt take me to thee as I am:
Nothing but sin have I to give,—
Nothing but love shall I receive.

Then will I tell to sinners round,
What a dear Saviour I have found;
I'll point to thy redeeming blood,
And say,—Behold the way to God.

While ye have Light.

"**Ephraim is joined to his idols,** *let him alone.*"—HOSEA.

THERE is a time, we know not when,
  A point, we know not where,
That marks the destiny of men
  To glory or despair.

There is a line, by us unseen,
  That crosses every path;
The hidden boundary between
  God's patience and his wrath.

To pass that limit is to die,
  To die as if by stealth;
It does not quench the beaming eye,
  Or pale the glow of health.

The conscience may be still at ease,
  The spirits light and gay;
That which is pleasing still may please,
  And care be thrust away.

But on that forehead God has set
  Indelibly a mark,
Unseen by man, for man as yet
  Is blind and in the dark.

And yet the doomed man's path below
  May bloom, as Eden bloomed;
He did not, does not, will not know,
  Or feel that he is doomed.

He knows, he feels that all is well,
  And every fear is calmed;
He lives, he dies, he wakes in hell,
  Not only doomed, but damned.

O where is this mysterious bourn,
  By which our path is crossed;
Beyond which, God himself hath sworn,
  That he who goes is lost?

How far may we go on in sin?
  How long will God forbear?
Where does hope end, and where begin
  The confines of despair?

An answer from the skies is sent:
  "Ye that from God depart,
While it is called TO-DAY repent,
  And harden not your heart."

Faith Conquering.

THE moment a sinner believes,
  And trusts in his crucified God,
His pardon at once he receives,—
  Redemption in full through his blood:
Though thousands and thousands of foes
  Against him in malice unite,
Their rage he through Christ can oppose,
  Led forth by the Spirit to fight.

The faith that unites to the Lamb,
  And brings such salvation as this,
Is more than mere notion or name,
  The work of God's Spirit it is;
A principle, active and young,
  That lives under pressure and load;
That makes out of weakness more strong,
  And draws the soul upward to God.

It treads on the world and on hell;
  It vanquishes death and despair;
And oh! let us wonder to tell,
  It overcomes heaven by prayer;
Permits a vile worm of the dust,
  With God to commune as a friend;
To hope his forgiveness as just,
  And look for his grace to the end.

It says to the mountains, "Depart,"
  That stand betwixt God and the soul;
It binds up the broken in heart,
  And makes wounded consciences whole;
Bids sins of a crimson-like dye
  Be spotless as snow, and as white;
And raises the sinner on high,
  To dwell with the angels of light.

Just as I am.

JUST as I am, without one plea,
But that thy blood was shed for me,
And that thou bidst me come to thee,
    O! Lamb of God, I come.

Just as I am, and waiting not
To rid my soul of one dark blot,
To thee, whose blood can cleanse each spot,
    O! Lamb of God, I come.

Just as I am, though tossed about,
With many a conflict, many a doubt,
With fears within, and wars without,
O! Lamb of God, I come.

Just as I am—poor, wretched, blind;
Sight, riches, healing of the mind,
Yea, all I need in thee to find,
O! Lamb of God, I come.

Just as I am thou wilt receive,
Wilt welcome, pardon, cleanse, relieve;
Because thy promise I believe,
O! Lamb of God, I come.

Just as I am—thy love unknown
Has broken every barrier down;
Now to be thine, yea, thine alone,
O! Lamb of God, I come.

Draw Me.

At anchor laid, remote from home,
Toiling, I cry, Sweet Spirit, come!
Celestial breeze, no longer stay,
But swell my sails, and speed my way!

Fain would I mount, fain would I glow,
And loose my cable from below;
But I can only spread my sail;
Thou, thou must breathe th' auspicious gale.

The Shadow of the Great Rock.

Sweet is the solace of thy love,
  My heavenly Friend, to me,
While through the hidden way of faith
  I journey home with thee,
Learning by quiet thankfulness
  As a dear child to be.

Though from the shadow of thy peace
  My feet would often stray,
Thy mercy follows all my steps,
  And will not turn away;
Yea, thou wilt comfort me at last,
  As none beneath thee may.

Oft in a dark and lonely place,
  I hush my hastened breath,
To hear the comfortable words
  Thy loving Spirit saith;
And feel my safety in thy hand
  From every kind of death.

O there is nothing in the world
  To weigh against thy will;
Even the dark times I dread the most,
  Thy covenant fulfil:
And when the pleasant morning dawns,
  I find thee with me still.

No other comforter I need,
  If thou, O Lord, be mine,—

Thy rod will bring my spirit low,
  Thy fire my heart refine,
And cause me pain that none can heal
  By other love than thine.

Then in the secret of my soul,
  Though hosts my peace invade,
Though through a waste and weary land
  My lonely way be made,
Thou, even thou, wilt comfort me,—
  I need not be afraid.

Still in the solitary place
  I would awhile abide,
Till with the solace of thy love
  My heart is satisfied;
And all my hopes of happiness
  Stay calmly at thy side.

Freedom from Care.

While I lived without the Lord,
  (If I might be said to live,)
Nothing could relief afford,
  Nothing satisfaction give.

Empty hopes and groundless fear
  Moved by turns my anxious mind;
Like a feather in the air,
  Made the sport of every wind.

Now I see, whate'er betide,
  All is well, if Christ be mine;
He has promised to provide,
  I have only to resign.

When a sense of sin and thrall
  Forced me to the sinner's Friend,
He engaged to manage all,
  By the way, and to the end.

"Cast," he said, "on me thy care,
  'Tis enough that I am nigh:
I will all thy burdens bear,
  I will all thy wants supply.

"Simply follow as I lead,
  Do not reason, but believe;
Call on me in time of need,
  Thou shalt surely help receive."

Lord, I would, I do submit,
  Gladly yield my all to thee;
What thy wisdom sees most fit,
  Must be, surely, best for me.

Only, when the way is rough,
  And the coward flesh would start,
Let thy promise and thy love
  Cheer and animate my heart.

My Cup Runneth over.

O LOOK, my soul, and see
  How thy cup doth overflow!
Think of the love so free,
  Which fills it for thee so!

Let fall no tears therein,
  Of self-will or of doubt,—
There may be tears for sin,
  But sinful tears keep out.

What lies within?—Life, health,
  Friends—here, or gone before,—
Promise of heavenly wealth—
  Of earthly, some small store,—

Power to act thy part
  In earth's great labour-field,—
Grace, which should make thy heart
  An hundred-fold to yield.

The drops that overflow,
  Shine in the morning sun,
And catch the evening glow
  When each day's work is done.

And if there mingle there
  Some drops of darker hue,—
What colour would all bear,
  If all were but thy due?

40*

These cannot now obtain
  A gleam from earthly light;
But look, my soul, again,—
  Use faith instead of sight.—

Are they not sinful tears
  Which weep for humbled pride?
Or even the hope of years—
  By perfect love denied?

What God's own wisdom planned,
  Is it not right and meet?
Shall aught come from his hand,
  And not to thee seem sweet?

Ah thankless heart! I feel
  It is thy unbelief!
For want of faith can steal
  The very joy of grief.

O Earth-perverted taste!
  Seek, seek, thy joys on high!
Lest my soul be a waste,
  With a river flowing by.

For what if from thy cup
  All Earth-joys dried away?
Can *God* not fill it up?
  Think, guilty soul, and say!

Providence.

GREAT God, we sing that mighty hand
By which supported still we stand:
The opening year thy mercy shows;
That mercy crowns it, till its close.

By day, by night, at home, abroad,
Still we are guarded by our God;
By his incessant bounty fed,
By his unerring counsel led.

With grateful hearts the past we own;
The future, all to us unknown,
We to thy guardian care commit,
And peaceful leave before thy feet.

In scenes exalted or depressed,
Thou art our joy, and thou our rest;
Thy goodness all our hopes shall raise,
Adored through all our changing days.

When death shall interrupt these songs,
And seal in silence mortal tongues;
Our helper God, in whom we trust,
In better worlds our souls shall boast

The Living—the Living; He shall Praise Thee.

HEALTH is a jewel dropt from heaven,
  Which money cannot buy,
The light of life, the body's peace
  And pleasant harmony.
Lord, who hath tuned my outward man
  To such a lively frame!
Renew my heart, in holiness
  To praise thy sacred name.

While others in distresses lie,
  Bound in affliction's chains,
I walk at large, secure and free
  From sickness and from pains:
Their life is death; their language groans;
  Their meat is juice of galls;
Their friends but strangers, wealth but want;
  Their houses prison-walls.

Their earnest cries do pierce the skies,
  And shall I silent be?
Lord, were I sick, as I am well,
  Thou shouldst have heard from me:
The sick have no more cause to pray
  Than I to praise my king:
Since nature teaches them to groan,
  Let grace teach me to sing.

I see my friends, I taste my meat,
  I'm free for mine employ;
But when I do enjoy my God,
  Then I myself enjoy:
Lord, thou dost keep me on my feet,
  Direct me in thy ways,—
O crown thy gift of health with grace,
  And turn it to thy praise.

Divine Mercy.

THY mercy, my God, is the theme of my song,
The joy of my heart, and the boast of my tongue;
Thy free grace alone, from the first to the last,
Hath won my affections and bound my soul fast.

Without thy sweet mercy, I could not live here,
Sin soon would reduce me to utter despair:
But through thy free goodness, my spirits revive,
And he that first made me still keeps me alive.

Thy mercy is more than a match for my heart,
Which wonders to feel its own hardness depart;
Dissolved by thy goodness, I fall to the ground,
And weep to the praise of the mercy I found.

The door of thy mercy stands open all day,
To the poor and the needy, who knock by the way;
No sinner shall ever be empty sent back,
Who comes seeking mercy for Jesus's sake.

Thy mercy in Jesus exempts me from hell;
Its glories I'll sing, and its wonders I'll tell:
'Twas Jesus, my friend, when he hung on the tree,
That opened the channel of mercies for me.

Great Father of mercies! thy goodness I own,
And the cov'nant of love in thy crucified Son;
All praise to the Spirit, whose witness divine
Seals mercy, and pardon, and righteousness mine.

In Sickness.

NOT more than I have strength to bear,
Thy mercy, Lord, will lay on me;
Pain shall not always last;
Sweet ease is coming fast.
On my sick bed, free from care,
Present Helper! praise I thee!

When me the world so much distraught,
Thy hand to solitude did bring;
And when the fight I fled,
To deeper warfare led;
And through pain my heart hath taught
A new and patient song to sing.

And shall I drain this cup of woe?
Ah, Lord! thou knowest flesh is weak!
Forgive the tears that start
From weary eyes and heart!
Now thy tender pity shew,
Give the patient faith I seek.

The pain which racks and weakens me,
  Drives far away my sleep's soft rest:
    The long dark nights may hear
    My groans of grief and fear.
How poor I find man's help to be!
  But thou canst still my throbbing breast!

Thy will may choose and give command,
  How long the trial hour shall last:
    And though on this dark field
    My whole life-strength should yield,
Passing to the better land,
  Still my heart shall hold thee fast!

The Sure Foundation

In every trying hour
  My soul to Jesus flies;
I trust in his almighty power,
  When swelling billows rise.

His comforts bear me up;
  I trust a faithful God;
The sure foundation of my hope
  Is in my Saviour's blood.

Loud hallelujahs sing,
  To our Redeemer's name;
In joy or sorrow—life or death—
  His love is still the same.

When I Walk in Darkness.

God doth not leave his own:
The night of weeping for a time may last,
Then, tears all past,
His going forth shall as the morning shine,
The sunrise of his favour shall be thine.
God doth not leave his own.

God doth not leave his own.
Though few and evil all their days appear,
Though grief and fear
Come in the train of earth and hell's dark crowd,—
The trusting heart says even in the cloud:
God doth not leave his own.

God doth not leave his own.
This sorrow in their life he doth permit—
Yea, chooseth it,
To speed his children on their heavenward way.
He guides the winds.—Faith, hope, and love all say,
God doth not leave his own.

He is Able to Keep.

My God, within thy hand
My helpless soul I trust!
Thy love shall ever stand,
Thy promise must.

To whom, Lord, should I go,
  To be upheld and blest?
Thine are all souls below,
  Mine with the rest.

Thou gavest it to me,
  And wilt call home above,
To live up there with thee,
  Whom here I love.

It is besprinkled o'er
  With blood of thy dear Son;
By this made clean, no more
  It shuns thy throne.

My faith doth wave its wings
  Already towards the skies,
And sealed for heavenly things
  To thee would rise.

O God, thou didst set free
  My soul from sin's distress,
So be thou near to me
  In death, to bless.

My God, within thy hand
  My helpless soul I trust!
Thy love shall ever stand—
  Thy promise must.

The Shepherd Boy.

HE that is down, needs fear no fall;
He that is low, no pride;
He that is humble ever shall
Have God to be his guide.
I am content with what I have,
Little be it or much:
And, Lord, contentment still I crave,
Because thou savest such.
Fulness to such a burden is
That go on pilgrimage:
Here little, and hereafter bliss,
Is best from age to age.

All for the Best.

MY soul now arise,
My passions take wing,
Look up to the skies,
And cheerfully sing;
Let God be the object,
In praises addressed,
And this be my subject,
'Tis all for the best.

Search all the world through,
Examine and see—
And what canst thou find
More suited to thee,

Than this declaration,
In Scripture expressed,
That God, thy salvation,
Does all for the best?

Though here day by day
His love shall see good,
Upon thee to lay
His Fatherly rod;
Yet be not dejected,
However oppressed;
Though sorely afflicted,
'Tis all for the best.

The beams of his grace
Are passing all worth;
The smiles of his face
Are heaven upon earth;
When to me he shews them
What joys fill my breast!
And when he withdraws them,
'Tis all for the best.

When conflicts begin
From various parts,
And Satan throws in
His fiery darts,
Though often full sorely
My soul he molests;
Yet this I know surely,
'Tis all for the best.

On creatures below
I'll not set my heart,
For surely I know
We shortly must part:
For though when God gives them
His name's to be blest,
Yet when he removes them
'Tis all for the best.

But O the blest day!
And soon 'twill arise,
When freed from my clay
I shall mount to the skies;
Then shall I recover
My heavenly rest,
And there sing for ever,
'Twas all for the best.

And thus through the whole
I meet with while here,
I'll comfort my soul,
And silence my fear,
In hoping and praying
Ere long to be blest;
In thinking and saying,
'Tis all for the best.

He Goeth before Them.

LORD, it belongs not to my care,
  Whether I die or live;
To love and serve thee is my share,
  And this thy grace must give.

If life be long, I will be glad
  That I may long obey;
If short, yet why should I be sad
  To soar to endless day?

Christ leads me through no darker rooms
  Than he went through before;
He that unto God's kingdom comes,
  Must enter by his door.

Come, Lord, when grace has made me meet
  Thy blessed face to see;
For if thy work on earth be sweet,
  What will thy glory be.

Then shall I end my sad complaints,
  And weary sinful days,
And join with the triumphant saints
  That sing Jehovah's praise.

My knowledge of that life is small,
  The eye of faith is dim;
But 'tis enough that Christ knows all,
  And I shall be with him.

He is not Here: He is Risen.

Hallelujah! Jesus lives!
Life, immortal life, he gives.—
Conquered now are death and hell!
Jesus pierced them, and they fell.
Heaven and earth the conquest tell!
Jesus lives!

Hallelujah! See his tomb!
Victory-lights prevent the gloom!
All your tears they shine away,
Poor mourners for the dead today;
Look in here where Jesus lay,—
Jesus lives!

Hallelujah! Seek no more
The Gone-to-life, at death's low door:
Now believe the joyful word
From the herald-angels heard,—
Heaven and earth the tidings stirred!—
Jesus lives!

Hallelujah! then will I
Dread no more in death to lie;
By his death my foes are slain,
From his grave I rise again;
Enough for me what faith makes plain,
Jesus lives!

Hallelujah! he to me
Life in death will surely be.

Joyfully I meet death here,
Christ, my life, shall soon appear,—
Faith looks up and sees him near!
Jesus lives!

The City of Refuge.

Now I have found the ground wherein
Sure my soul's anchor may remain;
The wounds of Jesus for my sin,
Before the world's foundation slain;
Whose mercy shall unshaken stay,
When heaven and earth are fled away.

Father, thine everlasting grace
Our scanty thought surpasses far:
Thy heart still melts with tenderness;
Thine arms of love still open are,
Returning sinners to receive,
That mercy they may taste and live,

O love, thou bottomless abyss!
My sins are swallowed up in thee;
Covered is my unrighteousness,
No spot of guilt remains in me;
While Jesus' blood, through earth and skies,
Mercy, free, boundless mercy, cries.

By faith I plunge me in this sea;
Here is my hope, my joy, my rest;
Hither, when hell assails, I flee,
And look unto my Saviour's breast;

Away, sad doubt and anxious fear!
Mercy is all that's written here.

Though waves and storms go o'er my head,
  Though strength, and health, and friends be gone;
Though joys be withered all, and dead,
  And every comfort be withdrawn;
On this my steadfast soul relies,—
Father, thy mercy never dies.

Fixed on this ground will I remain,
  Though my heart fail, and flesh decay;
This anchor shall my soul sustain,
  When earth's foundations melt away;
Mercy's full power I then shall prove,
Loved with an everlasting love.

Heavenly Rest.

JERUSALEM, my happy home!
  Name ever dear to me!
When shall my labours have an end,
  In joy, and peace, and thee?

When shall these eyes thy heaven-built walls
  And pearly gates behold?
Thy bulwarks, with salvation strong,
  And streets of shining gold?

O when, thou city of my God,
  Shall I thy courts ascend?
Where congregations ne'er break up,
  And Sabbaths have no end?

There happier bowers than Eden's bloom,
Nor sin nor sorrow know:
Blest seats! through rude and stormy scenes
I onward press to you.

Why should I shrink at pain and woe?
Or feel at death dismay?
I've Canaan's goodly land in view,
And realms of endless day.

Apostles, martyrs, prophets, there,
Around my Saviour stand;
And soon my friends in Christ below,
Will join the glorious band.

Jerusalem! my happy home!
My soul still pants for thee;
Then shall my labours have an end,
When I thy joys shall see.

The Christian's Home.

BRETHREN, while we sojourn here,
Fight we must, but should not fear;
Foes we have, but we've a Friend,
One that loves us to the end:
Forward, then, with courage go,
Long we shall not dwell below;
Soon the joyful news will come,
"Child, your Father calls, Come home."

In the way a thousand snares
Lie to take us unawares;
Satan with malicious art,
Watches each unguarded heart:
But from Satan's malice free,
Saints shall soon in glory be;
Soon the joyful news will come,
"Child, your Father calls, Come home."

But of all the foes we meet,
None so oft mislead our feet,
None betray us into sin,
Like the foes that dwell within:
Yet let nothing spoil your peace,
Christ shall also conquer these;
Then the joyful news will come,
"Child, your Father calls, Come home."

Try Me, and Know My Ways.

O THOU, to whose all-searching sight
The darkness shineth as the light,
Search, prove my heart, it pants for thee;
O burst these bonds, and set it free.

Wash out its stains, refine its dross;
Nail my affections to the cross;
Hallow each thought; let all within
Be clean, as thou, my Lord, art clean.

If in this darksome wild I stray,
Be thou my light, be thou my way:
No foes, no violence I fear,
No fraud, while thou, my God, art near.

When rising floods my soul o'erflow,—
When sinks my heart in waves of wo,—
Jesus, thy timely aid impart,
And raise my head, and cheer my heart.

Saviour, where'er thy steps I see,
Dauntless, untired, I follow thee;
O let thy hand support me still,
And lead me to thy holy hill.

If rough and thorny be the way,
My strength proportion to my day;
Till toil, and grief, and pain shall cease,
Where all is calm, and joy, and peace.

O that I were as in Months past.

SWEET was the time when first I felt
The Saviour's pardoning blood,
Applied to cleanse my soul from guilt,
And bring me home to God.

Soon as the morn the light revealed,
His praises tuned my tongue;
And when the evening shades prevailed,
His love was all my song.

In vain the tempter spread his wiles,
The world no more could charm;
I lived upon my Saviour's smiles,
And leaned upon his arm.

In prayer my soul drew near the Lord,
And saw his glory shine;
And when I read his holy word,
I called each promise mine.

Then to his saints I often spoke
Of what his love had done;
But now my heart is almost broke,
For all my joys are gone.

Now when the evening shade prevails,
My soul in darkness mourns;
And when the morn the light reveals,
No light to me returns.

My prayers are now a chattering noise,
For Jesus hides his face;
I read, the promise meets my eyes,
But wilt not reach my case.

Now Satan threatens to prevail,
And make my soul his prey;
Yet, Lord, thy mercies cannot fail:
O come without delay.

The Method.

POORE heart, lament.
For since thy God refuseth still,
There is some rub, some discontent,
Which cools his will.

Thy Father *could*
Quickly effect, what thou dost move;
For he is *Power:* and sure he *would;*
For he is *Love.*

Go search this thing,
Tumble thy breast, and turn thy book:
If thou hadst lost a glove or ring,
Wouldst not thou look?

What do I see
Written above there? *Yesterday*
I did behave me carelessly,
When I did pray.

And should God's care
To such indifferents chainèd be,
Who do not their own motions heare?
Is God lesse free?

But stay! what's there?
Late when I would have something done,
I had a motion to forbear,
Yet I went on.

And should God's eare,
Which needs not man, be tyed to those
Who heare not him, but quickly heare
His utter foes?

Then once more pray:
Down with thy knees, up with thy voice:
Seek pardon first, and God will say,
Glad heart rejoyce.

The Withered Hand.

LORD, can a soul like mine,
Unholy and unclean,
Dare venture near a throne of grace,
With such a load of sin?

When I attempt to pray,
And lisp thy holy name,
My thoughts are hurried soon away,
I know not where I am.

When in thy word I look,
Such darkness fills my mind,
I only read a sealed book,
And no relief I find.

Myself can hardly bear
This wretched heart of mine;
How hateful, then, must it appear
To those pure eyes of thine.

40

Low at thy feet I bow,
  Oh pity and forgive;
Here will I lie and wait till thou
  Shalt bid me rise and live.

Weary.

I AM weary of straying! O fain would I rest
In that far distant land of the pure and the blest!
Where sin can no longer its blandishments spread,
And tears and temptations for ever have fled.

I am weary of hoping—where hope is untrue,—
As fair, but as fleeting, as morning's bright dew.
I long for that land whose blest promise alone,
Is changeless and sure as eternity's throne.

I am weary of sighing o'er sorrows of earth,—
O'er joy's glowing visions, that fade at their birth.
O'er the pangs of the loved, that we cannot assuage;
O'er the blightings of youth, and the weakness of age.

I am weary of loving what passes away,—
The sweetest, the dearest, alas may not stay.
I long for that land where these partings are o'er,
And death and the tomb can divide hearts no more.

I am weary, my Saviour, of grieving thy love,—
Oh when shall I rest in thy presence above!
I am weary—but oh, let me never repine,
While thy word, and thy love, and thy promise are
  mine!

Impatience.

WHY thus impatient to be gone?
Such wishes breathe no more;
Let him who locked thy Spirit in,
When meet, unbolt the door.

Why wouldst thou snatch the victor's palm,
Before the conquest's won?
Or wish to seize th' immortal prize,
Ere yet the race is run?

Inglorious wish, to haste away,
And leave thy work undone!
To serve the Lord will please no less
Than praising round the throne.

While thou art standing in the field,
For bliss thou'lt riper grow;
Then wait the Lord's appointed time,
Till he shall bid thee go.

Perfect Peace.

PRINCE of Peace, control my will;
Bid this struggling heart be still;
Bid my fears and doubtings cease,—
Hush my spirit into peace.

Thou hast bought me with thy blood,
Opened wide the gate to God;

Peace I ask—but peace must be,
Lord, in being one with thee.

May thy will, not mine, be done;
May thy will and mine be one:
Chase these doubtings from my heart;
Now thy perfect peace impart.

Saviour! at thy feet I fall;
Thou, my life, my God, my all!
Let thy happy servant be
One forever more with thee!

Then would I Fly Away.

O FOR a breeze of heavenly love,
To waft my soul away,
To that celestial place above,
Where pleasures ne'er decay.
Come, my Saviour, O my Saviour,
Come and bless thy people now,
While at thy feet we humbly bow,
O come and save us now;
Then we will sing our sufferings o'er,
And praise thee evermore.

Eternal Spirit, deign to be
Our pilot here below,
To steer through life's tempestuous sea,
Where stormy winds do blow.

From rocks of pride on either hand,
From quicksands of despair—
O guide us safe to Canaan's land,
Through every latent snare.

Anchor us in that port above,
On that celestial shore,
Where dashing billows never move,
Where tempests never roar.

Following.

As God leads me, will I go,
Nor choose my way.
Let him choose the joy or woe
Of every day:
They cannot hurt my soul,
Because in his control:
I leave to him the whole,—
His children may.

As God leads me, I am still
Within his hand:
Though his purpose my self-will
Doth oft withstand.
Yet I wish that none
But his will be done,
Till the end be won
That he hath planned.

As God leads, I am content;
He will take care!
All things by his will are sent
That I must bear.
To him I take my fear,
My wishes while I'm here,—
The way will all seem clear,
When I am there!

As God leads me, it is mine
To follow him;
Soon all shall wonderfully shine,
Which now seems dim.
Fulfilled be his decree!
What he shall choose for me,
That shall my portion be,
Up to the brim!

As God leads me, so my heart
In faith shall rest.
No grief nor fear my soul shall part
From Jesus' breast.
In sweet belief I know,
What way my life doth go—
Since God permitteth so—
That must be best.

Heaven Below.

O HOW happy are they
Who the Saviour obey,
And have laid up their treasure above;

Tongue can never express
The sweet comfort and peace
Of a soul in its earliest love.

That sweet comfort was mine,
When the favour divine
I received through the blood of the Lamb;
When my heart first believed,
What a joy I received,—
What a heaven in Jesus's name!

'Twas a heaven below
My Redeemer to know;
And the angels could do nothing more,
Than to fall at his feet
And the story repeat,
And the Lover of sinners adore.

Jesus all the day long
Was my joy and my song:
O that all his salvation might see;
He hath loved me, I cried,
He hath suffered and died
To redeem even rebels like me.

On the wings of his love,
I was carried above
All sin, and temptation, and pain;
And I could not believe
That I ever should grieve,
That I ever should suffer again.

They shall Not Overflow.

In the floods of tribulation,
While the billows o'er me roll,
Jesus whispers consolation,
And supports my fainting soul;
Sweet affliction
That brings Jesus to my soul.

Thus the lion yields me honey,
From the eater food is given;
Strengthened thus I still press forward,
Singing as I wade to heaven,
Sweet affliction,
And my sins are all forgiven.

'Mid the gloom the vivid lightnings
With increasing brightness play:
'Mid the thorn-brake sweetest flowerets
Look more beautiful and gay:
Sweet affliction,
That brings Jesus to my soul.

So, in darkest dispensations,
Doth my faithful Lord appear,
With his richest consolations,
To reanimate and cheer:
Sweet affliction,
Thus to bring my Saviour near.

Floods of tribulation heighten,
  Billows still around me roar,
Those who know not Christ,—they frighten;
  But my soul defies their power:
    Sweet affliction,
  Thus to bring my Saviour near.

In the sacred page recorded,
  Thus his word securely stands,
"Fear not, I'm in trouble near thee,
  Nought shall pluck thee from my hands:"
    Sweet affliction,
  Every word my love demands.

All I meet, I find assists me
  In my path to heavenly joy.
Where, tho' trials now attend me,
  Trials never more annoy:
    Sweet affliction,
  Every promise gives me joy.

Wearing there a weight of glory,
  Still the path I'll ne'er forget,
But exulting, cry, it led me
  To my blessed Saviour's seat:
    Sweet affliction,
  Which hath brought me to his feet.

Zion's Children Rejoicing.

KING Jesus, reign for evermore,
Unrivalled in the courts above;
While we, with all thy saints, adore
The wonders of redeeming love.

No other Lord but thee we'll know,
No other power but thine confess;
We'll spread thine honours while below,
And heaven shall hear us shout thy grace.

We'll sing along the heavenly road
That leads us to our blest abode;
Till with the vast unnumbered throng,
On Zion's hill we join our song.

Then with pure hearts and voices sweet,
We'll cast our crowns at Jesus' feet;
And sing of everlasting love,
In everlasting strains above.

The Heavenly Pattern.

APPOINTED by thee, we meet in thy name,
And meekly agree to follow the Lamb;
To trace thy example, the world to disdain,
And constantly trample on pleasure and pain.

O what shall we do our Saviour to love?
To make us anew, come, Lord, from above;
The fruit of thy passion, thy holiness give;
Give us the salvation of all that believe.

O Jesus! appear; no longer delay,
To sanctify here, and bear us away;
The end of our meeting on earth let us see—
Triumphantly sitting in glory with thee.

Light in Darkness.

SOMETIMES a light surprises
The Christian while he sings;
It is the Lord who rises,
With healing on his wings:
Where comforts are declining,
He grants the soul again
A season of clear shining,
To cheer it after rain.

In holy contemplation,
We sweetly then pursue
The theme of God's salvation,
And find it ever new:
Set free from present sorrow,
We cheerfully can say,
E'en let the unknown tomorrow
Bring with it what it may.

It can bring with it nothing,
  But he will bear us through;—
Who gives the lilies clothing,
  Will clothe his people too:
Beneath the spreading heavens,
  No creature but is fed;
And he who feeds the ravens,
  Will give his children bread.

Though vine nor fig-tree neither
  Their wonted fruit shall bear,
Though all the fields should wither,
  Nor flocks nor herds be there;
Yet God the same abiding,
  His praise shall tune my voice;
For while in him confiding,
  I cannot but rejoice.

My only Happiness.

My God, my portion, and my love,
  My everlasting all,
I've none but thee in heaven above,
  Or on this earthly ball.

What empty things are all the skies,
  And this inferior clod!
There's nothing here deserves my joys,
  There's nothing like my God.

In vain the bright, the burning sun
  Scatters his feeble light:
'Tis thy sweet beams create my noon;
  If thou withdraw, 'tis night.

And whilst upon my restless bed
  Amongst the shades I roll,
If my Redeemer shows his head,
  'Tis morning with my soul.

To thee we owe our wealth and friends,
  And health and safe abode:
Thanks to thy name for meaner things,
  But they are not my God.

How vain a toy is glittering wealth,
  If once compared with thee!
Or what's my safety, or my health,
  Or all my friends to me?

Were I possessor of the earth,
  And called the stars my own:
Without thy graces and thyself,
  I were a wretch undone.

Let others stretch their arms like seas,
  And grasp in all the shore,
Grant me the visits of thy face,
  And I desire no more.

Temptation.

THE billows swell, the winds are high,
Clouds overcast my wintry sky;
Out of the depths to thee I call,
My fears are great, my strength is small.

O Lord, the pilot's part perform,
And guide and guard me through the storm;
Defend me from each threatening ill,
Control the waves, say, "Peace, be still!"

Amidst the roaring of the sea,
My soul still hangs her hopes on thee;
Thy constant love, thy faithful care,
Is all that saves me from despair.

Dangers of every shape and name
Attend the followers of the Lamb,
Who leave the world's deceitful shore,
And leave it to return no more.

Though tempest-tossed, and half a wreck,
My Saviour through the floods I seek;
Let neither winds nor stormy main
Force back my shattered bark again.

They Rest.

WEEP not for a brother deceased;
  Our loss is his infinite gain;
A soul out of prison released,
  And freed from its bodily chain;
With songs let us follow his flight,
  And mount with his spirit above,
Escaped to the mansions of light,
  And lodged in the Eden of love.

Our brother the haven hath gained,
  Outflying the tempest and wind;
His rest he hath sooner obtained,
  And left his companions behind:
Still tossed on a sea of distress,
  Hard toiling to make the blest shore,
Where all is assurance and peace,
  And sorrow and sin are no more.

There all the ship's company meet,
  Who sailed with the Saviour beneath;
With shouting each other they greet,
  And triumph o'er sorrow and death:
The voyage of life 's at an end;
  The mortal affliction is past:
The age that in heaven they spend,
  Forever and ever shall last.

My Heart is Fixed.

I'll not leave Jesus—never, never!
  Ah what can more precious be?
Rest and joy and light are ever
  In his hand to give to me.
All things that can satisfy,
Having Jesus, those have I.

Love has bound me fast unto him,
  I am his and he is mine;
Daily I for pardon sue him,
  Answers he with peace divine.
On that Rock my trust is laid,
And I rest beneath its shade.

Without Jesus, earth would weary,
  Seem almost like hell to be;
But if Jesus I see near me,
  Earth is almost heaven to me.
Am I hungry? he doth give
Bread on which my soul can live.

Spent with him, one little hour
  Giveth a year's worth of gain;
Grace and peace put forth their power,
  Joy doth wholly banish pain;
One faith-glance that findeth him,
Maketh earthly crowns look dim.

O how light upon my shoulder
  Lies my cross, now grown so small!
For the Lord is my upholder,
  Fits it to me, softens all;

Neither shall it always stay,—
Patience, it will pass away.

Now he leads me wonderfully,
Right and left, through sun and rain;
Yet I know, and trust him truly,
It is always for my gain.
Yes, his wonder-road indeed,
Always heavenward doth lead.

Those who faithfully go forward,
In his changeless care shall go;
Nothing's doubtful or untoward
To the flock who Jesus know.
Jesus always is the same;
True and faithful is his name.

Blinded world! if ye admire
Earthly trifles, ye are free!
Out of Jesus my desire
Never shall contented be:
I have sworn it in my heart,
I from Jesus will not part.

Morning Hymn.

Now the shades of night are gone;
Now the morning light is come;
Lord, may we be thine today,
Drive the shades of night away.

Fill our souls with heavenly light,
Banish doubt, and cleanse our sight;
In thy service, Lord, today,
Help us labour, help us pray.

Keep our haughty passions bound,
Save us from our foes around;
Going out, and coming in,
Keep us safe from every sin.

When our work of life is past,
O receive us then at last!
Night of sin will be no more,
When we reach the heavenly shore.

Their Works do Follow Them.

SERVANT of God, well done!
  Rest from thy loved employ!
The battle fought, the victory won,
  Enter thy Master's joy.

The voice at midnight came,
  He started up to hear;
A mortal arrow pierced his frame,
  He fell,—but felt no fear.

Tranquil amidst alarms,
  It found him on the field,
A veteran slumbering on his arms,
  Beneath his red-cross shield.

His sword was in his hand,
  Still warm with recent fight,
Ready that moment, at command,
  Through rock and steel to smite.

It was a two-edged blade,
  Of heavenly temper, keen;
And double were the wounds it made,
  Where'er it glanced between.

'Twas death to sin,—'twas life
  To all who mourned for sin;
It kindled and it silenced strife,
  Made war and peace within.

Oft with its fiery force
  His arm had quelled the foe,
And laid, resistless in his course,
  The alien armies low.

Bent on such glorious toils,
  The world to him was loss,
Yet all his trophies, all his spoils,
  He hung upon the Cross.

At midnight came the cry,
  "To meet thy God prepare!"
He woke,—and caught his Captain's eye;
  Then, strong in faith and prayer,—

His spirit, with a bound,
  Left its encumbering clay;
His tent, at sunrise, on the ground,
  A darkened ruin lay.

The pains of death are past,
Labour and sorrow cease;
And life's long warfare closed at last,
His soul is found in peace.

Soldier of Christ, well done!
Praise be thy new employ;
And while eternal ages run,
Rest in thy Saviour's joy.

Things Above.

Rise, my soul, and stretch thy wings,
Thy better portion trace;
Rise from transitory things,
Towards heaven thy dwelling-place.
Sun, and moon, and stars decay;
Time shall soon this earth remove:
Rise, my soul, and haste away,
To seats prepared above.

Rivers to the ocean run,
Nor stay in all their course;
Fire, ascending, seeks the sun;
Both speed them to their source:
So a soul that's born of God,
Pants to view his glorious face;
Upward tends to his abode,
To rest in his embrace.

Cease, ye pilgrims, cease to mourn;
  Press onward to the prize;
Soon your Saviour will return,
  Triumphant in the skies:
Yet a season, and you know
  Happy entrance will be given
All your sorrows left below,
  And earth exchanged for heaven.

Invitation.

COME ye sinners, poor and wretched,
  Weak and wounded, sick and sore,
Jesus ready stands to save you,
  Full of pity, love, and power:
    He is able,
  He is willing. Doubt no more!

Now ye needy, come and welcome,
  God's free bounty glorify;
True belief and true repentance,
  Every grace that brings us nigh,—
    Without money,
  Come to Jesus Christ and buy.

Let not conscience make you linger,
  Nor of fitness fondly dream;
All the *fitness* he requireth,
  Is to feel your need of him:
    This he gives you,—
  'Tis the Spirit's rising beam!

Come, ye weary, heavy laden,
  Lost and ruined by the fall!
If you tarry till you're better,
  You will never come at all.
    Not the righteous,
  Sinners Jesus came to call.

Agonizing in the garden,
  Your Redeemer prostrate lies;
On the bloody tree behold him;
  Hear him cry before he dies,
    IT IS FINISHED:
  Sinners, will not *this* suffice?

Lo! the incarnate God, ascended,
  Pleads the merit of his blood:
Venture on him—venture wholly:
  Let no other trust intrude:
    None but Jesus
  Can do helpless sinners good.

Saints and angels, joined in concert,
  Sing the praises of the Lamb;
While the blissful seats of heaven
  Sweetly echo with his name:
    Hallelujah!
  Sinners here may sing the same.

Remember not Our Offences.

STAY, thou insulted Spirit, stay,
Though I have done thee such despite;
Nor cast the sinner quite away,
Nor take thine everlasting flight.

Though I have steeled my stubborn heart,
And shaken off my guilty fears;
And vexed, and urged thee to depart,
For many long rebellious years.

Though I have most unfaithful been
Of all who e'er thy grace received;
Ten thousand times thy goodness seen,
Ten thousand times thy goodness grieved:

Yet, O! the chief of sinners spare,
In honour of my great High Priest;
Nor in thy righteous anger swear,
I shall not see thy people's rest.

This only woe I deprecate;
This only plague I pray remove;
Nor leave me in my lost estate,
Nor curse me with this want of love.

If yet thou canst my sins forgive,
E'en now, O Lord, relieve my woes;
Into thy rest of love receive,
And bless me with the calm repose

E'en now my weary soul release,
  And raise me with thy gracious hand;
Guide me into thy perfect peace,
  And bring me to the promised land.

Confidence.

Yes! since God himself hath said it,
  On the promise I'll rely;
His good word demands my credit,
  What can unbelief reply?
He is strong, and *can* fulfil;
He is truth and therefore *will*.

As to all the doubts and questions
  Which my spirit often grieve,
These are Satan's sly suggestions,
  And I need no answer give;
He would fain destroy my hope,
But the promise bears it up.

Sure the Lord thus far has brought me
  By his watchful tender care;
Sure 'tis he himself has taught me
  How to seek his face by prayer;
After so much mercy past,
Will he give me up at last?

True, I've been a foolish creature,
  And have sinned against his grace;
But forgiveness is his nature,
  Though he justly hides his face;

Ere he called me, well he knew
What a heart like mine would do.

In my Saviour's intercession
  Therefore I will still confide;
Lord, accept my free confession,
  I have sinned, but thou hast died:
This is all I have to plead,
This is all the plea I need.

Joy in the Holy Ghost.

GLORY to God the Father be,
  Glory to God the Son,
Glory to God the Holy Ghost,
  Glory to God alone.

My soul doth magnify the Lord,
  My spirit doth rejoice
In God, my Saviour and my God,
  I hear his joyful voice.

I need not go abroad for joy
  Who have a feast at home;
My sighs are turnèd into songs,
  The Comforter is come.

Down from on high the blessed Dove
  Is come into my breast;
To witness God's eternal love;
  This is my heavenly feast

This makes me, Abba Father, cry,
With confidence of soul;
It makes me cry, my Lord, my God,
And that without control.

There is a stream which issues forth
From God's eternal throne,
And from the Lamb, a living stream,
Clear as the crystal stone.

The stream doth water Paradise,
It makes the angels sing,
One cordial drop revives my heart;
Hence all my joys do spring.

Such joys as are unspeakable,
And full of glory too;
Such hidden manna, hidden pearls,
As wordlings do not know.

Eye hath not seen, nor ear hath heard,
From fancy 'tis concealed,
What thou, Lord, hast laid up for thine,
And hast to me revealed.

I see thy face, I hear thy voice,
I taste thy sweetest love;
My soul doth leap; but oh! for wings,
The wings of Noah's dove!

Then should I flee far hence away,
Leaving this world of sin;
Then should my Lord put forth his hand,
And kindly take me in.

Then should my soul with angels feast,
  On joys that always last:
Blessed be my God, the God of joy,
  Who gives me here a taste.

My Help Cometh from the Lord.

To the hills I lift mine eyes,
  The everlasting hills;
Streaming thence in fresh supplies,
  My soul the Spirit feels:
Will he not his help afford?
  Help, while yet I ask is given:
God comes down; the God and Lord
  Who made both earth and heaven.

Faithful soul, pray always; pray,
  And still in God confide;
He thy feeble steps shall stay,
  Nor suffer thee to slide.
Lean on thy Redeemer's breast;
  He thy quiet spirit keeps;
Rest in him, securely rest;
  Thy watchman never sleeps.

Neither sin, nor earth, nor hell,
  Thy Keeper can surprise;
Careless slumbers cannot steal
  On his all-seeing eyes;

He is Israel's sure defence;
  Israel all his care shall prove;
Kept by watchful Providence,
  And ever-waking Love.

See the Lord, thy Keeper, stand
  Omnipotently near:
Lo! he holds thee by thy hand,
  And banishes thy fear;
Shadows with his wings thy head;
  Guards from all impending harms;
Round thee and beneath are spread
  The everlasting arms.

Christ shall bless thy going out,
  Shall bless thy coming in;
Kindly compass thee about,
  Till thou art saved from sin;
Like thy spotless Master, thou,
  Filled with wisdom, love, and power;
Holy, pure, and perfect now,
  Henceforth, and evermore.

What Wait I for.

My times are in thy hand,—
  O God, I wish them there;
My life, my soul, my friends, I leave
  Entirely to thy care.

My times are in thy hand,
  Whatever they may be,
Pleasing or painful, dark or bright,
  As best may seem to thee.

My times are in thy hand,
  Why should I doubt or fear?
My Father's hand will never cause
  His child a needless tear.

My times are in thy hand
  Jesus the crucified;
The hand our many sins have pierced,
  Is now my guard and guide.

My times are in thy hand,—
  I'll always trust in thee;
Till I have left this weary land,
  And all thy glory see.

We would See Jesus.

"WE would see Jesus"—for the shadows lengthen
  Across this little landscape of our life:
We would see Jesus, our weak faith to strengthen
  For the last weariness—the final strife.

We would see Jesus—for life's hand hath rested
  With its dark touch upon both heart and brow;
And though our souls have many a billow breasted,
  Others are rising in the distance now.

We would see Jesus,—the great rock foundation,
  Whereon our feet were set by sovereign grace:
Not life nor death, with all their agitation,
  Can thence remove us if we see his face.

We would see Jesus!—other lights are paling
  Which for long years we have rejoiced to see:
The blessings of our pilgrimage are failing—
  We would not mourn them, for we go to thee!

We would see Jesus.—Yet the spirit lingers
  Round the dear objects it has loved so long,
And earth from earth can scarce unclose its fingers,—
  Our love to thee makes not this love less strong.

We would see Jesus.—Sense is all too blinding,
  And heaven appears too dim—too far away.
We would see thee, to gain a sweet reminding
  That thou hast promised our great debt to pay.

We would see Jesus! this is all we're needing,—
  Strength, joy, and willingness come with the sight,
We would see Jesus—dying, risen, pleading;—
  Then welcome day! and farewell mortal night!

I Wait for the Lord.

OH Jesus, leave not me,
Though full of sin I be—
  Love, love me yet!

Oh take me to thy breast,
For there I'll find true rest,
And with thy love possessed
All else forget.

When I'm with thee above,
I'll thank thee for the love
That sends this pain;
Though dark my way appear,
And washed with many a tear,
The prospect yet will clear,
When heaven I gain.

Oh guide me, Saviour, now!
Submissive may I bow
Unto thy will;
If trials be my lot—
My home a far-off spot—
Then, Saviour, leave me not!
Be near me still!

Why art Thou Cast Down?

BE still, my heart! these anxious cares
To thee are burdens, thorns, and snares;
They cast dishonour on thy Lord,
And contradict his gracious word.

Brought safely by his hand thus far,
Why wilt thou now give place to fear?
How canst thou want, if he provide,
Or lose thy way with such a guide?

When first before his mercy-seat
Thou didst to him thy all commit,
He gave thee warrant, from that hour,
To trust his wisdom, love, and power.

Did ever trouble yet befall,
And he refuse to hear thy call?
And has he not his promise passed,
That thou shalt overcome at last?

Like David, thou may'st comfort draw,
Saved from the bear and lion's paw;
Goliah's rage I may defy,
For God, my Saviour, still is nigh.

He who has helped me hitherto,
Will help me all my journey through,
And give me daily cause to raise
New Eben-ezers to his praise.

Though rough and thorny be the road,
It leads thee home, apace, to God;
Then count thy present trials small,
For heaven will make amends for all.

Why Take Ye Thought for the Rest?

But that thou art my wisdome, Lord,
 And both mine eyes are thine,
My minde would be extreamly stirred
 For missing my design.

Were it not better to bestow
  Some place and power on me?
Then should thy praises with me grow,
  And share in my degree.

But when I thus dispute and grieve,
  I do resume my sight,
And pilfring what I once did give,
  Disseize thee of thy right.

How know I, if thou shouldst me raise,
  That I should then raise thee?
Perhaps great places and thy praise
  Do not so well agree.

Wherefore unto my gift I stand;
  I will no more advise:
Only do thou lend me a hand,
  Since thou hast both mine eyes.

Fear Not, Little Flock.

"Poor and afflicted," Lord, are thine;
Among the great unfit to shine;
But though the world may think it strange,
They would not with the world exchange.

"Poor and afflicted." Yes they are;
They're not exempt from grief and care;
But he who saved them by his blood,
Makes every sorrow yield them good.

"Poor and afflicted." 'Tis their lot;
They know it, and they murmur not;
'Twould ill become them to refuse,
The state their Master deigned to choose.

"Poor and afflicted," yet they sing,
For Jesus is their glorious King:
"Through sufferings perfect," now he reigns:
And shares in all their griefs and pains.

"Poor and afflicted." But e'er long,
They'll join the bright celestial throng;
Their sufferings then will reach a close,
And heaven afford them sweet repose.

And while they walk the thorny way,
They're often heard to sigh and say;
"Dear Saviour, come, O quickly come!
And take thy mourning pilgrims home."

Foretaste of Endless Bliss.

My God, I am thine; what a comfort divine,
What a blessing, to know that my Jesus is mine!
In the heavenly Lamb, thrice happy I am;
And my heart doth rejoice at the sound of his name.

True pleasures abound in the rapturous sound,
And whoever hath found it, hath paradise found;
My Redeemer to know, to feel his blood flow,
This is life everlasting—'tis heaven below.

Yet onward I haste to the heavenly feast;
That indeed is the fulness, but this is the taste
And this I shall prove, till with joy I remove
To the heaven of heavens in Jesus's love.

God Liveth Ever.

God liveth ever!
Wherefore, soul, despair thou never!
Our God is good, in every place
His love is known, his help is found;
His mighty arm, and tender grace,
Bring good from ills that hem us round.
Easier than we think can he
Turn to joy our agony.
Soul, remember 'mid thy pains,
God o'er all for ever reigns.

God liveth ever!
Wherefore, soul, despair thou never!
Say, shall he slumber, shall he sleep,
Who gave the eye its power to see?
Shall he not hear his children weep,
Who made the ear so wondrously?
God is God; he sees and hears
All their troubles, all their tears.
Soul, forget not 'mid thy pains,
God o'er all for ever reigns.

God liveth ever!
Wherefore, soul, despair thou never!
He who can earth and heaven control,
Who spreads the clouds o'er sea and l
Whose presence fills the mighty whole,
In each true heart is close at hand.
Love him, he will surely send
Help and joy that never end.
Soul, remember in thy pains,
God o'er all for ever reigns.

God liveth ever!
Wherefore, soul, despair thou never!
Scarce canst thou bear thy cross? Then fly
To him where only rest is sweet;
Thy God is great, his mercy nigh,
His strength upholds the tottering feet.
Trust him, for his grace is sure,
Ever doth his truth endure.
Soul, forget not in thy pains,
God o'er all for ever reigns.

God liveth ever!
O my soul, despair thou never!
When sins and follies long forgot
Upon thy tortured conscience prey,
O come to God, and fear him not,
His love shall sweep them all away.
Pains of hell at look of his,
Change to calm content and bliss.
Soul, forget not in thy pain,
God o'er all doth ever reign.

God liveth ever!
Wherefore, soul, despair thou never!
Those whom the thoughtless world forsakes,
Who stand bewildered with their woe,
God gently to his bosom takes,
And bids them all his fulness know.
In thy sorrow's swelling flood
Own his hand who seeks thy good.
Soul, forget not in thy pains,
God o'er all for ever reigns.

God liveth ever!
Wherefore, soul, despair thou never!
Let earth and heaven outworn with age,
Sink to the chaos whence they came;
Let angry fears against us rage,
Let hell shoot forth his fiercest flame;
Fear not Death, nor Satan's thrusts,
God defends who in him trusts.
Soul, remember in thy pains,
God o'er all for ever reigns.

God liveth ever!
Wherefore, soul, despair thou never!
What though thou tread with bleeding feet
A thorny path of grief and gloom,
Thy God will choose the way most meet
To lead thee heavenwards, lead thee home.
For this life's long night of sadness
He will give thee peace and gladness.
Soul, forget not in thy pains,
God o'er all for ever reigns.

The Promised Land.

On Jordan's stormy banks I stand,
And cast a wishful eye
To Canaan's fair and happy land,
Where my possessions lie.

O the transporting, rapturous scene,
That rises to my sight!
Sweet fields arrayed in living green,
And rivers of delight.

There generous fruits that never fail,
On trees immortal grow;
There rock, and hill, and brook, and vale,
With milk and honey flow.

O'er all those wide extended plains
Shines one eternal day;
There God the Son forever reigns,
And scatters night away.

No chilling winds, or poisonous breath,
Can reach that healthful shore;
Sickness and sorrow, pain and death,
Are felt and feared no more.

When shall I reach that happy place,
And be forever blest?
When shall I see my Father's face,
And in his bosom rest?

Filled with delight, my raptured soul
Would here no longer stay:
Though Jordan's waves around me roll,
Fearless I'd launch away.

Unto Thee will I Cry.

O LORD, I pray thee comfort me,
In this my sore and deep distress
And let my troubled spirit see
The wonders of thy faithfulness.

Shine on this barren ground, that I
Lose not the fruits which should spring up;
Let me not pass thy mercy by,
Nor miss the sweetness in my cup.

Sweetness there is—I know it Lord,—
And otherwise it cannot be;
It is my Father's hand that poured
This mixture in the cup for me.

But much I fear lest my selfwill,
So disappointed and so blind,
Should overlook the sweet, or spill,
And nothing but the bitter find.

What is it Lord? dost thou intend
That patience should take root in me?
Is it thy will my will to bend,
That I more like a child may be?

Is it to raise my heart above
  All earthly joy and earthly pleasure,
And loose my hands from earthly love,
  To fill them full of heavenly treasure?

To hinder this poor mortal clinging,
  And set my heart from earth-bonds free?
O God, my spirit art thou bringing
  Nearer to leaving all for thee?

Whatever be thy gracious thought,
  Let me not lose its sweet design,—
Since Jesus hath the blessing bought,
  Oh for his sake may it be mine.

Alas, my unsubmissive heart,
  Believing its own aching sense,
Saith sweetness here can have no part—
  Or even that God hath caught it thence.

Ah Lord, my lesson lieth here—
  Faith should be eyes when eyes are dim.
Say to my doubts, "Thy God is near,"
  Say to my grief, "Hope thou in him."

Make Thy Way Plain

LIKE Israel, Lord, am I;
  My soul is at a stand;
A sea before, a host behind,
  And rocks on either hand.

O Lord, I cry to thee,
   And would thy word obey;
Bid me advance; and through the sea
   Create a new-made way.

The time of greatest strait
   Thy chosen time has been,
To manifest thy power is great,
   And make thy glory seen.

O send deliverance down;
   Display the arm divine;
So shall the praise be all thy own,
   And I be doubly thine.

Christ.

SWEETER sounds than music knows,
   Charm me in Emmanuel's name;
All her hopes my spirit owes
   To his birth, and cross, and shame.

When he came the angels sung,
   "Glory be to God on high;"
Lord, unloose my stammering tongue,
   Who shall louder sing than I?

Did the Lord a man become,
   That he might the law fulfil,
Bleed and suffer in my room,
   Canst thou then, my soul, be still?

No, I must my praises bring,
  Though they worthless are and weak
For should I refuse to sing,
  Sure the very stones would speak.

O my Saviour, Shield, and Sun,
  Shepherd, Brother, glorious Friend!
Every precious name in one,
  I will love thee without end.

Gethsemane.

Go to dark Gethsemane,
  Ye that feel the tempter's power,
Your Redeemer's conflict see,
  Watch with him one little hour:
Turn not from his griefs away,
Learn of Jesus Christ to pray.

Follow to the judgment-hall,
  View the Lord of Life arraigned;
O the wormwood and the gall!
  O the pangs his soul sustained!
Shun not suffering, shame, or loss:
Learn of him to bear the cross.

Calvary's mournful mountain climo,
  There, adoring at his feet,
Mark that miracle of time,
  God's own sacrifice complete:
"It is finished;"—hear the cry;
Learn of Jesus Christ to die.

Early hasten to the tomb,
  Where they laid his breathless clay:
All is solitude and gloom;
  Who hath taken him away?
Christ is risen! he meets our eyes.
Saviour, teach us so to rise.

Until the Day Dawn.

COMETH sunshine after rain,
After mourning joy again,
After heavy bitter grief
Dawneth surely sweet relief;
  And my soul, who from her height
  Sank to realms of woe and night,
  Wingeth now to heaven her flight.

He whom this world dares not face,
Hath refreshed me with his grace;
And his mighty hand unbound
Chains of hell about me wound;
  Quicker, stronger, leaps my blood,
  Since his mercy, like a flood,
  Poured o'er all my heart for good.

Bitter anguish have I borne,
Keen regret my heart hath torn,
Sorrow dimmed my weeping eyes,
Satan blinded me with lies;
  Yet at last I am set free,
  Help, protection, love, to me
  Once more true companions be.

Ne'er was left a helpless prey,
Ne'er with shame was turned away,
He who gave himself to God,
And on him had cast his load.
  Who in God his hope hath placed,
  Shall not life in pain outwaste,
  Fullest joy he yet shall taste.

Though today may not fulfil
All thy hopes, have patience still;
For perchance tomorrow's sun
Sees thy happier days begun.
  As God willeth march the hours,
  Bringing joy at last in showers,
  And whate'er we asked is ours.

When my heart was vexed with care,
Filled with fears well nigh despair;
When with watching many a night,
On me fell pale sickness' blight;
  When my courage failed me fast,
  Camest thou, my God, at last,
  And my woes were quickly past.

Now as long as here I roam,
On this earth have house and home,
Shall this wondrous gleam from thee
Shine through all my memory.
  To my God I yet will cling,
  All my life the praises sing
  That from thankful hearts outspring.

Every sorrow, every smart,
That the Eternal Father's heart
Hath appointed me of yore,
Or hath yet for me in store,
As my life flows on I'll take
Calmly, gladly, for his sake,
No more faithless murmurs make.

I will meet distress and pain,
I will greet e'en death's dark reign,
I will lay me in the grave
With a heart still glad and brave.
Whom the Strongest doth defend,
Whom the Highest counts his friend,
Cannot perish in the end.

The People of God.

PEOPLE, scattered abroad,
Poor people of God, who would fain see his face,
Hardly ye follow the road;
So much to hinder the race;
Poor people of God!

And yet why are ye weak?
This God whom ye serve, is not he your support?
Do not his promises speak?
Can ye not trust as ye ought?
Say, people of God!

What! has his hand lost power?
Is that arm shortened which holdeth the spheres?
Gives he a broken tower
To shelter ye from your fears?
Oh! no, people of God!

Wherefore then dread the foes,
That a word of his mouth can bring to dust?
When he can miracles do,
Why can ye not wait and trust?
Why not, people of God?

Yes, his promise shall stand,—
Yes, the Lord heareth his people's cry;
His grace shall reign in the land,
The power of hell shall die,
For thee, people of God!

People, fighting your way,
Poor people of God, let faith be your host.
Doubt not this war shall pay
Very much more than it cost.
Yes, believe, people of God!

Is This thy Kindness to thy Friend?

Poor, weak, and worthless though I am,
I have a rich, Almighty Friend;
Jesus, the Saviour, is his name,
He freely loves, and without end.

He ransomed me from hell with blood,
And by his power my foes controlled;
He found me wandering far from God,
And brought me to his chosen fold.

He cheers my heart, my wants supplies,
And says that I shall shortly be
Enthroned with him above the skies:
O what a friend is Christ to me!

But ah! my inmost spirit mourns,
And well my eyes with tears may swim,
To think of my perverse returns;
I've been a faithless friend to him.

Often my gracious friend I grieve,
Neglect, distrust, and disobey;
And often Satan's lies believe,
Sooner than all my friend can say.

He bids me always freely come,
And promises whate'er I ask;
But I am straitened, cold, and dumb,
And count my privilege a task.

Before the world that hates his cause,
My treacherous heart has throbbed with shame;
Loth to forego the world's applause,
I hardly dare avow his name.

Sure, were I not most vile and base,
I could not thus my friend requite;
And were not he the God of grace,
He'd frown, and spurn me from his sight.

It Wont Be Long.

ARISE, my soul, to Pisgah's height,
And view the promised land,
And see by faith the glorious sight,
Our heritage at hand.
We'll stem the storm, it wont be long;
The heavenly port is nigh;
We'll stem the storm, it wont be long;
We'll anchor by and by.

There endless springs of pleasure flow
At my Redeemer's side,
For all who live by faith below,
And in their Lord confide.
We'll stem the storm, &c.

Fair Salem's dazzling gates are seen,
Just o'er the narrow flood,
And fields adorned in living green,
The residence of God.

My conflicts here will soon be past,
Where wild distraction reigns;
Through toil and death I'll reach at last
Fair Canaan's happy plains.

O could I cross rough Jordan's wave,
No danger would I fear;
My bark would every tempest brave,
For O! my Captain's near.

My lamp of life will soon grow pale,
  The spark will soon decay;
And then my happy soul will sail
  To everlasting day.

The Issues of Life and Death.

O WHERE shall rest be found,
  Rest for the weary soul?
'Twere vain the ocean-depths to sound,
  Or pierce to either pole;
The world can never give
  The bliss for which we sigh;
'Tis not the *whole* of life to live;
  Nor *all* of death to die.

Beyond this vale of tears,
  There is a life above,
Unmeasured by the flight of years;
  And all that life is love;—
There is a death, whose pang
  Outlasts the fleeting breath;
O what eternal horrors hang
  Around "the second death!"

Lord God of truth and grace,
  Teach us that death to shun,
Lest we be banished from thy face,
  And evermore undone:

Here would we end our quest;
Alone are found in thee,
The life of perfect love,—the rest
Of immortality.

Goodnight.

I JOURNEY forth rejoicing,
From this dark vale of tears,
To heavenly joy and freedom,
From earthly bonds and fears :
Where Christ our Lord shall gather
All his redeemed again,
His kingdom to inherit.
Goodnight, till then!

Go to thy quiet resting,
Poor tenement of clay!
From all thy pain and weakness
I gladly haste away;
But still in faith confiding
To find thee yet again,
All glorious and immortal.
Goodnight, till then!

Why thus so sadly weeping,
Beloved ones of my heart?
The Lord is good and gracious,
Though now he bids us part.

Oft have we met in gladness,
And we shall meet again,
All sorrow left behind us.
Goodnight, till then!

I go to see his glory,
Whom we have loved below;
I go, the blessed angels,
The holy saints to know.
Our lovely ones departed,
I go to find again,
And wait for you to join us.
Goodnight, till then!

I hear the Saviour calling—
The joyful hour has come;
The angel-guards are ready
To guide me to our home,
Where Christ the Lord shall gather
All his redeemed again,
His kingdom to inherit.
Goodnight, till then!

The Further Shore.

PARTING soul! the floods await thee,
And the billows round thee roar;
Yet rejoice,—the holy city
Stands on yon celestial shore.

There are crowns and thrones of glory;
There the living waters glide;
There the just in shining raiment,
Standing by Immanuel's side.

Linger not,—the stream is narrow,
Though its cold dark waters rise;
He who passed the flood before thee,
Guides thy path to yonder skies.

Having a Desire to Depart.

I LONG to behold him arrayed
With glory and light from above;
The King in his beauty displayed,—
His beauty of holiest love:
I languish and sigh to be there,
Where Jesus has fixed his abode;
O when shall we meet in the air,
And fly to the mountain of God!

With him I on Zion shall stand,
For Jesus hath spoken the word;
The breadth of Immanuel's land
Survey by the light of my Lord:
But when, on thy bosom reclined,
Thy face I am strengthened to see,
My fulness of rapture I find,—
My heaven of heavens in thee.

How happy the people that dwell
  Secure in the city above!
No pain the inhabitants feel,
  No sickness or sorrow shall prove.
Physician of souls, unto me
  Forgiveness and holiness give;
And then from the body set free,
  And then to the city receive.

Hope.

In this world of sin and sorrow,
  Compassed round with many a care,
From eternity we borrow
  Hope that can exclude despair.

Thee, triumphant God and Saviour,
  In the glass of faith we see!
O assist each faint endeavour!
  Raise our earth-born souls to thee.

Place that awful scene before us,
  Of the last tremendous day,—
When to life thou wilt restore us;
  Lingering ages, haste away!

When this vile and sinful nature
  Incorruption shall put on:
Life renewing, glorious Saviour,
  Let thy glorious will be done.

What is Your Life.

AND am I only born to die?
And must I suddenly comply
With nature's stern decree?
What after death for me remains?
Celestial joys, or hellish pains,
To all eternity.

How then ought I on earth to live,
While God prolongs the kind reprieve,
And props the house of clay.
My sole concern, my single care,
To watch, and tremble, and prepare
Against that fatal day.

No room for mirth or trifling here,
For worldly hope, or worldly fear,
If life so soon is gone;
If now the Judge is at the door,
And all mankind must stand before
The inexorable throne!

No matter which my thoughts employ,
A moment's misery or joy;
But O, when life shall end,
Where shall I find my destined place?
Shall I my everlasting days
With fiends or angels spend?

Nothing is worth a thought beneath,
But how I may escape the death
That never, never dies!

How make mine own election sure;
And when I fall on earth, secure
 A mansion in the skies.

Jesus, vouchsafe a pitying ray;
Be thou my Guide, be thou my Way
 To glorious happiness.
Ah! write the pardon on my heart;
And whensoe'er I hence depart,
 Let me depart in peace.

Watchfulness and Prayer.

ALAS, what hourly dangers rise!
 What snares beset my way!
To heaven O let me lift my eyes,
 And hourly watch and pray.

How oft my mournful thoughts complain,
 And melt in flowing tears!
My weak resistance, ah, how vain!
 How strong my foes and fears!

O gracious God, in whom I live,
 My feeble efforts aid;
Help me to watch, and pray, and strive,
 Though trembling and afraid,

Increase my faith, increase my hope,
 When foes and fears prevail;
And bear my fainting spirit up,
 Or soon my strength will fail.

Whene'er temptations fright my heart,
Or lure my feet aside,
My God, thy powerful aid impart,
My guardian and my guide.

O keep me in thy heavenly way,
And bid the tempter flee;
And let me never, never stray
From happiness and thee.

Evening.

Now from the altar of our hearts,
Let warmest thanks arise;
Assist us, Lord, to offer up
Our evening sacrifice.

This day God was our sun and shield,
Our keeper and our guide;
His care was on our weakness shown,—
His mercies multiplied.

Minutes and mercies multiplied,
Have made up all this day;
Minutes came quick, but mercies were
More swift and free than they.

New time, new favours, and new joys,
Do a new song require:
Till we shall praise thee as we would,
Accept our heart's desire.

In the Field.

FIGHTING the Battle of Life !—
With a weary heart and head ;
For in the midst of the strife,
The banners of Joy are fled.

Fled and gone out of sight,
When I thought they were so near :
And the music of Hope, this night,
Is dying away on my ear.

Fighting the whole day long,
With a very tired hand,—
With only my armour strong—
The shelter in which I stand.

There is nothing left of *me*,—
If all *my* strength were shewn,
So small the amount would be,
Its presence could scarce be known.

Fighting alone tonight,—
With not even a stander-by
To cheer me on in the fight,
Or to hear me when I cry.

Only the Lord can hear—
Only the Lord can see
The struggle within how dark and drear,
Though quiet the outside be.

Fighting alone tonight!
With what a sinking heart,—
Lord Jesus, in the fight
Oh stand not thou apart!

Body and mind have tried
To make the field my own;
But when the Lord is on my side,
He doeth the work alone.

And when he hideth his face,
And the battle-clouds prevail,
It is only through his grace
If I do not utterly fail.

The word of old was true—
And its truth shall never cease,—
"The Lord shall fight for you,
And ye shall hold your peace."

Lord, I would fain be still
And quiet, behind my shield;
But make me to love thy will,
For fear I should ever yield.

For when to destroy my foes
Thou lettest them strike at me,
And fillest my heart with woes,
That joy may the purer be;—

Nothing but perfect trust,
And love of thy perfect will,
Can raise me out of the dust,
And bid my fears lie still.

Even as now my hands—
  So doth my folded will
Lie waiting thy commands,
  Without one anxious thrill.

But as with sudden pain
  My hands unfold, and clasp,—
So doth my will start up again,
  And taketh its old firm grasp.

Lord, fix my eyes upon thee,
  And fill my heart with thy love;
And keep my soul till the shadows flee,
  And the light breaks forth above.

Longings for the Blessing.

COME, O thou universal Good,
  Balm of the wounded conscience, come!
The hungry, dying spirit's food,
  The weary, wandering pilgrim's home;
Haven to take the shipwrecked in,
My everlasting rest from sin.

Come, O my comfort and delight;
  My strength and health, my shield and sun,
My boast, and confidence, and might,
  My joy, my glory, and my crown;
My Gospel hope, my calling's prize;
My tree of life, my paradise.

The Secret of the Lord thou art,
The mystery so long unknown;
Christ in a pure and perfect heart;
The name inscribed on the white stone:
The life divine, the little leaven,
My precious pearl, my present heaven.

Make Haste to Help.

O THOU from whom all mercy springs,
Compassionate my sufferings,
And pity me
That trust in thee!
O shelter with thy shady wings,
Until these stormes of woe
Cleare up, or overblowe.

Thee I invoke, O thou Most High,
Thou All-performer!—from the skie
Thy angels send;
Let them defend
My soule from him that would destroy.
O send thy mercy downe,—
With truth thy promise crowne!

Discipline.

TREMBLE not, though darkly gather
Clouds and tempests o'er thy sky,
Still believe thy Heavenly Father
Loves thee best when storms are nigh

When the sun of fortune shineth
  Long and brightly on the heart,
Soon its fruitfulness declineth,
  Parched and dry in every part.

Then the plants of grace have faded
  In the dry and burning soil;
Thorns and briers their growth have shaded—
  Earthly cares and earthly toil.

But the clouds are seen ascending;
  Soon the heavens are overcast;
And the weary heart is bending
  'Neath affliction's stormy blast.

Yet the Lord, on high presiding,
  Rules the storm with powerful hand;
He the shower of grace is guiding,
  To the dry and barren land.

See at length the clouds are breaking,—
  Tempests have not passed in vain;
For the soul, revived, awaking,
  Bears its fruits and flowers again.

Love divine has seen and counted
  Every tear it caused to fall,
And the storm which love appointed,
  Was its choicest gift of all.

As Thou Wilt.

My Jesus, as thou wilt!
  Oh! may thy will be mine!
Into thy hand of love
  I would my all resign.
Through sorrow, or through joy,
  Conduct me as thine own,
And help me still to say,
  My Lord, thy will be done!

My Jesus, as thou wilt!
  If needy here and poor,
Give me thy people's bread,
  Their portion rich and sure.
The manna of thy word
  Let my soul feed upon;
And if all else should fail—
  My Lord, thy will be done!

My Jesus, as thou wilt!
  If among thorns I go,
Still sometimes here and there
  Let a few roses blow.
But thou on earth along
  The thorny path hast gone,
Then lead me after thee;
  My Lord, thy will be done!

My Jesus, as thou wilt!
  Though seen through many a tear,
Let not my star of hope
  Grow dim or disappear.

Since thou on earth hast wept
  And sorrowed oft alone,
If I must weep with thee,
  My Lord, thy will be done!

My Jesus, as thou wilt!
  If loved ones must depart,
Suffer not sorrow's flood
  To overwhelm my heart.
For they are blest with thee,
  Their race and conflict won:
Let me but follow them.
  My Lord, thy will be done!

My Jesus, as thou wilt!
  When death itself draws nigh,
To thy dear wounded side
  I would for refuge fly.
Leaning on thee, to go
  Where thou before hast gone;
The rest as thou shalt please.
  My Lord, thy will be done!

My Jesus, as thou wilt!
  All shall be well for me:
Each changing future scene
  I gladly trust with thee.
Straight to my home above
  I travel calmly on,
And sing, in life or death,
  My Lord, thy will be done!

My Soul Thirsteth for God.

I THIRST, but not as once I did,
The vain delights of earth to share;
Thy wounds, Emmanuel, all forbid
That I should seek my pleasures there.

It was the sight of thy dear cross
First weaned my soul from earthly things;
And taught me to esteem as dross
The mirth of fools and pomp of kings.

I want that grace that springs from thee,
That quickens all things where it flows,
And makes a wretched thorn like me,
Bloom as the myrtle or the rose.

Dear fountain of delight unknown,
No longer sink beneath the brim:
But overflow, and pour me down
A living, and life-giving stream!

For sure, of all the plants that share
The notice of my Father's eye,
None proves less grateful to his care,
Or yields him meaner fruit than I.

I Would Not Live Alway.

I WOULD not live alway—live alway below!
O no, I'll not linger, when bidden to go.
The days of our pilgrimage granted us here,
Are enough for life's woes, full enough for its cheer.
Would I shrink from the path which the prophets of
God,
Apostles and martyrs, so joyfully trod?
While brethren and friends are all hasting home,
Like a spirit unblest o'er the earth would I roam?

I would not live alway—I ask not to stay,
Where storm after storm rises dark o'er the way;
Where seeking for peace, we but hover around,
Like the patriarch's bird, and no resting is found:
Where hope, when she paints her gay bow in the air,
Leaves its brilliance to fade in the night of despair,
And joy's fleeting angel ne'er sheds a glad ray,
Save the gleam of the plumage that bears him away.

I would not live alway—thus fettered by sin;
Temptation without, and corruption within:
In a moment of strength, if I sever the chain,
Scarce the victory is mine, ere I'm captive again.
E'en the rapture of pardon is mingled with fears,
And my cup of thanksgiving with penitent tears:
The festival trump calls for jubilant songs,
But my spirit her own *miserere* prolongs.

I would not live alway—no, welcome the tomb;
Immortality's lamp burns there bright mid the gloom;

There too is the pillow where Christ bowed his head;
O! soft are the slumbers on that holy bed,
And then the glad dawn soon to follow that night,
When the sunrise of glory shall beam on my sight,
When the full matin song as the sleepers arise,
To shout in the morning, shall peal through the skies.

Who, who would live alway, away from his God,
Away from yon heaven, that blissful abode,
Where the rivers of pleasure flow o'er the bright plains,
And the noontide of glory eternally reigns:
Where the saints of all ages in harmony meet,
Their Saviour and brethren transported to greet,
While the songs of salvation unceasingly roll,
And the smile of the Lord is the feast of the soul?

That heavenly music! what is it I hear?
The notes of the harpers ring sweet in the air:
And see, soft unfolding those portals of gold;
The King all arrayed in his beauty behold!
O! give me, O! give me the wings of a dove!
Let me hasten my flight to those mansions above:
Ay, 'tis now that my soul on swift pinions would soar,
And in ecstasy bid earth adieu evermore.

Peace in Believing.

O FOR a faith that will not shrink,
  Though pressed by every foe,
That will not tremble on the brink
  Of any earthly woe!—

That will not murmur nor complain,
  Beneath the chastening rod,
But in the hour of grief or pain
  Will lean upon its God;—

A faith that shines more bright and clear
  When tempests rage without;
That when in danger knows no fear,
  In darkness feels no doubt;—

That bears, unmoved, the world's dread frown,
  Nor heeds its scornful smile;
That seas of trouble cannot drown,
  Nor Satan's arts beguile;—

A faith that keeps the narrow way
  Till life's last hour is fled,
And with a pure and heavenly ray
  Lights up the dying bed.

Lord, give us such a faith as this,
  And then whate'er may come,
We'll taste, e'en here, the hallowed bliss
  Of our eternal home.

Ask what I shall Give Thee.

COME, my soul, thy suit prepare,
Jesus loves to answer prayer;
He himself has bid thee pray,
Therefore will not say thee nay.

Thou art coming to a King,
Large petitions with thee bring;
For his grace and power are such
None can ever ask too much.

With my burden I begin,
Lord, remove this load of sin!
Let thy blood, for sinners spilt,
Set my conscience free from guilt.

Lord! I come to thee for rest,
Take possession of my breast:
There thy blood-bought right maintain,
And without a rival reign.

As the image in the glass
Answers the beholder's face;
Thus unto my heart appear,
Print thine own resemblance there.

While I am a pilgrim here,
Let thy love my spirit cheer!
As my Guide, my Guard, my Friend,
Lead me to my journey's end.

Show me what I have to do,
Every hour my strength renew;
Let me live a life of faith,
Let me die thy people's death.

Our Guide.

GENTLY, Lord, oh gently lead us
  Through this gloomy vale of tears,
Through the changes thou'st decreed us,
  Till our last great change appears.
    O refresh us with thy blessing,
      O refresh us with thy grace,
    May thy mercies, never ceasing,
      Fit us for thy dwelling-place.

When temptation's darts assail us,
  When in devious paths we stray,
Let thy goodness never fail us,
  Lead us in thy perfect way.
    O refresh us with thy blessing.

In the hour of pain and anguish,
  In the hour when death draws near
Suffer not our hearts to languish,
  Suffer not our souls to fear.
    O refresh us with thy blessing.

When this mortal life is ended,
  Bid us in thine arms to rest,
Till by angel hands attended,
  We awake among the blest.
    O refresh us with thy blessing.

Then, O crown us with thy blessing,
  Through the triumphs of thy grace;
Then shall praises never ceasing
  Echo through thy dwelling-place.
    O refresh us with thy blessing.

The Contrite Heart.

THE Lord will happiness divine
  On contrite hearts bestow;
Then tell me, gracious God, is mine
  A contrite heart or no?

I hear, but seem to hear in vain,
  Insensible as steel;
If aught is felt, 'tis only pain,
  To find I cannot feel.

I sometimes think myself inclined
  To love thee, if I could;
But often feel another mind,
  Averse to all that's good.

My best desires are faint and few,
  I fain would strive for more;
But when I cry, "My strength renew,"
  Seem weaker than before.

Thy saints are comforted, I know,
  And love thy house of prayer;
I therefore go where others go,
  But find no comfort there.

O make this heart rejoice or ache;
  Decide this doubt for me;
And if it be not broken, break,
  And heal it, if it be.

The Effort.

APPROACH, my soul, the mercy-seat
  Where Jesus answers prayer;
There humbly fall before his feet,
  For none can perish there.

Thy promise is my only plea,
  With this I venture nigh;
Thou callest burdened souls to thee,
  And such, O Lord, am I.

Bowed down beneath a load of sin,
  By Satan sorely pressed;
By war without, and fears within,
  I come to thee for rest.

Be thou my shield and hiding-place!
  That, sheltered near thy side,
I may my fierce accuser face,
  And tell him, thou hast died.

Oh wondrous love! to bleed and die,
  To bear the cross and shame,
That guilty sinners, such as I,
  Might plead thy gracious name.

"Poor tempest-tossèd soul, be still,
  My promised grace receive:"
'Tis Jesus speaks—I must, I will,
  I can, I do believe.

Perfect that which Concerneth Me.

UNTIL thou didst comfort me
I had not one poor word to say :—
Thick busie clouds did multiply,
And said I was no child of day ;
They said, my own hands did remove
That candle given me from above.

O God ! I know and do confess
My sins are great and still prevail,
(Most heinous sins, and numberless ;)
But thy compassions cannot fail.
If thy sure mercies can be broken,
Then all is true my foes have spoken.

But while time runs, and after it
Eternity which never ends,
Quite through them both, still infinite,
Thy covenant by Christ extends ;
No sins of frailty, nor of youth,
Can foil his mercies, and thy truth.

And this I hourly finde, for thou
Dost still renew, and purge, and heal :
Thy care and love, which jointly flow,
New cordials, and new medicines, deal.
But were I once cast off by thee,
I know, my God, this would not be.

Wherefore with tears, tears by thee sent,
  I beg my faith may never faile!
And when in death my speech is spent,
  O let that silence then prevaile!
O chase in that cold calm my foes,
And hear my heart's last private throes!

So thou, who didst the work begin,
  For I, till drawn, came not to thee,
Wilt finish it, and by no sin
  Will thy free mercies hindered be.
For which, O God, I only can
Bless thee, and blame unthankful Man.

Prayer.

WHAT various hindrances we meet
In coming to the mercy-seat!
Yet who that knows the worth of prayer,
But wishes to be often there?

Prayer makes the darken'd cloud withdraw,
Prayer climbs the ladder Jacob saw,
Gives exercise to faith and love,
Brings every blessing from above.

Restraining prayer, we cease to fight,
Prayer makes the Christian's armour bright;
And Satan trembles when he sees
The weakest saint upon his knees.

When Moses stood with arms spread wide,
Success was found on Israel's side;
But when through weariness they failed,
That moment Amalek prevailed.

Have you no words? Ah! think again,
Words flow apace when you complain,
And fill your fellow-creature's ear,
With the sad tale of all your care.

Were half the breath thus vainly spent,
To Heaven in supplication sent,
Your cheerful song would oftener be,
"Hear what the Lord has done for me."

Trust in God Alone.

In true and patient hope,
  My soul, on God attend;
And calmly confident look up,
  Till he salvation send.

I shall his goodness see,
  While on his name I call;
He will defend and strengthen me,
  And I shall never fall.

Jesus, to thee I fly,
  My refuge and my tower;
Upon thy faithful love rely,
  And find thy saving power.

Trust in the Lord alone,
Who aids us from above;
In every strait surround his throne,
And hang upon his love.

I Press Towards the Mark.

'TIS not too hard, too high an aim,
Secure, thy part in Christ to claim;
The sensual instinct to control,
And warm with purer fires the soul.
Nature will raise up all her strife,
Foe to the self-abasing life,
Loth in a Saviour's death to share,
Her daily cross compelled to bear;
But grace omnipotent at length
Shall arm the saint with saving strength,
Through the sharp war with aid attend,
And his long conflict sweetly end

Act but the infant's gentle part,
Give up to love thy willing heart;
No fondest parent's tender breast
Yearns like thy God's to make thee blest:
Taught its dear mother soon to know,
The simplest babe its love can show.
Bid bashful, servile fear retire,
The task no labour will require.
The sovereign Father, good and kind,
Wants but to have his child resigned;

Wants but thy yielding heart, no more,—
With his rich gifts of grace to store.
He to thy soul no anguish brings,
From thy own stubborn will it springs;
That foe but crucify, thy bane,
Nought shalt thou know of frowns or pain.

Shake from thy soul, o'erwhelmed, deprest,
The encumbering load that galls its rest,
That wastes its strength with bondage vain;
With courage break the enslaving chain!
Let faith exert its conquering power,
Say, in thy fearing, trembling hour,
"Father, thy pitying aid impart!"
'Tis done! a sigh can reach his heart.
Yet if, more earnest plaints to raise,
Awhile his succours he delays;
Though his kind hand thou canst not feel,
The smart let lenient patience heal:
Or if corruption's strength prevail,
And oft thy pilgrim footsteps fail;
Lift for his grace thy louder cries,
So shalt thou cleansed and stronger rise.

If haply still thy mental shade
Deep as the midnight's gloom be made,
On the sure faithful arm divine,
Firm let thy fastening trust recline.
The gentlest Sire, the best of friends,
To thee nor loss nor harm intends;
Though tossed on the most boisterous main,
No wreck thy vessel shall sustain.

Should there remain of rescuing grace
No glimpse, no shadow left to trace,
Hear thy Lord's voice, " 'Tis Jesus' will"—
Believe, thou dark lost pilgrim, still!

Then, thy sad night of terrors past,
Though the dread season long may last,
Sweet peace shall from the smiling skies
Like a new dawn before thee rise;
Then shall thy faith's firm ground appear
Its eyes shall view salvation clear.

Be hence encouraged more, when tried,
On thy best Father to confide.
Oh! my too blind, but nobler part,
Be moved! Be won by these, my heart;
See of how rich a lot, how blest,
The true believer stands possest!

Come, backward soul, to God resign;
Peace, his best blessing, shall be thine!
Boldly recumbent on his care,
Cast thy full burden only there.

Rock of Defence.

JESUS, lover of my soul,
  Let me to thy bosom fly,
While the nearer waters roll,
  While the tempest still is high;

Hide me, O my Saviour, hide,
  Till the storm of life is past;
Safe into the haven guide,
  O receive my soul at last.

Other refuge have I none;
  Hangs my helpless soul on thee:
Leave, O leave me not alone;
  Still support and comfort me:
All my trust on thee is stayed;
  All my help from thee I bring;
Cover my defenceless head
  With the shadow of thy wing.

Thou, O Christ, art all I want:
  More than all in thee I find:
Raise the fallen, cheer the faint,
  Heal the sick, and lead the blind.
Just and holy is thy name;
  I am all unrighteousness;
Vile and full of sin I am;
  Thou art full of truth and grace.

Plenteous grace with thee is found,—
  Grace to cover all my sin:
Let the healing streams abound;
  Make and keep me pure within.
Thou of life the fountain art;
  Freely let me take of thee:
Spring thou up within my heart;
  Rise to all eternity.

Zion's Pilgrim.

PILGRIMS we are, to Canaan bound,
Our journey lies along this road;
This wilderness we travel round,
To reach the city of our God.
O happy pilgrims, spotless fair,
What makes your robes so white appear?
Our robes are washed in Jesus' blood,
And we are travelling home to God.

A few more days, or weeks, or years,
In this dark desert to complain;
A few more sighs, a few more tears,
And we shall bid adieu to pain.
O happy pilgrims, spotless fair,
What makes your robes so white appear?
Our robes are washed in Jesus' blood,
And we are travelling home to God.

Ark of Safety.

O CEASE, my wandering soul,
On restless wing to roam;
All this wide world, to either pole,
Has not for thee a home.

Behold the ark of God;
Behold the open door;
O haste to gain that dear abode,
And rove, my soul, no more.

There safe shalt thou abide,
  There sweet shall be thy rest,
And every longing satisfied,
  With full salvation blessed.

Strength Failed Me.

I FIND this trouble in my heart,—
That when the Lord saith unto me,
  "Arise, depart,
For here your rest can never be":—

To give up part, it would consent,—
To let all for the present go;—
  And be content
That for long years it should be so.

But never in this world to find
One thing of all that it might crave!
  Yea, not to bind
Its tendrils round the drift-wood in its cave!

Then doth my heart cry out in grief
And pain that it can hardly bear;
  Nor finds relief
In that drear moment, anywhere.

Those fair blue heavens so distant are,—
Their very clearness seems to say
  How far! how far!
They lie above man's stormy way.

And human weakness fain would rise
Not all at once, but by degrees;
And seek the skies
With gentle steps, and at its ease:

Would make its many tendrils fast
Round every thing of life and love,
And so at last,
Leave earth behind, and mount above.

But hast thou seen the child of earth
To whom all mortal helps were given,-
Whom from its birth,
God's blessings called to him and heaven;—

Hast thou not seen that soul twine round
These helps—yet use them not to rise,
But to the ground
Turn, and grow downward from the skies?

Hast seen the soul without one stay
Round which its tendrils might be cast,
Yet make its way
Up to God's throne, and there hold fast?

O God, thou knowest all—and me,—
What my heart bears, and what it needs!
My weakness see,—
Yet not my sins, for Jesus pleads.

So make me ever upward grow,
Mounting to thee by good and ill,—
So let me know
The strength of resting in thy will!

Submitting.

WEARY of struggling with my pain,
Hopeless to burst this sinful chain,
At length I give the contest o'er,
And seek to free myself no more.

From my own works at last I cease—
God, who creates, must seal my peace;
Fruitless my toil, and vain my care,
Unless thy sovereign grace I share.

Lord, I despair myself to heal,
I see my sin, but cannot feel;
I cannot, till thy Spirit blow,
And bid the obedient waters flow.

'Tis thine a heart of flesh to give,
Thy gifts I only can receive;
Here then to thee I all resign,
To draw, redeem, and seal, is thine.

With simple truth to thee I call,
My light, my life, my Lord, my all:
I wait the moving of the pool—
I wait the word that speaks me whole.

Speak, gracious Lord, my sickness cure,
Make my infected nature pure;
Peace, righteousness, and joy impart,
And pour thyself into my heart.

Guidance Through Life.

THOU who didst for Peter's faith
Kindly condescend to pray,
Thou, whose loving kindness hath
Kept me to the present day,
Kind Conductor,
Still direct my devious way!

When a tempting world in view
Gains upon my yielding heart,
When its pleasures I pursue,
Then one look of pity dart,—
Teach me pleasures
Which the world can ne'er impart.

When with horrid thoughts profane
Satan would my soul invade,
When he calls religion vain,
Mighty Victor! be my aid!
Send thy Spirit,
Bid me conflict undismayed.

When my unbelieving fear
Makes me think myself too vile,
When the legal curse I hear,
Cheer me with a gospel smile:
Or if hiding,
Hide thee only for a while.

When I listen to thy word,
In thy temple cold and dead,
When I cannot see my Lord,
All faith's little daylight fled,
Sun of glory,
Beam again around my head.

When thy statutes I forsake,
When my graces dimly shine,
When the covenant I break,
Jesus, then remember thine:
Check my wanderings
By a look of love divine.

Then if heavenly dews distil,
And my views are bright and clear,
While I sit on Zion's hill,
Temper joy with holy fear;
Keep me watchful,
Safe alone while thou art near.

When afflictions cloud my sky,
When the tide of sorrow flows,
When the rod is lifted high,
Let me on thy love repose;
Stay thy rough wind,
When thy chilling east wind blows.

When the vale of death appears,
Faint and cold this mortal clay,
Kind Forerunner, soothe my fears,
Light me through the darksome way:
Break the shadows,
Usher in eternal day.

Starting from this dying state,
  Upward bid my soul aspire,
Open thou the crystal gate,
  To thy praise attune my lyre;
    Dwell for ever,
  Dwell on each immortal wire.

From the sparkling turrets there,
  Oft I'll trace my pilgrim way,
Often bless thy guardian care,
  Fire by night, and cloud by day;
    While my triumphs
  At my Leader's feet I lay.

And when mighty trumpets blown,
  Shall the judgment dawn proclaim,
From the central burning throne,
  'Mid creation's final flame,
    With the ransomed,
  Judge and Saviour, own my name!

Prospects of Heaven.

WHAT must it be to dwell above,
  At God's right hand, where Jesus reigns,
Since the sweet earnest of his love
  O'erwhelms us on these earthly plains!
No heart can think, no tongue explain,
What bliss it is with Christ to reign.

When sin no more obstructs our sight,
  When sorrow pains our hearts no more,
How shall we view the Prince of Light,
  And all his works of grace explore!
What heights and depths of love divine
Will then through endless ages shine!

This is the heaven I long to know:
  For this with patience would I wait,
Till, weaned from earth and all below,
  I mount to my celestial seat,
And wave my palm, and wear my crown,
And with the elders cast them down.

Sleeping in Jesus.

Asleep in Jesus! blessed sleep!
From which none ever wakes to weep!
A calm and undisturbed repose,
Unbroken by the last of foes!

Asleep in Jesus! oh! how sweet
To be for such a slumber meet:
With holy confidence to sing
That death hath lost its venomed sting!

Asleep in Jesus! peaceful rest!
Whose waking is supremely blest;
No fear—no woe, shall dim that hour,
That manifests the Saviour's power.

Asleep in Jesus! oh, for me
May such a blissful refuge be:
Securely shall my ashes lie,
Waiting the summons from on high.

Asleep in Jesus! time nor space
Debars this precious "hiding place:"
On Indian plains, or Lapland snows,
Believers find the same repose.

Asleep in Jesus! far from thee
Thy kindred and their graves may be;
But there is still a blessed sleep,
From which none ever wakes to weep.

When?

WHEN shall I see the day
  That ends my woes;
When shall I victory gain
  O'er all my foes;
When will the trumpet sound
  That calls the exiles home,
The grand, sabbatic year,
  When will it come?

A crown of glory bright,
  By faith I see,
In yonder realms of light,
  Prepared for me.

O may I faithful prove,
  And keep the prize in view;
And through the storms of life
  My way pursue.

Jesus, be thou my guide,
  My steps attend;
O keep me near thy side,
  Be thou my friend;
Be thou my shield and sun,
  My Saviour and my guard;
And when my work is done,
  My great reward.

O how I long to see
  That happy day,
When sorrow, sin, and pain,
  Shall flee away;
When all the heavenly tribes
  Shall find their long sought home!
The Jubilee of Heaven,
  When will it come?

Reunion.

MEET again! yes, we shall meet again,
Though now we part in pain!
    His people all
    Together Christ shall call.
        Hallelujah!

Soon the days of absence shall be o'er,
And thou shalt weep no more;
    Our meeting day
    Shall wipe all tears away.
        Hallelujah!

Now I go with gladness to our home,
With gladness thou shalt come;
    There I will wait
    To meet thee at heaven's gate.
        Hallelujah!

Dearest! what delight again to share
Our sweet communion there!
    To walk among
    The holy ransomed throng.
        Hallelujah!

Here, in many a grief, our hearts were one,
But there in joys alone;
    Joy fading never,
    Increasing, deepening ever.
        Hallelujah!

Not to mortal sight can it be given
To know the bliss of heaven;
    But thou shalt be
    Soon there, and sing with me,
        Hallelujah!

Meet again! yes, we shall meet again,
Though now we part in pain!
    Together all
    His people Christ shall call.
        Hallelujah!

Yet Rejoicing.

FRIEND after friend departs:
   Who hath not lost a friend?
There is no union here of hearts,
   That finds not here an end:
Were this frail world our final rest,
Living or dying, none were blest.

Beyond the flight of time,
   Beyond this vale of death,
There surely is some blessed clime,
   Where life is not a breath;
Nor life's affections transient fire,
Whose sparks fly upward and expire!

There is a world above,
   Where parting is unknown;
A whole eternity of love,
   Formed for the good alone;
And faith beholds the dying here,
Translated to that happier sphere.

Thus star by star declines,
   Till all are passed away,
As morning high and higher shines
   To pure and perfect day;
Nor sink those stars in empty night,—
They hide themselves in heaven's own light.

Then Shall Come to Pass the Saying that is Written.

LET love weep,—
It cometh, that day of the Lord, divine;
And the morning-star will surely shine
On the long death-night of sleep.

Let faith fear,—
The unending light comes on apace;
The path leads homeward from this place;
Through the twilight home must appear.

Let hope despair,—
Let death and the grave shout victory,—
That flush of the morning yet shall be,
Which shall wake the slumberers there

The Days of the Years of My Pilgrimage.

NOT always on the journey, O my God!
Not always on the journey, when the home,
The place thou hast prepared for my abode,
Stands open to receive me when I come.
Why should I wish to linger in the wild,
When thou art waiting, Father, to receive thy child?

It is a weary way, and I am faint;
  I pant for purer air and fresher springs;
O Father, take me home! there is a taint,
  A shadow, on earth's purest, brightest things;
This world is but a wilderness to me;
There is no rest, my God! no peace apart from thee.

Come, gentle Death! though I have feared thee long,
  And thou art dreadful still to mortal sense;
Come! thou art stingless now. I did thee wrong;
  Thou shalt but aid me to escape from hence;
Come! I can meet thee; for the Conqueror's arm
Upholds my shrinking soul, and shields me from alarm.

Looking to Jesus with a steadfast eye,
  Clad in his righteousness, my robe divine,
Come! for thy boasted terrors I defy:
  Poor, harmless, shadowy phantom! *he* is mine.
My life is bound in *his*, whose living word
Cries that the dead are blest, when dying in the Lord.

I see him shining on his throne of light—
  The Lamb that hath been slain, and slain for me—
The King of glory! Of all power and might,
  The Lord and God; by whose most high decree
The vile, the guilty, trusting in his name,
A dying wretch like me, eternal life may claim.

This is my confidence, that I am his;
  That I believe, repent, and am forgiven;
That I adore, and love, and meekly kiss
  His garment's hem, and thus I look to heaven:
Lord, thou wilt not deceive me! Faithful Friend,
Wilt thou not take me home? When shall my journey end?

Evening Twilight.

Hail tranquil hour of closing day!
  Begone disturbing care!
And look, my soul, from earth away
  To him who heareth prayer.

How sweet the tear of penitence,
  Before his throne of grace,
While, to the contrite spirit's sense,
  He shows his smiling face.

How sweet, through long-remembered years,
  His mercies to recall,
And, pressed with wants and griefs and fears,
  To trust his love for all.

How sweet to look, in thoughtful hope,
  Beyond this fading sky,
And hear him call his children up
  To his fair home on high.

Calmly the day forsakes our heaven,
To dawn beyond the west;
So let my soul, in life's last even,
Retire to glorious rest.

My Shepherd.

O HAD I an angel's harp and tongue,
And a heart like that for which I pray,
The praise which has long through heaven rung,
Should be sounded forth on earth today!
The Lord my shepherd! who can make known
The love and pity that he hath shown?

When the ninety and nine were in the fold,
And I a poor wanderer far away;
In a region of sin and fears untold,
With every thought and wish astray:
The Lord my Shepherd, with tender care,
Sought me and found me, even there!

He set my feet in his chosen road,
And then the waters of joy and peace
He on my weary soul bestowed,
And bade their measure still increase.
The Lord my Shepherd! alas how far
Below his mercy my praises are!

For every day that has since gone by,
As well as the years that went before,
His love has followed my steps, but I
Have been a poor sinner, and no more!

Ready to rove and disobey,
And murmuring when he hedged my way.

The Lord my Shepherd! he is the same,—
He doth not measure his love by mine;
True and unchangeable is his name,
His love and pity are all divine:
He doth remember when I forget,—
And therefore I think he'll keep me yet.

I bless him now for that hedge of thorn!
Far better than flowers it was for me:
In every sorrow that I have borne,
I might, if I would, his blessing see.
The Lord my Shepherd! he hath done all
My wandering heart to him to call.

He ever leadeth his little flock,
He gave his life their life to buy,—
Their flowing fountain and shadowing rock—
They cannot faint, while he is nigh.
The Lord my Shepherd! O I will be
Forever devoted unto thee!

The Inward Warfare.

STRANGE and mysterious is my life,
What opposites I feel within!
A stable peace, a constant strife;
The rule of grace, the power of sin:
Too often I am captive led,
Yet daily triumph in my Head.

I prize the privilege of prayer,
  But oh! what backwardness to pray!
Though on the Lord I cast my care,
  I feel its burden every day;
    I seek his will in all I do,
    Yet find my own is working too.

I call the promises my own,
  And prize them more than mines of gold;
Yet though their sweetness I have known,
  They leave me unimpressed and cold:
    One hour upon the truth I feed,
    The next, I know not what I read.

I love the day of holy rest,
  When Jesus meets his gathered saints;
Sweet day, of all the week the best;
  For its return my spirit pants;
    Yet often through my unbelief,
    It proves a day of guilt and grief.

While on my Saviour I rely,
  I know my foes shall lose their aim;
And therefore dare their power defy,
  Assured of conquest through his name;
    But soon my confidence is slain,
    And all my fears return again.

Thus different powers within me strive,
  And grace and sin by turns prevail;
I grieve, rejoice, decline, revive,
  And victory hangs in doubtful scale:
    But Jesus has his promise passed,
    That grace shall overcome at last.

Hope in the Covenant.

How oft have sin and Satan strove
  To rend my soul from thee my God!
But everlasting is thy love,
  And Jesus seals it with his blood.

The oath and promise of the Lord,
  Join to confirm the wondrous grace;
Eternal power performs the word,
  And fills all heaven with endless praise.

Amidst temptations sharp and long,
  My soul to this dear refuge flies:
Hope is my anchor firm and strong,
  While tempests blow and billows rise.

The gospel bears my spirits up;
  A faithful and unchanging God
Lays the foundation for my hope,
  In oaths, and promises, and blood.

The Beggar.

ENCOURAGED by thy word,
  Of promise to the poor,
Behold a beggar, Lord,
  Waits at thy mercy's door!
No hand, no heart, O Lord, but thine,
Can help or pity wants like mine.

The beggar's usual plea,
  Relief from men to gain,
If offered unto thee,
  I know thou wouldst disdain;
And pleas which move thy gracious ear,
Are such as men would scorn to hear.

I have no right to say,
  That though I now am poor,
Yet once there was a day
  When I possessèd more:
Thou know'st that from my very birth
I've been the poorest wretch on earth.

Nor can I dare profess,
  As beggars often do,
Though great is my distress,
  My faults have been but few.
If thou shouldst leave my soul to starve,
It would be well what I deserve.

'Twere folly to pretend
  I never begged before;
Or if thou now befriend,
  I'll trouble thee no more:
Thou often hast relieved my pain,
And often I must come again.

Though crumbs are much too good
  For such a dog as I,
No less than children's food
  My soul can satisfy.

O do not frown and bid me go,
I must have all thou canst bestow.

Nor can I willing be
Thy bounty to conceal
From others, who like me,
Their wants and hunger feel:
I'll tell them of thy mercy's store,
And try to send a thousand more.

Thy thoughts, thou only wise!
Our thoughts and ways transcend,
Far as the archèd skies
Above the earth extend:
Such pleas as mine men would not bear,
But God receives a beggar's prayer.

Unto Jesus.

SEE a poor sinner, dearest Lord,
Whose soul encouraged by thy word,
At mercy's footstool would remain,
And then would look, "and look again."

How oft deceived by self and pride,
Has my poor heart been turned aside;
And, Jonah-like, has fled from thee,
Till thou hast looked again on me!

Ah! bring a wretched wanderer home
And to thy footstool let me come!

And tell thee all my grief and pain,
And wait, and look, and look again.

Do fears and doubts thy soul annoy,
Do thundering tempests drown thy joy?
And canst thou not one smile obtain?
Yet wait, and look, and look again.

Take courage then, my trembling soul,
One look from Christ will make thee whole,—
Trust thou in him, 'tis not in vain,
But wait, and look, and look again.

Look to the Lord, his word, his throne:
Look to his grace, and not your own:
There wait and look, and look again;
You shall not wait, nor look in vain.

Ere long that happy day will come,
When I shall reach my blissful home;
And when to glory I attain,
O then I'll look, and look again.

Faith Fainting.

ENCOMPASSED with clouds of distress,
Just ready all hope to resign,
I pant for the light of thy face,
And fear it will never be mine:

Disheartened with waiting so long,
  I sink at thy feet with my load,
All plaintive I pour out my song,
  And stretch forth my hands unto God.

Shine, Lord! and my terror shall cease;
  The blood of atonement apply;
And lead me to Jesus for peace,
  The rock that is higher than I:
Speak, Saviour, for sweet is thy voice,
  Thy presence is fair to behold;
I thirst for thy Spirit with cries
  And groanings that cannot be told.

If sometimes I strive, as I mourn,
  My hold of thy promise to keep,
The billows more fiercely return,
  And plunge me again in the deep:
While harassed and cast from thy sight,
  The tempter suggests with a roar,
"The Lord has forsaken thee quite;
  Thy God will be gracious no more."

Yet, Lord, if thy love hath designed
  No covenant blessing for me,
Ah, tell me, how is it I find
  Some pleasure in waiting for thee?
Almighty to rescue thou art;
  Thy grace is my only resource:
If e'er thou art Lord of my heart
  Thy Spirit must take it by force.

Our Surety.

ARISE, my soul, arise;
Shake off thy guilty fears;
The bleeding Sacrifice
In my behalf appears:
Before the throne my Surety stands,
My name is written on his hands.

He ever lives above,
For me to intercede;
His all-redeeming love,
His precious blood, to plead;
His blood atoned for all our race,
And sprinkles now the throne of grace.

Five bleeding wounds he bears,
Received on Calvary;
They pour effectual prayers,
They strongly plead for me;—
Forgive him, O forgive, they cry,
Nor let that ransomed sinner die.

The Father hears him pray,
His dear anointed One:
He cannot turn away
The presence of his Son:
His Spirit answers to the blood,
And tells me I am born of God.

My God is reconciled;
  His pardoning voice I hear:
He owns me for his child;
  I can no longer fear:
With confidence I now draw nigh,
And Father, Abba Father, cry.

Lead Me in Thy Truth.

LORD, my times are in thy hand;
All my fondest hopes have planned,
To thy wisdom I resign,
And would make thy purpose mine.

Thou my daily task shalt give;
Day by day to thee I live:
So shall added years fulfil
Not my own, my Father's will.

Fond ambition, whisper not;
Happy is my humble lot;
Anxious, busy cares, away;
I'm provided for, today.

O to live exempt from care,
By the energy of prayer,
Strong in faith, with mind subdued,
Yet elate with gratitude!

Will Ye also Go Away.

WHEN any turn from Zion's way,
  Alas! what numbers do!
Methinks I hear my Saviour say,
  "Wilt thou forsake me too?"

Ah, Lord! with such a heart as mine,
  Unless thou hold me fast,
I feel I must, I shall decline,
  And prove like them at last.

Yet thou alone hast power, I know,
  To save a wretch like me,
To whom or whither could I go,
  If I should turn from thee?

Beyond a doubt I rest assured
  Thou art the Christ of God,
Who hast eternal life secured
  By promise and by blood.

The help of men and angels joined
  Could never reach my case;
Nor can I hope relief to find,
  But in thy boundless grace.

No voice but thine can give me rest,
  And bid my fears depart;
No love like thine can make me blessed,
  And satisfy my heart.

What anguish has that question stirred,
If I will also go?
Yet, Lord, relying on thy word,
I humbly answer, No.

Bound for the Kingdom.

WHITHER goest thou, pilgrim, stranger,
Wandering through this gloomy vale?
Know'st thou not 'tis full of danger,
And will not thy courage fail?
No! I'm bound for the kingdom;
Will you go to glory with me?
Hallelujah! Praise ye the Lord.

Pilgrim thou dost justly call me,
Travelling through this lonely void;
But no ill shall e'er befall me,
While I'm blest with such a Guide.
O I'm bound for the kingdom.

Such a Guide! no guide attends thee,
Hence for thee my fears arise;
If some guardian power defends thee,
'Tis unseen by mortal eyes:
O I'm bound for the kingdom.

Yes, unseen; but still believe me,
Such a guide my steps attends;
He'll in every strait relieve me,
He will guide me to the end:
For I'm bound for the kingdom.

Leave thy folly, cease from crime,
From this hour redeem thy time;
Life secure without delay,
Evil is the mortal day.

Be not blind and foolish still,
Called of Jesus, learn his will:
Jesus calls from death and night,
Jesus waits to shed his light.

True Riches.

LORD, shall we part with gold for dross,
With solid good for show?
Outlive our bliss and mourn our loss
In everlasting woe?

Let us not lose the living God,
For one short dream of joy:
With fond embrace cling to a clod,
And fling all heaven away.

Vain world, thy weak attempts forbear,
We all thy charms defy;
And rate our precious souls too dear,
For all thy wealth to buy.

I Shall Not Want.

THOU All-sufficient One!
Who art
The chosen portion of my heart!
Other rejoicing need I none.
I can find all in thee,
Thou chiefest good to me!
Who has thee, is satisfied;
Who by thee doth still abide,
Is no more lonely, at thy side.

To whom thou dost reveal
Thy face,
He lives in joy in every place,—
In every time has what he will,
Who in his deep heart-ground
To thee is firmly bound,
Still and joyful, knows no fear.
Earth costs him no bitter tear—
Earth grows dim when thou art near.

O highest joy of joy!
True rest!
Comfort of every aching breast!
Whom can earth trouble or annoy,
Whom thou art near to bless—
Who does thy love possess?
All I seek for out of thee
Hindrance to my joy might be,
And diminish peace in me.

I Shall Not Want.

THOU All-sufficient One!
Who art
The chosen portion of my heart!
Other rejoicing need I none.
I can find all in thee,
Thou chiefest good to me!
Who has thee, is satisfied;
Who by thee doth still abide,
Is no more lonely, at thy side.

To whom thou dost reveal
Thy face,
He lives in joy in every place,—
In every time has what he will,
Who in his deep heart-ground
To thee is firmly bound,
Still and joyful, knows no fear.
Earth costs him no bitter tear—
Earth grows dim when thou art near.

O highest joy of joy!
True rest!
Comfort of every aching breast!
Whom can earth trouble or annoy,
Whom thou art near to bless—
Who does thy love possess?
All I seek for out of thee
Hindrance to my joy might be,
And diminish peace in me.

Whom thou dost call thy child,
Thine own,—
By all on earth may be unknown,
By all on earth may be reviled ;—
What then? if God be his,
He needs no other bliss.
If I know that I have thee,
Life and strength and joy may flee,
Griefs may come—they move not me.

Come, O thou Blessed One,
My choice!
Now in thy light make me rejoice.
Come, fill the soul which thou hast won.
Come take the whole, that I
To thee may live and die.
I am thine, O be thou mine,
Until in yonder life divine
Thy face shall on me fully shine!

Healed by Mercy.

SIN enslaved me many years,
And led me bound and blind;
Till at length a thousand fears
Came swarming o'er my mind.
Where, (said I in deep distress,)
Will these sinful pleasures end?
How shall I secure my peace,
And make the Lord my friend?

Friends and ministers said much
  The gospel to enforce;
But my blindness still was such,
  I chose a legal course:
Much I fasted, watched, and strove,
  Scarce would show my face abroad;
Feared almost to speak or move—
  A stranger still to God.

Thus afraid to trust his grace,
  Long time did I rebel;
Till despairing of my case,
  Down at his feet I fell:
Then my stubborn heart he broke,
  And subdued me to his sway;
By a simple word he spoke—
  "Thy sins are done away."

The Atonement of Christ.

In vain we seek for peace with God
  By methods of our own:
Jesus, there's nothing but thy blood
  Can bring us near the throne.

The threatenings of thy broken law
  Impress our souls with dread:
If God his sword of vengance draw,
  It strikes our spirits dead.

But thine illustrious sacrifice,
  Hath answered these demands,
And peace and pardon from the skies
  Come down by Jesus' hands.

Here all the ancient types agree,—
  The altar and the lamb;
And prophets in their visions see
  Salvation through his name.

'Tis by thy death we live, O Lord;
  'Tis on thy cross we rest;
For ever be thy love adored,
  Thy name for ever blest.

The Only Plea.

JESUS, the sinner's friend, to thee,
Lost and undone, for aid I flee;
Weary of earth, myself, and sin:
Open thine arms, and take me in.

Pity and save my sin-sick soul;
'Tis thou alone canst make me whole;
Dark, till in me thine image shine,
And lost, I am, till thou art mine.

At last I own it cannot be
That I should fit myself for thee:
Here, then, to thee I all resign;
Thine is the work and only thine.

What can I say thy grace to move?
Lord, I am sin,—but thou art love:
I give up every plea beside,—
Lord, I am lost—but thou hast died.

This Earthly House.

Lord, my house of clay
Doth crumble every day;
Hear me, thou in whom I trust,
Bring me gently unto dust.

Let my end be peace,
Let eyesight softly cease,
And these failing hands of mine
Gently be unclasped by thine.

When I come to die,
Then let me quiet lie
Even as one gone to sleep,
In that other rest more deep.

Yet thy will be done!
For when the fight is won
I shall be in endless rest,
I shall be forever blest.

Stay thou in my heart,
Who its sole portion art:
Even death-pains then shall be
Good and welcome unto me.

Jesus' blood applied,
My soul hath justified;
Flesh and heart may sunder then—
They shall be made one again.

For thy mercy's sake,
My spirit, Jesus, take;
Now death breaks its house away,
And would fain the inmate slay.

Yet this dust shall rise
In glory to the skies:
There shall I my Jesus see,
And his face will shine on me!

The Dying Christian.

My soul's full of glory, inspiring my tongue,
Could I meet with the angels, I'd sing them a song;
I'd sing of my Jesus, and tell of his charms,
And beg them to bear me to his loving arms.

Methinks they're descending to hear while I sing,
Well pleasèd to hear mortals praising their king;
O! angels,—O! angels, my soul's in a flame·
I faint in sweet rapture at Jesus's name.

Oh, Jesus! oh Jesus! thou balm of my soul,
'Twas thou, my dear Jesus, that made my heart whole;
Oh bring me to view thee, thou precious sweet King,
In oceans of glory thy praises to sing.

Sweet Spirit! attend me, till Jesus shall come,
Protect and defend me until I'm called home;
Though worms my poor body may claim as their prey,
'Twill outshine, when rising, the sun at noonday.

The sun shall be darkened, the moon turned to blood,
The mountains all melt at the presence of God;
Red lightnings may flash, and loud thunders may roar,
All this cannot daunt me on Canaan's blest shore.

A glimpse of bright glory surprises my soul,
I sink in sweet visions to view the bright goal;
My soul, while I'm singing, is leaping to go,
This moment for heaven I'd leave all below.

Farewell, my dear brethren,—my Lord bids me come;
Farewell, my dear sisters,—I'm now going home;
Bright angels are whispering so sweet in my ear,—
Away to my Saviour my spirit they'll bear.

I'm going,—I'm going; but what do I see!
'Tis Jesus in glory appears unto me.
I'm going,—I'm going,—I'm going,—I'm gone!—
Oh glory! oh glory!—'tis done,—it is done.—

To the regions of glory the spirit is fled,
And left this poor body inactive and dead;
With angelic armies for ever to blaze,
On Jesus's beauties for ever to gaze.

When the six seals shall open, the trumpet shall sound
To awake God's dear children, that sleep under ground;
Their souls and their bodies shall then join in one,
And each from their Saviour receive a bright crown.

Thy Comforts.

I JOURNEY through a desert drear and wild;
Yet is my heart by such sweet thoughts beguiled,
Of him on whom I lean—my strength, my stay,—
I can forget the sorrows of the way.

Thoughts of his love!—the root of every grace
Which finds in this poor heart a dwelling-place;
The sunshine of my soul, than day more bright,
And my calm pillow of repose by night.

Thoughts of his sojourn in this vale of tears!—
The tale of love unfolded in those years
Of sinless suffering, and of patient grace,
I love again, and yet again, to trace.

Thoughts of his glory!—on the cross I gaze,
And there behold its sad, yet healing rays;
Beacon of hope, which, lifted up on high,
Illumes with heavenly light the tear-dimmed eye.

Thoughts of his coming! for that joyful day
In patient hope I watch, and wait, and pray;
The dawn draws nigh, the midnight shadows flee,—
And what a sunrise will that advent be!

Thus while I journey on, my Lord to meet,
My thoughts and meditations are so sweet—
Of him on whom I lean—my strength, my stay,
I can forget the sorrows of the way.

Jesus, the Pilot.

JESUS, at thy command,
I launch into the deep;
And leave my native land,
Where sin lulls all asleep:
For thee I fain would all resign,
And sail to heaven with thee and thine.

What tho' the seas are broad?
What tho' the waves are strong?
What tho' tempestuous storms
Distress me all along?
Yet what are seas or stormy wind,
Compared to Christ, the sinner's friend.

Thou art my Pilot wise;
My compass is thy word;
My soul each storm defies,
While I have such a Lord!
I trust thy faithfulness and power,
To save me in the trying hour.

Through rocks and quicksands deep,
Though all my passage lie;
Yet thou wilt safely keep,
And guide me with thine eye;
My anchor, hope, shall firm abide,
And I each boisterous storm outride.

By faith I see the land,
  The port of endless rest;
My soul, thy sails expand,
  And fly to Jesus' breast.
Oh may I reach the heavenly shore,
Where winds and waves distress no more!

Whene'er becalmed I lie,
  And storms and winds subside;
Lord, to my succour fly,
  And keep me near thy side:
For more the treacherous calm I dread,
Than tempests bursting o'er my head.

Come, heavenly Wind, and blow
  A prosperous gale of grace,
To waft me from below,
  To heaven, my destined place:
Then in full sail, my port I'll find,
And leave the world and sin behind.

Even So.

STEP by step my course doth tend
To the grave, its final end;
Thence by Jesus I shall rise,
With glancing plumage to the skies!
How heavy my sin-burden lies!
  Oh that my Lord would come!

Here for every hour and day
Measure full of care I pay;

Yonder opens to my sight
An unclouded morning light.
Eternity is still and bright.
Oh that my Lord would come!

Here the flowers bloom and fall,
Precious things fade first of all:
Yonder, in the heavenly land,
Our treasures shall immortal stand;
There joy-harvests wait our hand;
Oh that my Lord would come!

Here our springs of water fail—
Frost doth freeze, and drought prevail.
There a river sweet and clear,
Wherein falleth not one tear,
By the throne of God flows near.
Oh that my Lord would come!

Lord, thou buildest this weak clay
To thy hidden life, today;
Yonder, from thy throne, wilt thou
Crown with glory each poor brow.
Oh that I were with angels now!
Oh that my Lord would come!

The Discharge in that War.

It is not death to die—
To leave this weary road,
And, 'midst the brotherhood on high,
To be at home with God.

It is not death to close
The eye long dimmed by tears,
And wake, in glorious repose
To spend eternal years.

It is not death to bear
The wrench that sets us free
From dungeon chain, to breathe the air
Of boundless liberty.

It is not death to fling
Aside this sinful dust,
And rise, on strong exulting wing,
To live among the just.

Jesus, thou Prince of Life!
Thy chosen cannot die;
Like thee, they conquer in the strife,
To reign with thee on high.

Strength Promised.

WAIT, my soul, upon the Lord,
To his gracious promise flee,
Laying hold upon this word,
"As thy days, thy strength shall be."

If the sorrows of thy case
Seem peculiar still to thee,
God has promised needful grace—
"As thy days, thy strength shall be."

Days of trial, days of grief,
  In succession thou mayst see;
This is still my sweet relief—
  "As thy days, thy strength shall be."

Rock of ages, I'm secure,
  With thy promise, full and free,
Faithful, positive, and sure;
  "As thy days, thy strength shall be."

The Border-land.

FATHER, into thy loving hands
  My feeble spirit I commit,
While wandering in these Border-lands,
  Until thy voice shall summon it.

Father, I would not dare to choose
  A longer life,—an earlier death;
I know not what my soul might lose
  By shortened, or protracted breath.

These Border-lands are calm and still,
  And solemn are their silent shades;
And my heart welcomes them, until
  The light of life's long evening fades.

I heard them spoken of with dread,
  As fearful, and unquiet places;
Shades, where the living and the dead
  Look sadly in each other's faces,

But since thy hand hath led me here,
  And I have seen the Border-land;
Seen the dark river flowing near;
  Stood on its brink, as now I stand:

There has been nothing to alarm
  My trembling soul; how could I fear
While thus encircled with thine arm?
  I never felt thee half so near.

What should appal me in a place
  That brings me hourly nearer thee,
Where I may almost see thy face—
  Surely 'tis here my soul would be!

They say the waves are dark and deep,—
  That faith hath perished in the river;
They speak of death with fear,—and weep;
  Shall my soul perish? Never, never!

I know that thou wilt never leave
  The soul that trembles while it clings
To thee; I know thou wilt achieve
  Its passage on thine outstretched wings.

I cannot see the golden gate
  Unfolding yet to welcome me;
I cannot yet anticipate
  The joy of heaven's jubilee.

But I will calmly watch and pray
  Until I hear my Saviour's voice
Calling my happy soul away,
  To see his glory, and rejoice.

The Ninety-first Psalm.

Whence doth come my peace, my joy?
  Sorrows everywhere abound,—
God in anger doth destroy,
  And his judgments earth confound;
    Fears are rife in every part.
Whence doth come my peace, my joy?
    Jesus dwelleth in my heart.

How am I so calm and still
  When destruction walks abroad?
Thousands here the grave do fill,
  Thousands there are on the road.
    Over all death shakes his dart!
How am I so calm and still?
    Jesus dwelleth in my heart.

What can keep away my fear?
  Passing on from door to door
Pestilence flies far and near,
  Slaying daily more and more,
    Making the strong-hearted start.
What can keep away my fear?
    Jesus dwelleth in my heart.

And my soul more tender grows
  For the fearful things I see;
I the dying eyes can close,
  Go to all that send for me,
    All the help I can, impart:
Yes, my soul more tender grows:
    Jesus dwelleth in my heart.

Let death come, and vanquish me,
  Death cannot my soul alarm;
Though the city I can see
  Hung with mourning by his arm.
    Conquering Death, thou conquered art!
Let him come and vanquish me,
    Jesus dwelleth in my heart.

I have treasures more than earth,
  In a casket valueless.
I was poor and nothing worth,
  I am rich, and all possess.
    Never can my wealth depart,
I have treasures more than earth.
    Jesus dwelleth in my heart.

A Sight of Heaven in Sickness.

OFT have I sat in secret sighs,
  To feel my flesh decay,
Then groaned aloud with frightened eyes,
  To view the tottering clay.

But I forbid my sorrows now,
  Nor dares the flesh complain:
Diseases bring their profit too;
  The joy o'ercomes the pain.

My cheerful soul now all the day
  Sits waiting here and sings;
Looks through the ruins of her clay,
  And practises her wings.

Faith almost changes into sight,
  While from afar she spies
Her fair inheritance in light
  Above created skies.

Had but the prison walls been strong,
  And firm without a flaw,
In darkness she had dwelt too long,
  And less of glory saw.

But now the everlasting hills
  Through every chink appear,
And something of the joy she feels
  While she's a prisoner here.

The shines of heaven rush sweetly in
  At all the gaping flaws:
Visions of endless bliss are seen;
  And native air she draws.

O may these walls stand tottering still,
  The breaches never close,
If I must here in darkness dwell,
  And all this glory lose.

Or rather let this flesh decay,
  The ruins wider grow,
Till glad to see the enlargèd way,
  I stretch my pinions through.

Christ, the First-fruits.

SING praise! the tomb is void
  Where the Redeemer lay;
Sing of our bonds destroyed,
  Our darkness turned to day.

Weep for your dead no more;
  Friends, be of joyful cheer;
Our Star moves on before,
  Our narrow path shines clear.

He who, so patiently,
  The crown of thorns did wear,—
He hath gone up on high;
  Our hope is with him there.

Now is his truth revealed,
  His majesty and might;
The grave has been unsealed;
  Christ is our life and light.

He who for men did weep,
  Suffer, and bleed, and die,—
First-fruits of them that sleep,—
  Christ has gone up on high.

His victory hath destroyed
  The shafts that once could slay:
Sing praise! the tomb is void
  Where the Redeemer lay.

Fear Not.

YE trembling souls, dismiss your fears,
Be mercy all your theme;
Mercy, which like a river flows
In one continual stream.

Fear not the powers of earth and hell,
God will these powers restrain;
His mighty arm their rage repel,
And make their efforts vain.

Fear not the want of outward good,
He will for his provide;
Grant them supplies of daily food,
And all they need beside.

Fear not that he will e'er forsake,
Or leave his work undone;
He's faithful to his promises,
And faithful to his Son.

Fear not the terrors of the grave,
Or death's tremendous sting;
He will from endless wrath preserve,
To endless glory bring.

You in his wisdom, power, and grace,
May confidently trust;
His wisdom guides, his power protects,
His grace rewards the just.

Weep Not.

WEEP not—Jesus lives on high,
O sad and wearied one!
If thou with the burden sigh
Of grief thou canst not shun,
Trust him still,
Soon there will
Roses in the thicket stand,
Goshen smile in Egypt's land.

Weep not—Jesus thinks of thee
When all beside forget,
And on thee so lovingly
His faithfulness hath set,
That though all
Ruined fall,
Every thing on earth be shaken,
Thou wilt never be forsaken.

Weep not—Jesus heareth thee,
Hears thy moanings broken,
Hears when thou right wearily
All thy grief hast spoken.
Raise thy cry,
He is nigh,
And when waves roll full in view,
He shall fix their "Hitherto."

Weep not—Jesus loveth thee,
  Though all around may scorn,
And though poisoned arrows be
  Upon thy buckler borne.
    With his love,
    Nought can move;
All may fail—yet only wait,
He shall make the crooked straight.

Weep not—Jesus cares for thee,
  Then what of good can fail?
Why shouldst thou thus gloomily
  At thought of trouble quail?
    He will bear
    All thy care;
And if he the burden take,
He will all things perfect make.

Weep not—Jesus comforts thee,
  He yet shall come and save,
And each sorrow thou shalt see
  Lie buried in thy grave.
    Sin shall die,
    Grief shall fly,
Thou hast wept thy latest tears
When the Lord of life appears!

Song of the Hundred and Forty and Four Thousand.

WHAT are these in bright array,
  This innumerable throng,
Round the altar night and day
  Hymning one triumphant song:
" Worthy is the Lamb once slain,
  Blessing, honour, glory, power,
Wisdom, riches, to obtain,
  New dominion every hour."

These through fiery trials trod;
  These from great affliction came;
Now before the throne of God,
  Sealed with his almighty name:
Clad in raiment pure and white,
  Victor palms in every hand,
Through their dear Redeemer's might,
  More than conquerors they stand.

Hunger, thirst, disease unknown,
  On immortal fruits they feed;
Them the Lamb amidst the throne,
  Shall to living fountains lead;
Joy and gladness banish sighs,
  Perfect love dispels all fears,
And for ever from their eyes,
  God shall wipe away the tears.

At Home in Heaven.

"For ever with the Lord!"
Amen; so let it be;
Life from the dead is in that word,
'Tis immortality.

Here in the body pent,
Absent from him I roam,
Yet nightly pitch my moving tent
A day's march nearer home.

My Father's house on high,
Home of my soul, how near,
At times, to faith's far-seeing eye,
Thy golden gates appear!

Ah! then my spirit faints
To reach the land I love,
The bright inheritance of saints,
Jerusalem above.

Yet clouds will intervene,
And all my prospect flies,
Like Noah's dove, I flit between
Rough seas and stormy skies.

Anon the clouds depart,
The winds and waters cease,
While sweetly o'er my gladdened heart,
Expands the bow of peace.

Beneath its glowing arch,
Along the hallowed ground,
I see cherubic armies march,
A camp of fire around.

I hear at morn and even,
At noon and midnight hour,
The choral harmonies of heaven
Earth's Babel tongues o'erpower.

Then, then I feel that he,
(Remembered or forgot,)
The LORD, is never far from me,
Though I perceive him not.

In darkness as in light,
Hidden alike from view,
I sleep, I wake, as in *his* sight,
Who looks all nature through.

All that I am, have been,
All that I yet may be,
He sees at once, as he hath seen,
And shall for ever see.

How can I meet his eyes?
Mine on the cross I cast
And own my life a Saviour's prize,
Mercy from first to last.

"For ever with the Lord!"
—Father, if 'tis thy will,

The promise of that faithful word,
Even here to me fulfil.

Be thou at my right hand,
Then can I never fail;
Uphold thou me, and I shall stand,
Fight, and I must prevail.

So when my latest breath
Shall rend the veil in twain,
By death I shall escape from death,
And life eternal gain.

Knowing as I am known,
How shall I love that word,
And oft repeat before the throne,
"For ever with the Lord!"

Then, though the soul enjoy
Communion high and sweet,
While worms this body must destroy,
Both shall in glory meet.

The trump of final doom
Will speak the selfsame word,
And Heaven's voice thunder through the tomb,
"For ever with the LORD!"

The tomb shall echo deep
That death-awakening sound;
The saints shall hear it in their sleep,
And answer from the ground.

Then, upward as they fly,
  That resurrection-word,
Shall be their shout of victory,
  "For ever with the LORD!"

That resurrection-word,
  That shout of victory,
Once more,—"*For ever with the Lord!*"
  Amen: *so let it be!*

INDEX OF FIRST LINES.

www.ingramcontent.com/pod-product-compliance
Lightning Source LLC
LaVergne TN
LVHW021056110826
845150LV00001B/87

9781425566777